Maki

i

Andrew Azzopardi

Making Sense of Inclusive Education

Where Everyone Belongs

VDM Verlag Dr. Müller

Impressum/Imprint (nur für Deutschland/ only for Germany)

Bibliografische Information der Deutschen Nationalbibliothek: Die Deutsche Nationalbibliothek verzeichnet diese Publikation in der Deutschen Nationalbibliografie; detaillierte bibliografische Daten sind im Internet über http://dnb.d-nb.de abrufbar.
Alle in diesem Buch genannten Marken und Produktnamen unterliegen warenzeichen-, marken- oder patentrechtlichem Schutz bzw. sind Warenzeichen oder eingetragene Warenzeichen der jeweiligen Inhaber. Die Wiedergabe von Marken, Produktnamen, Gebrauchsnamen, Handelsnamen, Warenbezeichnungen u.s.w. in diesem Werk berechtigt auch ohne besondere Kennzeichnung nicht zu der Annahme, dass solche Namen im Sinne der Warenzeichen- und Markenschutzgesetzgebung als frei zu betrachten wären und daher von jedermann benutzt werden dürften.

Coverbild: www.ingimage.com

Verlag: VDM Verlag Dr. Müller Aktiengesellschaft & Co. KG
Dudweiler Landstr. 99, 66123 Saarbrücken, Deutschland
Telefon +49 681 9100-698, Telefax +49 681 9100-988
Email: info@vdm-verlag.de

Herstellung in Deutschland:
Schaltungsdienst Lange o.H.G., Berlin
Books on Demand GmbH, Norderstedt
Reha GmbH, Saarbrücken
Amazon Distribution GmbH, Leipzig
ISBN: 978-3-639-22323-1

Imprint (only for USA, GB)

Bibliographic information published by the Deutsche Nationalbibliothek: The Deutsche Nationalbibliothek lists this publication in the Deutsche Nationalbibliografie; detailed bibliographic data are available in the Internet at http://dnb.d-nb.de.
Any brand names and product names mentioned in this book are subject to trademark, brand or patent protection and are trademarks or registered trademarks of their respective holders. The use of brand names, product names, common names, trade names, product descriptions etc. even without a particular marking in this works is in no way to be construed to mean that such names may be regarded as unrestricted in respect of trademark and brand protection legislation and could thus be used by anyone.

Cover image: www.ingimage.com

Publisher: VDM Verlag Dr. Müller Aktiengesellschaft & Co. KG
Dudweiler Landstr. 99, 66123 Saarbrücken, Germany
Phone +49 681 9100-698, Fax +49 681 9100-988
Email: info@vdm-publishing.com

Printed in the U.S.A.
Printed in the U.K. by (see last page)
ISBN: 978-3-639-22323-1

TABLE OF CONTENTS

Charmaine Agius Ferrante has been working in the field of early intervention, disability and inclusion for over twenty years. Ms. Agius Ferrante is a Portage Trainer for the Mediterranean region. She in presently the Teaching Support Consultant of a Maltese Boys' Church school, as well as an Advisor and Vice-President to a Parents' run NGO, *Equal Partners Foundation*. She is also closely involved in lecturing with the *Programme for Inclusive Education*, within the *Department of Psychology* at the *University of Malta*. Ms. Agius Ferrante is a Member of the *Malta Association of the Counselling Profession* and a Member of the *Malta Psychological Association*. She can be reached at ferrante@waldonet.net.mt

Dr Andrew Azzopardi is a Lecturer at the *University of Malta*. His lecturing & research focus on inclusive education, sociology, critical pedagogy, disability politics, youth & community studies. He is currently coordinating a *Masters in Inclusive Education & Communities*. He has published extensively in the field of disability studies and inclusive education. He is a Member of the Editorial Panel of the highly acclaimed *International Journal of Inclusive Education* and has edited a special edition called *Creating Inclusive Communities*. He has contributed extensively in a number of other applauded journals. He has published three texts so far, *Career Guidance for Persons with Disability (2008) (JP Advertising), Reading Stories of Inclusion – Engaging with different perspectives towards an agenda for inclusion (2009)* and *Understanding disability politics in Malta (2009) (VDM Verlag Dr. Müller)*. In the coming months he will be publishing the following texts; Co-Editor of *Inclusive Communities: A Reader (Sense Publishers)*, Editor of *Roots to Inclusive Education* and Co-Author of *Sounds of Silence*. He can be reached at andrew.azzopardi@um.edu.mt

Claire Lucille Azzopardi Lane started working with people with learning and physical disability in 1996. She is currently reading a Ph.D. in *Sexuality and People with Learning Disability* with the *University of Kent* in the U.K. and working on issues of sexuality with parents of and young people with learning disability in Malta. She can be reached at klerdrama@gmail.com

Ronald Balzan studied *Public Policy and Management (University of Malta)* at undergraduate level, which studies were then furthered at postgraduate level. He currently works for a State-Funded Agency which provides services to disabled people and their families. He is a regular contributor in *Disability Equality Training* sessions. He has also lectured at the *University of Malta on numerous occassions*. He can be reached at ronabalz@gmail.com

Dr Paul A. Bartolo is Senior Lecturer in Educational Psychology at the University of Malta with a special interest in learner diversity. He has developed and tutored Masters programmes for educational psychologists and for teachers in *Responding to Diversity*. He coordinates the *Programme for Culturally Responsive Education*, Chaired the *National Curriculum Focus Group for Inclusive Education* and a *Comenius 2.1 Project* among seven European higher education institutions which produced multilingual training materials for preparing teachers to respond to diversity (www.dtmp.org). Before moving to University, Dr Bartolo had worked as a teacher and later set up the government School Psychology Service. He was also the first Consultant Psychologist in the setting up of *Eden Foundation,* now *Foundation Inspire* and is the psychologist for the programme for children with autism. Recent publications include: *Responding to Student Diversity: Teacher's Handbook, Tutor's Manual*, and a reader (2007): *Responding to student diversity: Teacher education and classroom practice* (2008) in the *Special Issue on Culturally Responsive Education* of the *Malta Review of Educational Research*; *Teacher Education for Diversity* in the *Becoming a Teacher Educator* (Springer) (2009) and *Teacher education online: Towards inclusive virtual learning communities* in *Teacher Education for Inclusion*: *Changing Paradigms and Innovative Approaches* (Routledge) (2010). He can be reached at paul.a.bartolo@um.edu.mt

George Borg read his first Degree in Education at the *University of Malta*. He pursued his studies at the same University and was awarded a *Post-Graduate Diploma* in the E*ducation of Children with Special Educational Needs*. In 2000 he was conferred with the *Masters Degree in Education (Special Educational Needs)* from Northern College Aberdeen, Scotland. His career in the education sector started in 1980 as a Teacher at various Primary and Special Schools and was promoted to Headmaster of *San Miguel School*, Principal Education Officer, Assistant Director and is currently the Director of Student Services within the *Directorate for Educational Services*. Mr. Borg is a member of *National Association for Special Educational Needs* and represents the Ministry of Education on the *National Commission for Persons with Disability* and is the Representative Board Member on the *European Agency for Development of Special Needs Education*. He can be reached at borgg@maltanet.net

Dr Toby Brandon conducted his *Economic and Social Research Council* funded PhD into *'Power and Disability'* at the *London School of Economics*. He went on to become a Senior Researcher at the *University of Durham*, primarily working in the field of mental health. He has published extensively in advocacy and mental health service evaluations, and more recently around disability. He now works as a Reader leading in *Disability Studies* at *Northumbria University* while developing a profile of participatory research utilising the social model of disability. Dr Brandon is also an editor for the journal *Disability and Society* and a trustee of the charity *Disability North*. He can be reached at toby.brandon@northumbria.ac.uk

Dr Carmel Cefai is the Director of the *European Centre for Educational Resilience and Socio-Emotional Health*, Lecturer in Psychology at the *University of Malta*, and visiting fellow at the *School of Education, University of Leicester*, UK. His most recent publications include; *Promoting Resilience in the Classroom: Guide to Developing Pupils Emotional and Cognitive Skills* (2008); *Promoting Emotional Education; Engaging Children and Young People with Social, Emotional and Behaviour Difficulties* (co-edited with P. Cooper, 2009); *Healthy Students Healthy Lives* (with L. Camilleri, 2009); and *Engagement Time: A National Study of Students with Social, Emotional, and Behaviour Difficulties in Maltese schools* (with P. Cooper and L. Camilleri). He is co–editor of the *International Journal of Emotional Education*, Associate Editor of the *Emotional and Behaviour Difficulties Journal* (Routledge) and book reviews editor of the *Maltese Review of Educational Research*. He is *Joint Chair of the European Network for Social and Emotional Competence* and the coordinator of the *Masters Programme in Social, Emotional and Behavioural Difficulties* at the *Faculty of Education, University of Malta*. He can be reached at carmel.cefai@um.edu.mt

Ruth Falzon is a Lecturer within the *Department of Psychology* at the *University of Malta*. Her areas of interest include Personal and Social Development (PSD), Inclusion and Dyslexia. She co-ordinates PSD seminars and PSD Initial Teacher Training. She is also currently reading for her Doctorate and has published papers on PSD and Dyslexia, Self esteem and Counselling. Ms. Falzon believes in the importance of voluntary work and is on the Executive Council of a number of associations: *PSD Association, Malta Dyslexia Association, Malta Association for the Counselling Profession* and the *National Council of Women*. As from April 2010, she has been asked to be the Treasurer of the *International Association for Counselling* and to be the President of the *Association for Professionals in Learning Disabilities* (Malta). She can be reached at ruth.falzon@um.edu.mt

Louisa Grech graduated in 1977 with a B.A.Gen. (History & Philosophy) and in 2005 completed her PGCE. She was appointed a Member of the Focus Group on the review of the *National Minimum Curriculum on Inclusive Education*. She is a Teacher by profession and also lectures at the *University of Malta* in the *Diploma in Facilitating Inclusive Education*. Ms. Grech is Executive Manager of *Equal Partners Foundation* and a parent activist for the rights of persons with an intellectual disability. She can be reached at louisagrech@onvol.net

Philip Grech is an Architect and Civil Engineer by profession. He graduated in 1982 with a B.E.&A.(Hons.) and in 1985 completed his M.Sc.. In 2001-2003 he occupied the post of President of the *Malta Federation of Organisations of Persons with Disability*. He was a Member of the Committee of *Down Syndrome Association, National Commission Persons with Disability* and *Equal Partners Foundation*. He is a parent activist for the rights of persons with an intellectual disability. He can be reached at philipgrech@onvol.net

Shaun Grech is an independent researcher and PhD candidate at the *Faculty of Health, Psychology and Social Care, Manchester Metropolitan University* UK. Shaun's research focuses on disability, poverty and international development in Latin America, especially on the interactions and dynamics between disability and poverty. Shaun has extensive field research experience predominantly in Guatemala, as well as other locations including Malaysia and Malta. Other areas of interest include: post/neocolonial approaches to the study of disability across cultures, decolonising research methodologies, and poverty and migration. He has published extensively in journals, contributed chapters in books, and is also co-editor of the forthcoming book *Inclusive Communities: A Reader (Sense Publishers)*. He can be reached at shaungrech@gmail.com

Lara Jane Grillo is a qualified LSA currently working at *St Joseph School, Blata l-Bajda*. Her interest in inclusive education was born from the experience she had with her own daughter, oppressed and voiceless in the educational system. Subsequently her daughter was statemented and supported, which improved the quality of life of all the family unit. Deep concern and awareness pushed Ms. Grillo to enrich herself on the subject of inclusive education and consequently read and successfully completed a *Diploma in Facilitating Inclusive Education* at the University of Malta. She can be reached at lagrillo@maltanet.net

Liliana Maric was awarded a B.Ed. (Hons.) in *Home Economics and Early and Middle Years* by the *University of Malta* and went on to get an *M.Ed. in Assessment and Evaluation*. For twelve years she taught Home Economics in a Maltese Independent co-ed Secondary school. These years contributed to the application and appreciation of differentiated teaching and assessment techniques. Since January 2008 she has been teaching at Post-Secondary level, at the *Gian Frangisk Abela, University of Malta, Junior College* teaching Nutrition, Family and Consumer Studies at Advanced Level. She is a Visiting Lecturer at the *University of Malta*. Her interest is to develop inclusive education in local schools, develop her competencies in disability studies and improve her teaching and learning skills at Higher Education Level. She is currently reading for a Doctorate in Inclusive Education. She can be reached at liliana.maric@um.edu.mt

Dr Duncan Mercieca is currently teaching Philosophy of Education at the *Faculty of Education, University of Malta*. Trained as a teacher, he has had experience teaching in mainstream and special schools. His interests are in the links between 'Education and Continental Philosophy', particularly in the issues of the 'Other' and 'Becoming'. In his current work with student teachers, he is interested in research which focuses on becoming-teacher. He has also done some work on how marginalised groups transgress boundaries. He can be reached at duncan.mercieca@um.edu.mt

Amanda Muscat is a Senior Speech and Language Pathologist by profession, who worked within the education as well as the health sector for the past five years. She currently holds the position of Resource Worker within the Student Services Department, working directly in the area of Inclusion and Special Education with special focus on developing Early Intervention Services and supporting educators in Curriculum Differentiation. Throughout the years, she has developed an expertise, provides training and lectures at a Certificate level on areas including disability, Complex Communication Difficulties, inclusive curriculum, pedagogy, Augmentative and Alternative Communication, IEPs and literacy. She also had a key role in the development of the *Inclusive Curriculum Project* and the publishing of Attainment Levels in Malta. She is currently completing a *Masters in Inclusive Education and Communities* and specialising in the creation of an inclusive curriculum, literacy and Autism Spectrum Disorders. She can be reached at mandymus@gmail.com

Sue Anne Pizzuto graduated with a B.Ed. (Hons.) *Primary Education* in 2005, and M.Ed. in *Social, Emotional and Behavioural Difficulties* in 2009 at the *University of Malta*. She has worked as a Primary Class Teacher for these last three years. During 2008 and 2009 she was involved with the running of a *Pilot Nurture Group Project* as part of the *College Behaviour Support Strategy*. She presently works as a Nurture Group Teacher. The work involves early intervention and inclusive strategies for students experiencing Social, Emotional and Behavioural difficulties in Primary Mainstream Schools. She can be reached at sue@euroweb.net.mt

Dr Elena Tanti Burlò graduated in Philosophy from the *University of Malta* and read a Doctorate in Applied Psychology at the *University of Padova, Italy*. She was greatly influenced by Dr Franco Basaglia and the Italian system of 'integrazione' of students with disabilities. Returning to Malta, she has worked as Clinical Psychologist at the *Child Guidance Clinic* at the Psychiatric Hospital in Malta. She has been teaching at the *University of Malta* since 1983 and was involved in designing undergraduate and post-graduate programmes in *inclusive education and communities*. She has presented various *papers* at local and international conferences; acted as external examiner for the *International Masters* organized by the newly established *Universita' Foro Italico*, in Rome. Dr Tanti Burlo' also contributed towards the International Ph.D. programme on *culture, disability and inclusion: education and formation* at the same University. She is also involved in a number of EU projects. Dr Tanti Burlo' was the *Head* of *Department of Psychology* till 2010 and is presently Coordinator of the *Programme for Inclusive Education* and Consultant Psychologist, Founder and Council Member of the *Equal Partners Foundation* an NGO supporting persons with disability in inclusive settings. Her present research is focusing on 'When educating becomes difficult' and this has led to her interest in Universal Design for Learning. She can be reached at elena.tanti-burlo@um.edu.mt

*I dedicate this book to all the students
whose lives have been turned upside
down by inclusive education*

and to

*Karl and Claire, my children,
who have taught me that change
comes from children themselves*

MAKING SENSE OF INCLUSIVE EDUCATION: WHERE EVERYONE BELONGS

The rationale of this Text is to provide a critical understanding of 'inclusive education' and 'disability issues' for those professionals, practitioners and researchers that may/not be, until now, directly (or closely) affianced with the disability field but may in the future consider taking up a role within this subject matter.

Inclusive education can be understood within a number of varied frameworks, namely, the cultural, historical, political and social paradigm keeping in mind that 'inclusion' is an elaborate interaction that is taking place within social structures and policy enactment. This Text will endeavour to interpret this combination of issues and decipher emerging problems contained in this complex intermix of inclusive education discourses. The educational experience which for a long time has been forced on the children seems to reproduce a social experience, which many a times is lacking educational worth. Members of the school community are unanimous that struggling to achieve an inclusive community is no easy task. Lack of resources and adequate debates within a school community occasionally wrapped in low morale lead to a significant contradiction that schools have the exclusive endeavour of representing standards and configurations that are there solely to enthral the bureaucrats and academics. The essence of inclusive education is the ability to respond to diversity. It is a process whereby children are given a voice. The *National Minimum Curriculum* (Ministry of Education 1999) and other reforms at State level have been responsible for the restructuring in the educational system conditioned by a competitive stance. 'Inclusion' needs to find its position primarily within this trajectory. *Making Sense of Inclusive Education: Where Everyone Belongs* incorporates a political dialogue situated within the principles of emancipation and respect.

Authors in this edited work, regardless of their field of expertise, training and specialization, have articulated notions about inclusive education within the following concepts; voices of disabled students and parents, policy concerns, problematising 'inclusion' and 'exclusion', challenging the notions of professionalism and professionalisation, contesting curriculum stances, deconstructing stereotypical constructions of identity, converging insider perspective with curriculum discourses, exploring the mechanisms of 'moving schools' and 'school communities' and notionalising collaborative inquiry.

Finally, the exciting experience of this Text lies in the fact that people come with very different positons, epistemologies and beliefs. Together with its 'sister' publication, *Roots to Inclusive Education* (2010) this Text is a continuation of this process thus ensuring that most if not all professionals, academics, practitioners and activists from the disabled people and parents movement are represented. I may not agree with some or most contributions – but it is so fascinating that as an Editor I have managed to converge so many assorted discourses and positions.

MAKING SENSE OF INCLUSIVE EDUCATION

Inclusion has to be won, classroom by classroom, school by school. Once won, it can also be lost again if a dedicated teacher leaves or other circumstances change.
Gordon & Morton (2008, p. 246).

Regular schools with an inclusive orientation are the most effective means of…building an inclusive society and achieving education for all.
Salamanca Statement (1994, p. 2).

Armstrong and Barton (2007) call inclusion a "flagship idea" that "transform[s] cultures and practices…in celebration of diversity" while it simultaneously has been "colonized, hollowed out and transformed into an empty signifier" (p. 5). In fact, over twenty-five years after the crafting of the *Salamanca Statement*, inclusion remains elusive and empty and has an international and an intergenerational impact on disabled people. Exclusion starts well before children attend school and continues through adulthood. Dóra Bjarnason (2008), in Iceland, documents how prenatal testing can construct the fetus as disabled and Geert vanHove (2008) and his colleagues describe how disabled infants are pigeonholed in Belgium. By the time disabled individuals reach the age of tertiary education, access and inclusion can be extraordinarily difficult (Reid & Knight, 2006; Marshall, 2008) in spite of the fact that the *World Declaration on Higher Education* (1998) states that higher education should provide equity of access and should involve a "seamless system starting with early childhood and primary education and should continue throughout life" (§ 3.b.). Gordon & Morton find inclusion "slippery and difficult" (2008, p. 246) even when State mandates require it, as in New Zealand, where parents have to search for a school that will take in their disabled children as students. The same holds true in the United States, where many publicly funded charter schools find creative ways of avoiding the enrollment of disabled students even though federal law requires that public schools admit students on an equitable basis. More discouraging is the evidence of losing ground on a wholesale level, as in the case of students with intellectual disabilities. Phil Smith (2010) documents the 1980's rise and 1990's decline in inclusion of these students, who remain the most segregated of all school age children in the United States. Given the reality of the above, how do we celebrate diversity and transform culture and practices, as Armstrong and Barton claim is the possibility of inclusion? The authors in this volume demonstrate that this depends on who we are and where and with whom we live and work. They also demonstrate the importance of a volume like this. Their stories, reflections, and recommendations offer me hope, particularly given the positions and relationships these authors represent. As someone steeped in the critical tradition, I too often dwell on the discouraging facts I report above. So I thank Dr Azzopardi for giving me the opportunity to write this Forward and I thank these chapter authors for their work and their commitment to inclusive education.

REFERENCES

Armstrong, F., & Barton, L. (2007). Introduction. In Armstrong, F. & Barton, L. (Eds.), *Policy, experience, and change: Cross-cultural reflections on inclusive education, p. 5-8.* Dordrecht: Springer.

Bjarnason, D. (2008). Private troubles or public issues? The social construction of the "disabled baby" in the context of social policy. In Gabel, S. L. & Danforth, S. (Eds.), *Disability and the politics of education: An international reader, p. 251-274.* New York: Peter Lang.

Gordon, L., & Morton, M. (2008). Inclusive education and school choice: Democratic rights in a devolved system. In Gabel, S. L. & Danforth, S. (Eds.), *Disability and the politics of education: An international reader, p. 237-250.* New York: Peter Lang.

Marshall, K. (2008). The reasonable adjustments duty for higher education in England and Wales. In Gabel, S. & Danforth, S. L. (Eds.), *Disability and the politics of education: An international reader, pp. 541-560.* New York: Peter Lang.

Reid, D. K., & Knight, M. G. (2006). Disability justifies exclusion of disabled students: A critical history grounded in disability studies. *Educational Researcher 35, 6, 18-23.*

Smith, P. (2010). (Ed.). *Whatever happened to inclusion? The place of students with intellectual disabilities in education.* New York: Peter Lang.

UNESCO. (1994). *Salamanca Statement and Framework for Action on Special Needs Education.* Salamanca, Spain. Retrieved July 10, 2007 from http://www.un.org/esa/socdev/enable/disovlf.html.

UNESC. (1998). *World Declaration on Higher Education for the Twenty-First Century: Vision and Action.* Retrieved July 8th, 2007 from http://www.unesco.org/education/educprog/wche/declaration_eng.htm.

VanHove, G., Roets, G., Mortier, K., DeSchauwer, E., Leroy, M., & Broekaert, E. (2008). Research in inclusive education as a possible opening to disability studies in education. In Gabel, S. L. & Danforth, S. (Eds.), *Disability and the politics of education: An international reader, p. 121-140.* New York: Peter Lang.

OF RAMPS AND REVOLVING DOORS: MY STORY

ABSTRACT

This Chapter attempts to convey to the reader a 'raw' account of my personal experience of 'inclusion'. The account touches on different aspects of my life; family, education, relationships. I do not delve into too much analysis of my own experience as i prefer to let the experience touch the reader in such a way that he/she can draw his/her own conclusions. I hope that the use of narrative "makes it possible to render [my life] in such a way that others might access something of the raw truths of [my life]" (Goodley *et al.*, 2004, p. 184). The story is narrated by me but the Editor of this Text has contributed a Preamble.

Preamble

This is the story of a 34-year-old physically disabled man.

The story of Ronald lies coated in pliability. His thinking is tremendously and excitingly elastic. He stands through with his principles, core values and beliefs. He does not compromise with his Christian values. He practices his faith ardently and enthusiastically. Ronald would also attend prayer group and Bible study sessions. He is no exhibitionist. He is low profile, but 'everyone' seems to know him! He is a symbol of success to many, especially to other disabled people. He doesn't fit the 'super-disabled' mould although he has said that he feels that he has been used as a token disabled person in the past. This chap keeps strong and is unwavering in what he believes in. It seems that his inability to change physically in certain aspects has been transferred in his ability to adapt himself. On the other hand he loves an audience if it gives him the opportunity to debate on the social paraphernalia he is entrapped in. This may sound like a freedom story but in reality Ronald makes the most complex of complexities, the most tough of harsh experiences sound simple and straightforward. He is one to reckon with.

New Born Baby

I was born 28 years ago. I was my parents' first and only child after my mother had three miscarriages. Her gynaecologist suggested that she spends most of her pregnancy in absolute bed rest, which she did.

I was born by a Caesarean section. Since my mother was still under the effect of the anaesthetic, my father was the first to know about my impairment, a medical condition known as Spina Bifida. He was also given the option to consent to an immediate surgical intervention, which I needed, without which I could not have survived for more than a couple of weeks. What was 'interesting' was the way he was 'advised' about this...although rather implicitly, he was encouraged to "let nature take its course" because..."*anyway...with or without the operation, my life in the future will not be anything similar to what parents dream for their children...he would not be able to do this, that and the other".* Thankfully, my father, in spite of this 'wise talk', consented to the surgery.

The surgery entailed, that I had to be transferred to another hospital. Before I was relocated to this other hospital, my father wanted my mother to see me and hold me at least a couple of minutes (this could have been the last time she had the opportunity to do so). As I already said, she was still under the effect of the anaesthetic, but she remembers seeing my feet a little bit bluish! This little incident was relevant, because when my father, eventually told her that I was transferred to the general hospital, he did not tell her immediately about my condition, but told her that I needed a little bit of oxygen. Having observed my bluish feet, she believed this story.

My mother had to stay in hospital for some more days. One fine day, she asked my father to bring her something to read. He went home to my grandma and asked one of my mother's sisters to give her some stuff to read. She had just bought a *Reader's Digest* edition, which she gave him to give it to my mum (without having read it herself yet).

When my mother was reading this *Reader's Digest*, she came across a story about a couple who had just had a baby with a 'strange condition' known as 'Spina Bifida'. This story was about the struggle with coming to terms with the fact that they did not consent for a surgery, which was required for their son's survival. Eventually, the baby died. This story set my mum thinking about what she would have done where she in their situation! She thought she would surely have given the baby the chance to live, to survive.

That day, my father went to visit her as usual and she started discussing this story with him...one can imagine what my father felt when hearing this! Obviously, he could not tell her all this, there and then! When, eventually, it was time for her to leave hospital and she asked my father to take her to see me, he had to tell her that "something was wrong"...when she asked him what was it that I had, his answer was: *"Bhal tal-ktieb!* (The book's same story!)" Eventually, she interpreted the *"Reader's Digest"* incident as the way through which God prepared her for what was to come!

The Patient

It was obvious that I needed frequent medical attention, and my parents used to take me to hospital to visit various consultants, at least three times a week. In spite of this, my parents were never really informed about my needs and most of the things they had to learn themselves. They could sense an almost total lack of support. I was very often quite sick, and when I was eleven months old, they could not take it any longer, and decided to seek consultation abroad. Obviously, they needed some sort of referral, or at least some medical information about my condition. The Consultant they sought advice from listened to their story and to their concerns, and eventually gave them his feedback: "Listen...he's got so many problems, it's just no use wasting money on him!" No need to comment further on this statement!

My parents persisted, and eventually I was taken to *Queen Mary's University Hospital*, in Roehampton, UK. What immediately struck my parents was the completely different approach adopted by the doctors and other professionals there...what was important was not that the 'glass was half empty', but that 'it was half full'. I was a human being who had a potential to lead a fulfilling life if only I had the necessary support, something which my parents were all for giving me!

I was taken to that same hospital one other time with my parents paying all the expenses. In 1977, I needed another urgent operation, and since the doctors in Malta were on industrial action, the government had no alternative other than to send me to have the operation abroad. I was taken to the same hospital I had been before. I remained their patient for the years to come, and the government used to send me for check-ups and/or interventions at least once a year, up till 1992, when my condition was considered stable, and when the UK doctors decided that I could be adequately followed by doctors, surgeons, and other professionals locally.

Breaking a Leg or Two

When it was time for me to start my schooling, my parents opted for mainstream schooling, again in spite of going against what was being suggested to them by some local professionals. The people at the first kindergarten school they went to, were not too keen to accept me (the nun 'could not cope with my needs', even though my mother offered all her help and support), and another school in the vicinity was approached. This time the problem was that the class was already full, but I was accepted anyway. My mother used to come to school every single day during mid-day break to see to my needs. Although the concept was not at all known at the time, she was fulfilling the role of my Learning Support Assistant. A very good "working relationship" was developed between my mother and the nun who was teaching me, so that my personal, social and educational needs could be addressed adequately.

After a scholastic year in this kindergarten school, it was time for me to move to a primary school. Again a school in the vicinity was chosen. Yet again, my mother went to the school before the beginning of the scholastic year to speak to the person who was to be my teacher. She was hesitant in the beginning because it was her first such experience, but seeing that my mother was willing to offer all her support, she decided to give me a chance. What was fascinating was the fact that after about three weeks of me being in her class, my teacher felt that she had to apologise with my mother for being so hesitant initially. Again, even during this year, my mother used to come to school every single day during mid-day break to see to my personal needs. Moreover, I had absolutely no problem in participating in all the activities in class. My classmates did not only 'accept' me as one of them, it was simply natural for them to give me the support in those circumstances - I wanted it from them. What was sometimes annoying were the comments my mother used to hear from some of my classmates' parents - concerns that my presence in their children's classroom could in a way hinder the fast and steady progress of their children's education.

Things proceeded well for the next two years. I was just a typical boy. I participated in class activities and always found ways to do things my own way. I once 'defended' myself from one of my classmates by almost running over his feet with my wheelchair, with all the strength I had. Were it not for the fact that my mother was watching, this poor fellow, would surely have ended with a broken leg or two!

13

Speaking of my mother, it is important for me to point out that both my parents disciplined me whenever it was necessary (the above example was a case in point!). They always demanded from teachers that I be given the grades and marks that I deserved, no more, no less!

When I was to start my fourth year at primary school, the first major difficulty with physical accessibility arose. My classroom was to be in the second floor. There was no lift installed in the school. When my mother went to speak to the Headmaster to see what support we could get, this guy was anything but helpful! His solution was for me to move to a 'special school' where I could have all the necessary support. Obviously, my mother was furious, but at the same time she felt helpless! Going out of the school after the meeting, she coincidentally met a friend of hers, who happened to have her husband who worked with the *Education Department*. She offered her help and later during the day phoned my mother to tell her that according to an *Education Department* official, it was my right that my classroom is moved to the ground floor in the same school. The headmaster had no option other than to accept this decision, and things proceeded smoothly from then on.

The Piano

My life, even then, did not consist of just hospitals and schools. Through the constant encouragement I received from my parents to try and develop my potential as much as possible, I was always very eager to participate in extra-curricular activities.

One fine day, I announced to my mother that I wanted to play the piano. She said, "OK…fine!" She approached one music teacher:

"My son wants to learn the piano. Would you teach him?"
"Can he make any use of his legs?"
"No"
"A piano has pedals…they are important! If he can't use them, I can't see how he'll be able to study the instrument effectively".
"Oh…really!?! OK…thank you very much then!"
Obviously, my mother being the way she is, was not to be discouraged so easily. She approached another teacher:
"My son wants to learn the piano. Would you teach him?"
"Of course! Can he read the alphabet?"
"Not yet."
"When he is able to do so, please contact me".
"What about the pedals?"
"What about them?"
"He can't use his legs."
"Let's take things one step at a time. Pedals are important for higher grades…we'll see what we can do about them, when we get there!"
Eventually, I learnt the alphabet, and eventually I started my piano lessons. When I reached the point where I was to use the pedals, my teacher wrote to the Examining Board abroad and explained the situation. Their reply was:

"OK, no problem, he can sit for examinations just the same. The examiner will be informed about the situation and will examine him on other important aspects of piano playing".

I managed to reach Grade 8 level, and had to stop only because of other commitments.

I Want to Play Soccer!

Piano lessons were not my only extra curricular activity. I was involved in quite a number of other things. This meant that I needed support especially from both my parents. My father was taking me here and there himself. The lack of an adequate transport service, which was accessible for my needs, proved to be a problem when I started schooling at a Church run College after my first four years at a State School.

My father used to take me to school himself, before he started work at 7:00am. This meant that I usually had to be at school by about 6:40am every single day. Thus at a young age, I had to get used to getting up really early so that my parents could help me get organised for school.

Life at secondary school was fun although not barrier-free. I had problems with accessibility. My classroom was situated in the second floor. However, this time, I had the support to make way there because older boys were given a roster to help me to get to wherever I needed to go. There were occasional problems. I remember being carried by one of my teachers single-handedly (a very frightening experience I must say!) down two flights of stairs because the people who were supposed to come to help somehow did not turn up!

Apart from the accessibility issue, I had all the necessary support from all the teachers. Again, my mother used to come to school every day for the first four years I remained at College. This helped in building a relationship with my teachers, enabling problems to be sorted out as soon as they cropped up.

Again, I was actively involved in extra curricular activities. A particular experience is worth mentioning. It was my first year at secondary school and the PE teacher came in class to take the names of those boys who were interested in taking part in the soccer league. Obviously, I put up my hand! He started taking names and left me to the very end. When it was finally my turn, he looked at me perplexed! I read his mind and anticipated whatever he was going to say; *"please sir, may I be the Team Coach?"*, irrespective of the fact that I hardly knew that a football is a round object made of leather, and that a soccer team is made up of 11 players. What was important for me was that I participate in as many activities as possible - which I did!

Writing Like a Hen!

When I was in my second year at College, I needed to undergo a major surgery in my back. I had to be taken to the UK for this to be done, and we knew that our stay there would not have been a brief one.

I was almost eleven years old at the time and so I was to be admitted to a children's ward in the hospital. However, when I was to be admitted, there was a boy who had chicken pox or measles or whatever, and so they couldn't admit new patients there. I was placed in the teenagers ward. It was a blessing in disguise! I was the youngest among them all, but I managed to integrate fully with all my fellow patients in the Ward. The staff there was fantastic! We used to be given syringes to play with, which we used to fill with whatever liquid we had on our bedside, after which we all engaged in 'fierce' water fights!

What was important in the experience was the fact that the doctors and other professionals always and unfailingly explained to me clearly and with a language I could understand, whatever was going to happen to me. This gave me my dignity and helped me understand.

Although I have beautiful memories of the experience at Stanmore, it was not all plain-sailing. During the operation, I had a cardiac arrest, which according to the doctors lasted for five-and-a-half minutes. When they finally managed to resuscitate me, the doctors were more than 100% positive that I had brain damage, considering the length of time that my brain was starved of oxygen. According to my parents, I did show signs of brain damage, but with their perseverance, and with them continuously talking to me not to let my brain go to sleep, I somehow managed to get over it in 10 days. Even after that, my motor skills were affected (my handwriting looked more like the 'finger' printing of a hen left to roam about on a piece of paper). It required hard work and constant support to get back to almost the same point I was before.

Some Teachers are Good

When we got back to Malta, I had to make up what I had lost in school. It is worth mentioning here, that while I was in the UK, one thing that helped me tremendously was the fact that some teachers used to write to me frequently, informing me what they were doing in class. This helped me tremendously both as a means of keeping in touch and also as a means of keeping my morale high!

When I was back in Malta, teachers used to come to us at home to help me make up for what I had lost. Although it was hard work, considering that it was a very hot summer and that I had a plaster jacket from neck to waist, we managed to get through as well.

Eventually, it was time for me to start preparing for my O-levels. One particular teacher offered to coach me through this "ordeal". He helped me prepare a plan so as not to sit for the examinations all in one setting. He helped me get the necessary support in the subjects I needed most. He also made me aware that I had a right for extra time during examinations to compensate for my slow writing. This proved to be very useful. Eventually, I sat for the examinations successfully. Often, other arrangements had to be made, especially when it came to choosing examination venues that were accessible to me.

Chemical Ron

My natural next step was to start studying for my A-levels. I chose the science subjects. I had decided to remain at the sixth form of the same school I was in. I must say I was a bit angry, because the sixth form complex had just been built, but it lacked necessary amenities for people with a physical disability. The biggest problem was that there was no lift. I had to be carried one or two flights of steps two or three times a week because the laboratories and the library were in the upper floors.

This time the problem of accessibility was a little bit more complex for me. At that age, I was becoming more self-conscious then when I was a child and the fact that I had to be carried in front of other students that also included girls, was sometimes a bit difficult to handle.

As I said, I had chosen to study the sciences. When it came to chemistry, the teachers taught that it would be too dangerous for me to handle certain chemicals because of my reduced manual dexterity. So, their solution to the problem, was for me to drop chemistry and choose another subject (for example, religious studies or philosophy). They summoned my parents to tell them about their suggestion, without me knowing, even though I was 16 years old!

We refused to give in to their pressure and wrote to the examining board abroad. They replied saying that there was absolutely no ground for me to be asked to drop a subject I wanted to study. They suggested that I participate in all the practical sessions like other students with one of my classmates helping me to handle the chemicals, which could be dangerous for me, were they to make contact with my skin. They also granted me exemption from the practical sessions of the A-level examinations. The marks allotted for the practical sessions where distributed evenly among the other papers.

Eventually, I successfully obtained my A-levels in Maths, Physics, Chemistry and Biology.

Of Ramps and Revolving Doors

After Sixth Form, I wanted to go to University to study Physics and computer science. I knew that the place was not very accessible, and thus the summer before the commencement of the academic year, we went to meet the people responsible to see what arrangements needed to be done. This exercise proved to be very useful. I was given a power wheelchair because the ramps were steep due to the limitations imposed by the infrastructure.

We made sure that I had access to whatever I needed for my academic work. The apparatus I needed was transferred from a laboratory in an upper floor to another one in ground floor. My father, for the umpteenth time throughout my school years, made another desk, which was accessible and comfortable for me. Lecturers made themselves available to help me sort out any problems I might have encountered.

In spite of all this, there were some problems that remained with me till the very end. Access to the student house was non-existent and when a lift was finally installed, it was used as a service lift. This meant that to access it I had to use a back door, pass through an area where garbage bags were stacked, and when I finally made it to the lift, I often found myself accompanied by a tray or two of pizzas and Maltese pastries.

Another problem was the University Library. A revolving door had just been installed. There was no way I could pass through it with my wheelchair and so, every time I needed to go into the Library, I had to wait for someone to go get the key to a side-door, a key which was very often misplaced. This meant that most often, I could not manage to get to do the work I needed to do because of the time wasted prior to my even getting into the library.

There were problems that were slightly beyond my control. For example, I often found myself blocked, because I needed to use a ramp, after having found that 'some kind-hearted' individual parked immediately in front of it; when I wanted to use the ATM, which was way too high for me; when I wanted to use a newly installed lift in which I barely managed to get in it being so narrow.

At University I also had my first formal IEP (Individual Educational Programme). Since the Course I opted for was proving to be a bit too taxing on my physical stamina, I asked that something be done about it. I was eventually given the opportunity to finish the course in twice the amount of years, and also to be assessed by whatever the individual Lecturer deemed fit, and not necessarily by test or examination. These arrangements proved to be very useful.

Eventually, I opted to change course, to study management and public policy, getting the degree after three years. The constant support I received from most of the Lecturers was amazing. My graduation day was an important landmark, because it was my way of reaping the fruits of all the effort over the years, and my way of showing appreciation to my parents and to all those individuals who supported me in one way or another. Another issue worth mentioning was the fact that by the time I started my University degree, an accessible transport service was set up, which proved to be crucial for me to be able to pursue my dream of getting the degree I was after. Even though I must say, the service was not completely hassle-free!

Saturday Night Fever

Over the years, one thing that I always felt missing as I started growing up, was a group of peers, especially for Saturday night activities. University life helped in this respect as well. One of my extra curricular activities at University was my involvement with the *Catholic Movement*. Through this involvement, I managed to build a circle of friends. This circle of friends is important to me up to this very day.

What I miss sometimes is a lack of close disabled friends. I have always grown up in an almost exclusively non-disabled environment. Although this had it's positive aspect, it also had its negatives. I always 'competed' with non-disabled people, and my targets were those that were important for other non-disabled persons. As a consequence, such issues as being able to do certain important things (e.g. self-care) on my own, were never given importance, and I found myself lagging behind in these areas up to this very day.

Bridging the Gap

A very important landmark in my life is when eventually, about four months after I graduated, I found the job I am in now.

I must say that I am very lucky to be in this job. I enjoy the contact with the disability field; I greatly appreciate the constant support from my colleagues and friends; I am continuously challenged to work towards becoming a better, more efficient, more-capable-of-doing-it-on-my-own person; to develop my potential further. My colleagues understand the needs that arise from my physical condition and were/are willing to accommodate for them when this was/is necessary. All this has helped me to eventually start thinking seriously about starting to develop further support systems, such as the recruitment of a personal assistant and getting my own transport organised.

Feelings

Having a disability for me does not mean that one is condemned to a tragic life, as my parents were made to believe as soon as I was born. Challenges exist all the time, but every hurdle one manages to surpass, makes one stronger. One hurdle I am working towards at the moment, is giving myself permission to feel. More importantly doing something about those 'feelings' - all the range of possible human emotions, be it anger, loneliness, sadness or love. I still have a long way to go, but I will get there - eventually!

Thinking Point 1:
After having read the chapter, what are your thoughts about the 'voice' of the protagonist in relation to his story? Do you think the protagonist feels that his 'voice' has been respected in the course of his life story?
Thinking Point 2:
Now think about the relationships which the protagonist had with the various individuals he encountered in the course of his life story? What was the nature of these relationships?
Thinking Point 3:
Think about the influence which society's cultural (e.g. general attitude towards disabled people) and structural (e.g. accessibility) aspects had on the quality of life of the protagonist in the story.

REFERENCE

Goodley, D., Lawthom, R., Clough, P., & Moore, M. (2004). *Researching life stories – method, theory and analysis in a biographical.* London: Routledge & Falmer Press.

THE DISABILITY MOVEMENT IN THE MAKING
(AND INCLUSIVE EDUCATION)

ABSTRACT

Education keeps featuring as a crucial constituent in our social fabric due to the ever increasing demands in the industry and services sector. It has often been claimed by politicians and policy makers that our main and probably only resource is the 'individual's skills and competencies. Inclusive education and the broader disability issues are fundamental ingredients in the weaving of this tapestry. An important question that all students and their parents ask is 'what will I do in the future?' The school community needs to endeavor to make inclusion work within a school environment that is conducive to the learning and growth of all.

Introduction: Conceptualising Disability Studies

Disability Studies applies social, cultural, historical, and philosophical perspectives to the study of disability in society. The *Fundamental Principles of Disability* (UPIAS & The Disability Alliance, 1976) is a major piece of writing that has influenced greatly our thinking and perception of disability studies all over the Western hemisphere. It is a colossal piece of work with a vision that can still be considered valid even some thirty-five years after its publication. Way back in the mid-70's the UPIAS was already proposing a social theory of disability that had the objective of transforming the landscape of our understanding of disability (UPIAS & The Disability Alliance, 1976; Barnes & Oliver, 1995; Drewett, 1999).

> the alternative struggle proposed by the Union is logically developed from a social theory of disability ... We ourselves look for our expertise to the wealth of talent and intellectual imagination of disabled people, which will be freed for expression once we contemplate our own situation from our own collective experience (UPIAS & The Disability Alliance, 1976, p. 20).

Disability Studies to my understanding is:
- based on the experiences of disabled people;
- relates to the NGOs that represent this minority;
- adopts a cross-disability perspective;
- views disability as a social construct;
- adopts a transdisciplinarity approach;
- recognises the role of family members;
- interprets social needs and emancipates in its teaching and research;
- adopts the social model of disability as its foremost theoretical paradigm.

Disabled people continue to be excluded from mainstream society. This is particularly apparent in education and employment where disabled people remain under-represented. World estimates indicate there are 500 million disabled people. The disabled population is characterized by unemployed and/or unemployable people who lack formal qualifications. For this to change we require political will, coming from politicians and policy makers but most notably from disabled people themselves (and their organisations). Disability studies is a call to remind disabled people that they deserve and have a right to have a place in society, that they are valued and significant citizens and that society must change to embrace their needs - rather than having to adapt to a disabling environment. Disability studies is also about a commitment to the social model of disability, a political concern that embraces inclusion.

> Independent Living means that we demand the same choices and control in our every-day lives that our non-disabled brothers and sisters, neighbours and friends take for granted. We want to grow up in our families, go to the neighbourhood school, use the same bus as our neighbours, work in jobs that are in line with our education and interests, and start families of our own. Since we are the best experts on our needs, we need to show the solutions we want, need to be in charge of our lives, think and speak for ourselves - just as everybody else. To this end we must support and learn from each other, organize ourselves and work for political changes that lead to the legal protection of our human and civil rights. As long as we regard our disabilities as tragedies, we will be pitied. As long as we feel ashamed of who we are, our lives will be regarded as useless. As long as we remain silent, we will be told by others what to do (Adolf Ratzka, 2003, http://www.independentliving.org, Accessed 8/7/2004).

Positioning Education

Culture and interpretation is at the foundation of understanding the symbols that the school institution is engrossed in (Ritzer, 1996). The educational structures have always been thought of as developing a model of adult behaviour. The centrality of the notion of culture depends on its rapport with understanding meaning, positionality and the relationship that develops between power and ideology (Allies, 1999; Goodson & Sikes, 2001). The ethos, or rather the range of values and beliefs, which identify the atmosphere in a school, is central to the understanding of school life. The values we tend to disseminate in our schools are infused by Catholic influences.

The Agenda

There are two important annotations I need to make at this point. Firstly, inclusive education is turning out to be a cliché - a politically correct term that is used for speeches and for policy-makers to silence all woes. Secondly, 'inclusion' is an encompassing term. This word is full to capacity with arguments, disputes and contestations. But what is inclusion fundamentally? Is 'inclusion' an end in itself or is it a process that starts in school but has to find its fulfillment in adult life? What audit processes do we need to engage in to have apposite 'inclusion'? Using the term 'inconclusive education' as opposed to 'inclusive education' is no wisecrack. The debate on 'inclusion' is an ongoing, eternal process. This in itself can have its positives, but it is also a situation, which brings to my mind circumstances whereby 'inclusion' has a preface but no end to it. It very often turns out to be a philosophical debate rather than a strategic framework. It is described by Allan (1999) as 'a state of unsettled uncertainty'. 'Inclusion' is also about positioning the special school debate. I feel that in the local context we may still look down on special schools and on the virtuous work they have been responsible for in the past. This is not right. We need to look at educational processes as all chipping into the weaving of this educational fabric. However, special schooling, in my estimation, is diametrically opposed to having an inclusion strategy that teaches in remoteness rather than enclosure, in privacy rather than attachment. Children learn when they are together, encapsulated in the same experiences, interacting together (Salend, 2006). Having said all this, what are the arguments that will help us iron these folds? These are some fundamental questions we need to ask in the 'inclusion' debate: In what way can the stories of children at the margins expose issues of 'inclusion' and exclusion? What are the different perspectives of parent and disabled activists, teachers, academics, labeled students, para-professionals and others in relation to presenting a transformative agenda for 'inclusion'? Are we pinning our ears back to parental expertise? It is necessary to create an 'inclusion' movement. This is no longer an isolated issue that interests the few. It is a debate that has a great deal of social and economic implications on the Island. Inclusive education can be analysed within a number of varied frameworks; the cultural, historical, political and social (Armstrong, 1999). However, 'inclusion' is fundamentally an elaborate interaction that is taking place within the social structures we are engaged in. We need to interpret this combination of issues and decipher emerging problems contained in this complex intermix of 'inclusion' discourses. 'Inclusion' even in Malta is a contemporary debate in education that raises noticeable discussion and argumentation but regrettably remains a dispassionate topic, with shallow exchanges. Policymakers, politicians, academics, service providers, disabled activists and parents appear to be at different polarities.

Lack of public education and the invisibility of disability from the public sphere is still rampant. This is compounded by an often patronizing and charitable media representation of disability, a media hardly up to date on current terminology. Genuine spaces need to be created for the articulation of disabled people's voices. Across-ministerial, across-sectorial and across-stakeholder collaborations are required to tackle the current fragmentation. A research agenda needs to be developed via a strategic alliance with the *University of Malta* so that the latter will take on board the responsibility of coordinating emancipatory funded research to partner this minority.

Disability Issues: Salient Characteristics and Milestones

> I don't think anyone knows for sure what a disability movement is but essentially what we are talking about is a set of ideas and an analysis which people can then support in different ways. I always think of the movement as a set of people that have somehow made a connection with a set of ideas (Lisicki cited in Campbell & Oliver, 1997, p. 21).

In Malta, going by WHO estimates, over 30,000 people have an impairment and some 80,000 family members are directly or indirectly impacted by this reality. The visibility of disabled people in the public sphere is a relatively recent phenomenon. The influence of Catholicism and the dominance of its institutions in the 'treatment and care' of disabled people has left an indelible mark. This influence is prevailing in the charitable views of disability that persist till this day with a staunch medicalised view alongside charity. In this last decade, the disability community in Malta has made significant progress on the "services" dimension but has fallen short in policy (Fulcher, 1999). What previously focused on charity-based and individualised initiatives, is now emerging as a package of community services and new plans in the health, social and educational spheres. There has been an interesting increase in public awareness with certain disability issues finding their way onto the national agenda. However, locally we look as if we have given a lot of impetus to "needs based initiatives" and focused almost exclusively on the manufacturing of new services, whereby versatility and individuality have been sacrificed for cubby hole provision.

Disabled people in Malta have also been silenced by the fears that non-disabled citizens have created. The politics of "difference" within the disability community began to be recognised only very recently most notably following the establishment of the *National Commission Persons with Disability* in 1987, even though the *National Parents' Society for Persons with Disability* and the *Federation of Organisation for Disabled Persons* were quite active in their own right, but steered mainly by the parent activist lobby. Locally, 1980 has been taken as the pivotal year because of the *UN Decade for Disabled Persons (1981-1990)*.

Despite the changing discourse around disability, the disability act, the *UN Convention*, the situation of disabled people in Malta seems to be still precarious in the social, economic and political sphere. Although this may sound like a broad generalistion, really and truly this is a very typical situation for disabled people. The situation of disabled people's employment is typified by long-term unemployment or unemployability. The perception is that disabled people are unproductive and dangerous to have around. Physical barriers, lack of transportation, over dependence on family members and perceived excessive protection keep disabled people in a rut. Children missing school repeatedly because of clinics and therapeutic sessions and the fact that programs are held during school hours with no proof of an organised and structured system. There seems to be a general unwillingness by the community to make public services accessible physically. Welfare benefits and non-contributory pensions are attractive as alternatives to effective engagement in the country's economy. Lack of public education on disability issues tops the list. To add insult to injury our lack of resources is further perpetuated by lack of cooperation between different stakeholders involved in disabled people's lives.

Disabled people remain particularly disadvantaged in the area of education. Unequal access and inferior quality of education for disabled people, despite the frequent reference to inclusive education, is very evident. Many parents are often forced to place their children in segregated schools because there is a lack of alternatives or else mainstream schools are not equipped well-enough to see to the needs of these students. Lack of trained teachers and often inadequately trained learning support assistants in mainstream schools is another weak link in the system. The frequent assignment of an LSA to an individual child rather than cooperating with the class teacher, means the child is further isolated from the rest of the class. Fragmented coordination between the school, teachers and other parties is also a characteristic we could do without. On one hand policy-makers and politicians petition for a different type of learning, the eradication of segregation and a never ending list of proposals and on the other hand, provisions and structures seem to favour exclusion (Thomas & Loxely, 2001).

The following are the salient milestones in the disability field in Malta. In this way one can get an overview of the way disability related services, policy and provision have developed over the years.

Table 1: Disability Milestones in Malta

1890s	The first charitable organisations with a strong religious foundation started opening their doors to disability but focusing largely on people with social problems, with the objective of moral regeneration.
1953	The *Education Division* opens the first Educational Sub-Normal (ESN) school.
1956	The *Education Division* opens a special school for deaf children.
1963	The Catholic Church opens a large residential hospital for persons with disability based on charity funding (*Dar tal-Providenza* – 'House of Providence').
1964	The *Department of Social Security* starts giving a non-contributory pension to blind people.
1966	The *Education Division* opens a school for emotionally disturbed children.
1966	The *Ministry of Finance* starts offering tax exemption for persons with disability and their families on the purchase of a new private car that would have required specialised adaptations.
1969	The *Department of Employment* enacted a law called *Disabled Persons (Employment) Act, 1969*, which in essence states that all companies having more than 20 people are to employ a person with a disability for every 20 people employed. The application of this legislation fails despondently.
1970	The *Education Division* opens a special unit/class within a mainstream primary school in Gozo. This service is till being offered to date.
1973	The *Police Force* started issuing the Blue Sticker for all cars that are used by persons with disability or/and their families. These sticker holders are allowed to park in reserved parking bays.
1974	The *Department of Social Security* extended the non-contributory pension to more "categories" of persons with disability.
1976	The *Kindergarten for the Handicapped* (Parents' Group) was established. In 1987. The group changed its name to the *Parents' Society for Handicapped Children* and later of to the *National Parents Society for Persons with Disability*.
1979	The *Department of Social Security* opens the first Adult Training Centre for people with learning disabilities and for blind people.
1982	The *Department of Social Security* opens another *Adult training Centre* for persons with disability in Gozo.

24

1982	The *Education Division* opens a new ESN (Educational Sub-Normal) special school.
1984	A consultative committee is set up between the *Federation of Organisations for Persons with Disability*, the *Ministry of Education*, the *Ministry of Health* and the *Ministry of Social Policy*.
1986	The *Department of Housing* inaugurates a scheme for persons with disability to improve their home.
1987	Two more *Adult Training Centres* for persons with disability are inaugurated.
1987	The *National Commission for the Handicapped* is set up later changed its name to the *National Commission Persons with Disability*.
1988	The *Department of Social Security* introduces a special allowance for children with disability.
1988	People with disability started being entitled to have a keep clear parking bay in front of their house following application.
1988	The *National Commission Persons with Disability (NCPD)* and the *Federation of Organisations for Persons with Disability* start organising a week of activities to focus attention on disability issues.
1989	The *Education Division* launches another special school, this time for children with severe learning and physical disabilities.
1989	A Non-Governmental Organisation, *Corradino Physically Rehabilitation Fund* (PHRF), is given the funds by Government to start a computer lab for the training of people with disability.
1989	Persons with disability are positively discriminated in housing schemes to encourage them to live independently. Community services are not developed in tandem making the scheme another 'white elephant'.
1989	A national seminar, "The Journey Ahead: Principles and Policies for Disabled Persons and their Families" was organised by the *Parents' Society for Handicapped Children*, the *Health Department and the NCPD*.
1989	A community home, *Dar il-Wens* (meaning, Home of Support), on the initiative of a voluntary organisation of persons with disability, started offering services to ten people with learning difficulties.
1990	The national telephone company introduces new specialised services for the deaf community.
1990	The *NCPD* introduces the Special Identity Card for people with disability.
1990	The *NCPD* publishes an information booklet, which brings together benefits and services for people with disability and their families.
1990	The *Ministry of Social Policy* signs an agreement to set up the first community home (ten residents) for people with learning difficulties.
1990	A support group, *Katina ('Chain')*, was formed. It was controlled and managed by persons with disability.
1990	Polices on accessibility, were introduced in a National Structure Plan.
1991	The *NCPD* and the *National Parents' Society for People with Disability* established the *Foundation for Respite Care Services*.
1991	The *NCPD* set up a special assistance scheme to provide financial support for persons with disability hoping that more persons with disability live independently.

1991	An in-home care support service, emergency round the clock telephone service and a handyman service started being offered.
1992	The *Education Division* opened a new special school for the blind, visually impaired and deaf students.
1992	The *NCPD* starts publishing a newsletter bi-annually.
1992	The *Ministry of Finance* starts giving tax exemption on computers purchased by persons with disability.
1992	An *Action Research Project* started. It was a programme that saw the Institute of Health Care at the *University of Malta* researching disability "needs" and providing services or *ad hoc* action plans as required. This project came to an end in 1994.
1992	The *Ministry of Social Policy* provided funds for the purchasing of a computer lab for the *Muscular Dystrophy Support Group*.
1992	The *NCPD* organises a national survey to provide data that would assist planning and implementation of policy. A national register of persons with disability is set up.
1993	The *NCPD* published a national policy on special education.
1993	A computer lab for blind disabled people started operating.
1993	A disability studies program started being offered at *University* at across-faculty level. This course is co-ordinated and delivered primarily by persons with disability, parent activists and a few professional allies.
1993	Malta signed the *Standard Rules on the Equalisation of Opportunities for Persons with Disabilities*.
1994	A new *Foundation for Independent Living*, which focused on offering specialised transportation services was established.
1995	The *NCPD* published a national policy on employment for persons with disability. The *1969 Employment Act* was amended to incorporate the responsibilities of the newly set up *Employment and Training Corporation (*ETC*)*.
1995	A *Child Development Assessment Unit* (CDAU) started offering services to assess children. The *Department of Health* is running this service.
1995	*Dar Nazareth ('Nazareth Home')*, a community home based on the principles of Jean Vanier was inaugurated. This home is administered by a clergyman.
1995	A specialised unit within the *ETC* was set up to monitor employment needs and issues related.
1996	The *Transport Authority* decided that all new public transport vehicles are to be accessible for people with disability. A committee was created to monitor all developments in this regard.
1996	A social work service for persons with disability and their families was set up within the *Social Welfare Development Programme* (SWDP).
1997	The Catholic Church opened a new community home, *Dar iz-Zerniq*.
1998	The Minister of Education Hon. Evarist Bartolo MP set up a Ministerial Committee on Inclusive Education which brought together all "parties" involved in inclusive education, the CDAU, the *Education Division*, NGO's, *Health Department* and voluntary groups for disabled people.
1998	A "legal notice" officially established *Statementing*. Another important milestone in service provision.

1998	"Teachers, change and the struggle or inclusive education", a presentation by Professor Len Barton at a Conference held by the *Malta Union of Teachers*.
1999	A comprehensive report delineating the residential services was presented to Government.
1999	The *Ministry of Education* commissioned a report on the status and future role of special schools.
1999	Professor Mike Oliver, Professor in disability studies at the *University of Greenwich*, Professor Len Barton from the *University of Sheffield*, author and editor of various writings on disability and Ms. Joy Oliver a trained counsellor, who is particularly interested in working with disabled people gave a one week seminar on disability issues. This was a landmark Conference especially when it came to disabled people leading activism.
2000	An *Equal Opportunities Act (Persons with Disability, 2000)* was enacted through Parliament.
2000	The *NCPD* participated in the screening process prior to starting negotiations with the European Union. An "EU desk" was set up within the *Federation of Organisations for Persons with Disability*. Mr. Joe Bugeja, a disabled person with a Masters in European Studies, manages this "desk".
2004	An *Inclusive and Special Education Review* (Spiteri Report) was unveiled following wide ranging consultation.
2008	Malta is the signatory of the Optional Protocol of the *UN Convention on the rights of Persons with Disability*.
2009	A report on 'Special Schools Reform' prompted by the *Education Department*.

Where to from here?

Finkelstein & Stuart (1996) define the Social Model of Disability as a model that:

> Incorporates a holistic interpretation of the situation facing disabled people. It suggests that people with physical and mental impairments can have satisfying life-styles as disabled people if the focus of attention is shifted towards the removal of disabling barriers rather than concentration only on the rehabilitation of disabled individuals (p. 171).

We need to get away from pathologizing disability and perceiving it as a welfare dilemma. Disability is an experience of social oppression through political and economic factors that seem to be influenced by a capitalist and consumer-driven paradigm. Disability is also interpreted as being a symptom of social oppression and impairment is the physical representation of this dimension. This social construction is not about or caused by the body (or some impairment), but it collides on the body. Impairment and discrimination have a massive impact on the life of this minority - in different proportions at different times.

The disabled community essentially requires a stronger disability voice at all levels and a forceful presence of parent and student participation in the organisation of school communities. Schools need to contribute to create an inclusion policy that starts from school and continues in 'adult' society. The purposes and the values of inclusive education are to be re-examined and re-thought but at the same time intertwined in the creation of new strategies for more effective provision. We need to develop new creative relationships in a very different World and diverse communities with dissimilar pressures and realities. Inclusion is at the core in initiating and bargaining active and effective citizenship.

Thinking Point 1:
In what way are the 'principles of inclusion' relevant to the school community? How would you describe a culture of inclusion?
Thinking Point 2:
What are the factors that perpetuate oppression?
Thinking Point 3:
'I believe in *inclusion'*. Discuss.

REFERENCES

Ainscow, M. (1995). Special needs through school improvement: School improvement through special needs. In Clark, C., Dysonm A. & Millward, A. (Eds.). *Towards inclusive schools.* London: David Fulton Publishers.

Ainscow, M. (1999). *Understanding the development of inclusive schools.* London: Routledge/Falmer Press.

Ainscow, M., Booth T & Dyson, A. (1999). Inclusion and exclusion in schools: Listening to some hidden voices. In Ballard, K. (Ed.). *Inclusive education: International voices on disability and justice.* London: Falmer Press.

Allan, J. (1999). I don't need this: Acts of transgression by students with special educational needs. In Ballard, K. *Inclusive education - international voices on disability and justice.* London: Falmer Press.

Allyn, J. (2000). Journeys in inclusive education: profiles. In Clough, P. & Corbett, J. *Theories of inclusive education - a student's guide.* London: Paul Chapman Publishing Limited.

Appelbee, E. (1998). Inclusive learning - a community approach. Proceedings of the North of England Education Conference Bradford, 5-9th January 1998.

Armstrong, F. (1999). Inclusion, curriculum and the struggle for space in school *International Journal of Inclusive Education, Volume 3 (1), 75-87.*

Armstrong, F. & Barton, L. (1999). (Eds.). *Difference and difficulty: Insights, issues and dilemmas.* London: Impact Graphics.

Armstrong, F., Armstrong, D. & Barton, L. (2000). (Eds.). *Inclusive education - policy, contexts and perspectives.* London: David Fulton Publications.

Avramadis, E. & Norwich, B. (2002). Teachers attitudes towards integration/inclusion: review of the literature. *The European Journal of Special Needs Education, Volume 17 (2), 129-147.*

Azzopardi, A. (2000). *Understanding disability politics in Malta: New directions explored.* Unpublished Masters Dissertation, University of Sheffield.

Azzopardi, A. (2003). *A case study of a Parents' support group in Malta. The concepts of 'Inclusion. Exclusion and disabling barriers' are analysed in the relationship that parents have with professionals. Disability and Society Volume 15 (7). 1065-1072.*

Azzopardi, A. (2003b). Inclusive education and the denial of difference: Is this the Cottonera experience? Exploring whether the discourse of inclusive education has been hijacked over standards. *International Journal of Inclusive Education Volume 7(2). April-June 2003, 159-174.*

Ballard, K. (1999). (Ed.). *Inclusive education: International voices on disability and justice.* London: Falmer Press.

Ballard, K. & MacDonald, T. (1998). New Zealand: Inclusive school, inclusive philosophy. In Booth, T. & Ainscow, M. *From them to us - an international study of inclusive education.* London: Routledge.

Barnes, C. (1997). A legacy of oppression: A history of disability in western culture. In Barton L and Oliver M (Eds.). *Disability studies: Past, present and future.* Leeds: The Disability Press.

Barnes, C. & Mercer, G. (1997). (Eds.). *Doing disability research.* Leeds: The Disability Press.

Barnes, C. & Mercer, G. (2003). *Disability.* Cambridge: Polity Press.

Barnes, C., Oliver, M. & Barton, L. (2002). (Eds.). *Disability studies today.* Cambridge: Polity Press.

Bartolo, P. (2001). Meeting the diversity of student needs: the development of policy and provisions for the education of children with disability in Malta. In Sultana R G *Yesterday's schools - readings in Maltese educational history.* San Gwann: PEG Limited (p. 203-233).

Bartolo, P. (2003). *Inclusive education is for all students.* The Times of Malta, Friday September 26th, 2003, 11.

Bartolo, P., Agius Ferrante, C., Azzopardi, A., Bason, L., Grech, L. & King, M. A. (2002). *Creating inclusive schools - guidelines for the implementation of the National Minimum Curriculum policy on inclusive education.* Sliema: Salesian Press.

Barton, L. (2000). Journeys to inclusive education: profiles and reflections. In Clough P and Corbett, J. (Eds.). *Theories of inclusive education - a students' guide.* London: Paul Chapman Publishing.

Barton, L. (2001). (Ed.). *Disability politics and the struggle for change.* London: David Fulton Publishers.

Barton, L. & Armstrong, F. (1999). (Eds.). *Difference and difficulty: Insights, issues and dilemmas.* Sheffield: University of Sheffield Press.

Barton, L. & Oliver, M. (1997). (Eds.). *Disability studies: Past, present and future.* Leeds: The Disability Press.

Bayliss, P. (2004). *'Sam': Proceedings of the 2004 Conference: Disability Studies: Putting theory into practice* held at Lancaster University. Exeter, University of Exeter.

Bernstein, B. (1999). Class, pedagogies: Visible and invisible. In Halsey A H, Lauder, H, Brown, P. & Wells, A. S. (Eds.). *Education: Culture, economy, society.* Oxford: Oxford University Press.

Bines, H, Swain, J. & Kaye, J. (1998). 'Once upon a time': Teamwork for complimentary perspectives and critique in research on special educational needs. In Clough, P. & Barton. L, (Eds.). *Articulating with difficulty: Research voices in inclusive education.* London: Paul Chapman Publishing Limited.

Black-Hawkings, K. (1999). *Close encounters of the cultural kind: The significance of culture in understanding processes of inclusion and exclusion in schools.* Paper presented at the British Educational Research Association Conference held at the University of Sussex. Sussex, University of Sussex.

Bonal, X. & Rambla, X. (1999). The recontextualisation process of educational diversity: New forms to legitimise pedagogic practice. *International Studies in Sociology of Education, Volume 9 (3), 293-313.*

Booth, T. & Ainscow, M. (1998). *From them to us - an international study of inclusion in education.* London: Routledge.

Booth, T. & Booth, W. (1993). Accentuating the positive: A personal profile of a parent with learning difficulties. *Disability, Handicap and Society, Volume 8(4).*

Booth, T. & Booth, W. (1997). Making connections: A narrative study of adult children of parents with learning disabilities. In Barnes, C. & Mercer, G. (Eds.). *Doing disability research.* Leeds: The Disability Press (p.123-141).

Booth, T., Swainm W., Mastertonm M. & Potts, P. (1992). (Eds.). *Learning for all 1 - Curricula for diversity in education.* London: Routledge and Falmer.

Boswell D M (1994). The social prestige of residential areas. In Sultana, R. G. & Baldacchino, G. (Eds.). *Maltese society: A sociological enquiry* Malta: Mireva Publications.

Bourdeau, A. & Passeron, J. (1977). *Reproduction in education, society and culture.* London: Sage.

Campbell, J. & Oliver, M. (1996). *Disability politics: Understanding our past, changing our future.* London: Routledge.

Clough, P (1998). (Ed.). *Managing inclusive education: From policy to experience.* London: Paul Chapman Publishing Limited.

Clough, P. (2002). *Narratives and fictions in educational research.* Buckingham: Open University Press.

Clough, P. & Barton, L. (1995). (Eds.). *Making difficulties: Research and the construction of SEN.* London: Paul Chapman Publishing Ltd.

Clough, P. & Barton, L. (1998). (Eds.). *Articulating with difficulty - research voices in inclusive education.* London: Paul Chapman Publishing Limited.

Clough, P. & Corbett, J. (2000). (Eds.). *Theories of inclusive education.* London: Paul Chapman Publications.

Corbett, J. (1996). *Bad-mouthing - The language of special needs.* London: the Falmer Press.

Corbett, J. (1997). Independent, proud and special: Celebrating our differences. In Barton, L. & Oliver, M. *Disability studies: Past, present and future.* Leeds: The Disability Press.

Corbett, J. (1998). *Special education needs in the twentieth century - a cultural analysis.* London: Cassell.

Corbett, J. & Slee, R. (2000). An international conversation on inclusive education. In Armstrong, F., Armstrong, D. & Barton, L. (Eds.). *Inclusive education: Policy, contexts and comparative perspectives.* London: David Fulton Publishers.

Finkelstein, V. (1987). *The naked truth* In DAIL Magazine February, 1987.

Finkelstein, V. (1991). *Working with able-bodied people* presented by Link TV, May 2nd 1991.

Finkelstein, V. (1999). A profession allied to the community: the disabled people's trade union. In Stone E *Disability and development - learning from action and research on disability in the majority world.* Leeds: The Disability Press.

Finkelstein, V. (2001). *A personal journey in to disability politics.* Paper presented at Leeds University centre for disability studies Leeds: University of Leeds.

Fulcher, G. (1999). *Disabling polices? A comparative approach to education policy and disability* Sheffield: Philip Armstrong Publications.

Goodson, I. & Sikes, P. (2001). *Life history research in educational settings.* Buckingham: Open University Press.

Moore, M. (2000). (Ed.). *Insider perspectives on inclusion - raising voices, raising issues.* Sheffield: Philip Armstrong Publications.

Morris, J. (2002). *People with physical impairments and mental health support needs: A critical review of the literature.* Unpublished.

Oliver, M. (1988). The social and political context of educational policy: the case of special needs. In Barton, L. (Ed.). *The politics of special educational needs.* London: Falmer Press.

Oliver, M. (1990). *The politics of disablement: Critical texts in social work and the welfare state.* London: Macmillan.

Oliver, M. (1996). *Understanding disability - from theory to practice.* London: Macmillan Press Limited.

Oliver, M. & Barnes, C. (1998). *Disabled people and social policy: From exclusion to inclusion.* London: Longman.

Oliver, M. & Sapey, B. (1999). (2nd edition). *Social work with disabled people.* London: Macmillan Press Limited.

Sacks, O. (1985). *The man who mistook his wife for a hat and other clinical tales.* New York: Summit Books.

Salend, S. J. (2001). (4th Edition). *Creating inclusive classrooms - effective and reflective practices.* New Jersey: Merrill Prentice Hall.

Shakespeare, T. (1998). (Ed.). *The disability reader - social science perspectives.* London: Cassell.

Sikes, P. (1997). *Parents who teach - stories from home and school.* London: Cassell.

Slee, R. (1993). (Ed.). *Is there a desk with my name on it? The politics of integration.* London: The Falmer Press.

Tregaskis, C. (2000). Interviewing non-disabled people about their disability-related attitudes: seeking methodologies. *Disability and Society, Volume 15 (2)., 343-353.*

Tregaskis, C. (2003). *Constructions of disability.* Paper presented at the Disability Studies Conference 2003 at the University of Lancaster. Sheffield: University of Sheffield.

'TO GIVE' AND THE 'SOCIAL MODEL':
TO THINK THE IMPOSSIBLE

ABSTRACT

Jacques Derrida reminds us that 'giving' is economical. Several variations of giving and receiving make true 'giving' impossible. In this Chapter I argue that discourses of models of disability and inclusion are caught in this 'giving' debate. While 'giving' is at the backbone of the Charity and Medical models, I think that very often 'giving' is the process that regulates the Social Model. It is thinking of the gift as an impossibility that allows us to reconsider the Social Model.

Introduction

> Pathway to Independent Living Programme: This is a course for school leavers with moderate learning difficulties. The course will teach independent living skills together with other basic skills and will give students the opportunity to sample areas of vocational interest to them. Throughout the programme emphasis is placed on independent living and the possibility of working in the wider community or where suitable follow another course
> (http://www.mcast.edu.mt/support_pathwaycourse.asp).

and

> Parents must be given the opportunity and supported to actively participate in the planning process and the IEP should serve as a tool for the ongoing collaboration between the school and the student's home (Ministry of Education, 2000).

The above are two examples taken from educational contexts to introduce and situate this Chapter. The *Pathway to Independent Living Programme* is a programme offered by a vocational College in Malta that has the aim of providing "universally accessible vocational and professional education and training with an international dimension, responsive to the needs of the individual and the economy" (http://www.mcast.edu.mt). Young adults with disability who have finished compulsory secondary education, often have to face the dilemma of the 'what now' question. What is next (if there is a next) in our educational journey? Are there opportunities they can relate to in their life-long learning? Such a programme is one of the answers to these questions.

The second quotation refers to the formulation of a document called *Individualised Education Programme* (IEP) which practical written plan, developed for (and hopefully with) a student with a disability, that describes the modifications and adaptations for a student's educational programme and the services necessary to ensure full access to educational entitlements according to the

National Minimum Curriculum. The IEP is a primary tool for ensuring equal opportunities, as laid out in the *National Minimum Curriculum* (see p. 1).

The accessibility of learning for all students requires tools like IEPs to ensure that the learning experience is tangible. In a content and exam oriented educational journey that characterizes the Maltese educational system, having a document that clearly summarises the student's modifications, adaptations and key stakeholders in the process is fundamental. In this way, students with an impairment have the tools to overcome some of the barriers that exclude students from full participation in learning.

If we have to leave aside the limitations, criticisms and evaluations of both examples, it can be argued that both the *Pathway to Independent Living Programme* and IEPs are working within the Social Model of Disability rationale. They are attempting to support students with impairment in participating as fully as possible in the life of Society. They are programmes aimed to break and/or compensate for some of the social and attitudinal barriers that prevent students with impairment from maximising their participation in educational contexts.

The focus of this Chapter is not to problematise these programmes but to engage with the concept of 'giving' that features regularly in these examples. As can be seen from the opening quotations, the 'Pathway to Independent Living Programme' will 'give' students the skills and opportunity to experience different vocational interests, while parents of students with impairment are given the opportunity and support to participate in IEP process and document formation. The Medical, Professional, Tragedy and Charity models work on the assumption of 'giving'. However, one needs to ask if the Social Model is also founded on the concept of 'giving'. Or is the 'giving' that takes place within the Social Model different from that which works with the other models? What is this 'giving' that is referred to by the 'Pathway to Independent Living Programme' and the IEPs? What follows in this Chapter is a problematisation of this 'giving' as very often it is assumed to be good and is taken for granted. In the following section I will show that 'giving' is a core component of the educational process and not just in the education of students with impairment. I will conceptualise this debate by making reference to some ideas from the French philosopher Jacques Derrida (1930-2004) which will be used to help unpack the idea of 'giving' in relation to the Social Model of Disability.

'Giving' in Educational Contexts: An Example

The examples of *Pathway* and *IEPs* are both taken from educational contexts, and this Chapter focuses on trying to understand the concept of 'giving' within the Social Model within the education contexts.

Following the European Parliament and Council of the 18 December 2006 (http://eurlex.europa.eu/LexUriServ/LexUriServ.do?uri=OJ:L:2006:394:0010:0018: en:PDF) which established a list of key competences for lifelong learning, the *Directorate for Quality and Standards in Education* in Malta in 2009 developed a policy entitled *National Policy and Strategy for the Attainment of Core Competences in Primary Education.* The focus of this policy is on students attending the primary cycle of education (early years) acquiring "skills, knowledge and attitudes" (p.13) in Maltese and English Literacy, eLiteracy and Numeracy

Literacy. As the opening lines of the Director of *Quality and Standards in Education* states:

> this policy [National Policy and Strategy for the Attainment of Core Competences in Primary Education] invites us all to give renewed attention to the challenges surrounding the acquisition of core competences by all learners. There are good reasons why we consider literacy, eLiteracy and mathematics at the core of a quality education (Directorate for Quality and Standards in Education, 2009).

While one may question why only four of the eight core competences, suggested by the *European Parliament and Council*, are taken into consideration within the *National Policy and Strategy for the Attainment of Core Competences in Primary Education*, and why priority is given to cognitive development (see p. 6), the argument is on the strategy of how these four core competences are carried out. As outlined by the policy the strategy has the following priorities:

- the prevention of attainment deficit in Core Competences through EARLY SUPPORT;
- the EARLY IDENTIFICATION of Core Competences attainment deficit;
- the INTEGRATION into mainstream teaching;
- the INTERVENTION with respect to Core Competences attainment deficit in early primary (emphasis in original, p. 8).

The process of early identification, then early support, intervention and integration are all based on a foundational concept of 'giving'. Parents and teachers 'give' competences to students, and they measure the students' perception and understanding of these competences. The competences suggested in the four areas are all performative, in the sense that one can measure the outcome of what is being given in instruction. One can say how far or near this student is to the desired teaching competence. As these competences are based on developmental criteria (by the age of three a child should be able to..., by the age of four a child should be able to..., and so on), measurement is facilitated. Therefore it is always a question of 'giving': how much is going to be 'given', by whom, and when. Certainly, the process, especially for those who manifest "attainment deficit", is imbued with 'givings'. The language/numeracy specialist, the educational psychologist, and other therapists are involved and often labels are given to what is lacking and difficult in the learning process. To compensate for this lack or difficulty, complementary teaching, specialised tutoring and an array of various techniques are called in to be given to students. Rather than highlighting how social and political structures debilitate children, this response further medicalises, labels and pathologises them.

This focus on the *National Policy and Strategy for the Attainment of Core Competences in Primary Education* (2009) is an example which demonstrates that policy documents in education work around this concept of 'giving'. It is an assumption which is taken for granted. It could be argued that it is the concept of education *per se* that is based on 'giving': the teacher who 'gives' guidance to his/her students. 'Giving' is not just related to the disability arena but has a wider context. Perhaps, in disability circles, 'giving' is magnified.

Problematising '*Givings*'

> What do the following have in common: on the one hand, to give a ring, a bracelet, to give something to drink and to eat and, on the other hand, to give an impression, to give a feeling, to give a show or play? (Derrida, 1992, p. 49).

The complexity that we are faced with in this Chapter when considering the concept of 'giving', is that we all appear to have an understanding of this notion. There seems to be a 'transcendental' aspect in the verb 'giving', which aspect is found in all our acts of 'giving' and the understanding of 'giving'. So when we are offering skills, or give to a particular student the support of a Classroom Assistant (in some countries known as Learning Support Assistant), or providing a particular ICT adaptive hardware, or making available opportunities, there seems to be a core understanding of the concept of 'giving'. However, we are aware that this notion has multiple meanings. There is a double bind that needs to kept in mind when reading texts that mention 'giving' and when actively involved in 'giving'.

This concept implies a 'gift'. The idea of gifts in disability discourse (as well as other minority group discourses) is seen as suspect and dangerous, as, very often, it starts a process of victimisation of people with impairment who are constructed as disabled people. These deserve pity and hence charity acts of 'givings' are necessary to compensate for disablement or to alleviate some of this pity. Therefore, this process transforms persons with impairment into "icons of pity". The focus is again on the limitations imposed by the impairment (as in the charity model) rather than on society that operates in ways which exclude persons with impairment.

The Social Model incorporates Human Rights discourse that embodies the values of respect for differences, equality of opportunity, and full participation in all aspects of social life. The argument is thus that a person with impairment is entitled to a service/adaptation and that one is not 'giving' but is providing that which is his/her right. However I think that the concept of gift still finds itself within these discourses. The question of 'who gives?' and 'why?' are important. The givers are not a group of people who give gifts to those who are perceived as less fortunate. It is their humanity which qualifies them as recipients of these gifts. It is the fact that all human beings have basic rights and freedoms that makes possible the 'giving' of gifts. I am aware of the complexity of the argument here and it is here that the fragility of our language and concepts is at stake. While many use the term Human Rights in inclusive argumentation, we rarely stop to think about the complexity of such discourses.

Derrida (1992) argues that giving is "related to economy" (p. 7). Let us assume that A gives B to C. As I have already stated above, we know what 'giving' is. Therefore, if I am A and I give a gift then there is some element of expectation that at one stage in my life I will be repaid back by C for the gift that I have given to him/her. If C can never reciprocate the gift, then I have the feeling of satisfaction and pleasure in my action of giving. If, on the other hand, I am C and received a gift, then I am caught up in a process of retribution to A; or if I cannot reciprocate the gift, then I am eternally grateful to the giver. This is why Derrida argues that giving is related to economy. The etymology of the word 'economy' goes back to the Greek word 'oikonomos' meaning 'one who manages a household'. There is the emphasis on the house, one's dwelling, a return home, and how this home is to be managed. There is, Derrida (1992) argues, a circular movement in giving. The gift always returns home annulling the gift. Following Derrida, it is legitimate to ask; What will return home will be given back by the fact that students attend the *Pathway to Independent Living Programme*, or else by the parents who are given the opportunity and supported to actively participate in the planning the IEP process? Are our 'givings' neutral, or are they political in nature? 'Giving' is not innocent. It will require a return to the giver. Therefore, why do we give if the countergift, debt, compensation, symbolic recognition and memory of giving or receiving are at play the moment a giver gives comes into action? What is expected as a return if giving is so fundamental in the area of education? These may seem just rhetorical questions posed by those interested in philosophy, but these are questions that require our attention, recognition and our engagement. This is because in my opinion there is the mistaken idea that such giving is neutral and is the result of objective entitlement.

Conclusion

Derrida (1992) engages with the idea of 'giving' and gifts a step further and argues that a gift is only a gift when the giver and receiver do not know that it is a gift, when not even the intention of 'giving' is conceived. He therefore sees that 'giving' and the gift are an impossibility. A true gift must be a-economical and escape the logic of the circle – it must never return home. Of course the question is how can this 'giving' be sustained? Can we think of education that does not give? Can we think of inclusive education that does not conceive of 'giving'?

The quandary is that we give and carry out acts of 'givings', but we know the impossibility of our 'givings'. It is precisely this impossibility, with its desire to escape being identified in performative terms that could help us think further about the Social Model of Disability. The Social Model focuses on the changes required from Society. These are changes of attitudes, support, information and physical structures. The risk is that this complex and rich discourse of change with its elements of uncertainty is very often closed down into acts of 'givings', which only serve to emphasise the children's deficits (in terms filling up what is lacking). Society justifies its changes through the amounts of 'givings' it can carry out. This is a watering down of the impetus of the Social Model. If we keep in mind that 'giving' returns, then we are aware of the limitations of our 'givings'. There is therefore a need for constant vigil of our thoughts and actions in continuing change for an inclusive society. So next time you think of 'giving' something (a gift) to someone, and next time you read in a policy document about provisions being made to meet identified needs, think about the impossibility of such thinking and acting.

Thinking Point 1:
Reflect on when you attended school as a student, or when you worked as a member of staff in an educational environment. What 'givings' occur in the educational environment? Who were the actors in these 'givings' and receiving?
Thinking Point 2:
We all give! Have you ever stopped and thought about the concept of 'giving'? Derrida is trying to argue that 'giving' for the sake of 'giving' is impossible. Do you agree with his ideas? How do you explain your concept of giving?
Thinking Point 3:
How are 'giving' and change that is required by the Social Model related? What tensions do they create for each other?
Thinking Point 4:
Get hold of a policy document that focuses on Inclusive Education. Read this document from the perspective of 'giving'. Is 'giving' mentioned? What does it promise to 'give'? To whom? By whom? What are your immediate reactions (feelings) when encountering the concept of 'giving' in this document?

REFERENCES

Derrida, J. (1992). *Given Time 1: Counterfeit money.* Chicago: The University of Chicago Press.

Directorate for Quality and Standards in Education, Malta (2009). *National Policy and Strategy for the Attainment of Core Competences in Primary Education.*

MCAST, Malta. *Pathway to Independent Living Programme.* Accessed http://www.mcast.edu.mt/support_pathwaycourse.asp on 15th January 2010.

Ministry of Education, Malta. (1999). *National Minimum Curriculum – Creating the future together.* Malta: Klabb Kotba Maltin.

Ministry of Education, Malta. (2000). *Inclusive Education Policy regarding students with a disability.*

Recommendations of the European Parliament and of the Council (2006). On Key Competences for Lifelong Learning (2006/962/EC).

POLICY INFORMING PRACTICE *OR* PRACTICE FORMING POLICY?

ABSTRACT
Inclusive education is high on the agenda in the Maltese Islands. Legislation with embedded inclusive and clear policy statements has an undeniable positive effect on inclusive practices. Day-to-day practice in regular schools is evidence that efforts at macro-levels do not always ensure a cultural change and equitable access to curriculum for the diverse populations in school communities. The discussion will allow us, policy makers, professionals, educators and students to reflect on the benefits and shortcomings of adopting a top down (policy informing practice) versus a bottom up (practice forming policy) approach to creating change and more inclusive practices. A joint contribution of stakeholders at macro and micro levels suggests a way forward to an enduring change and paradigm shift towards inclusive thinking.

Introduction

Policy is what generates entitlement (Rix, Simmons, Nind & Sheehy, 2005). It is the intention of the authors of this Chapter to allow us to debate the symbiotic role of policy and practice in creating communities and an education system which is more inclusive.

The Venture for Achieving Inclusion

For the past years, a common quest amongst nations has been that of creating inclusive learning communities characterised by high quality equitable education. The pursuit of achieving this is justifiable educationally, socially and economically for nations embracing this philosophy. Educating children together conceive pedagogies responsive to diverse characteristics of students which benefit all. Inclusive education has the power to create more positive attitudes to diversity forming a sound and just society limiting the occurrence of discrimination. Delivering inclusive education is a more effective option rather than the specialisation of schools to educate specific groups of children (UNESCO, 2003).

Through the analyses of issues of equity it is opportune to recognise how the educational system provides a nexus with policy. Policy and practice may often appear divergent in their functional role however both should operate within a framework imbued with principles and moral values which seeks to abolish blatant and concealed educational exclusion. Policy is intended to filter from a macro context, that of a national legislation framework into the micro contexts of schools and classrooms. This should reflect a lifelong vision of education as individuals may risk social exclusion from cradle to grave.

The notion of equity is a crux to policy development on inclusive education as it promotes social justice. It may be appropriate at this stage to provide the distinctive definition of equality versus equity. The concept of equality is rooted in egalitarian political thinking in that people should get the same and be treated the same. This is a problematic concept to be applied to inclusive education in that it creates a paradox in acknowledging that all individual are diverse and yet providing the same opportunities to all. Equity, can be placed on two dimensions which are closely intertwined; the first, one of fairness in that personal and social factors for example gender and race shall not be a barrier to achieve educational potential and secondly, it implies a basic minimum standard of education for all i.e. a set of competencies such as reading and simple arithmetic which should be common to all (OECD, 2007).

In the context of referring to a school as equitable and inclusive, it is intended to encompass the whole process of challenging inequalities that could possibly arise through sexuality, gender, disability, class as well as ethnicity. Locally this has an implication of mainstream schools accommodating and providing for all children regardless of any perceived difference, disability, social, emotional, cultural or linguistic differences. The successful implementation of inclusive education and community building is reflected by the ability of the educational system to minimise these inequalities whilst fostering equity and participation in society and employment (OECD, 2008). It is an equality of opportunity that is a fundamental human right and demands access and equity in education. This should inform all educational policies and practices (Florian, 2008).

The Development of Policy in Relation to Inclusive Education

On developing policies on Inclusion whereby access and equity are on the agenda, the terminology employed and discourse practiced has a particular weighing in the message that the policy is attempting to convey. This attentive choice of words supports the beliefs, values and attitudes that needs to transpire a dignity for the individual. One mode of ensuring this is through 'people first' language rather than 'disability first' language as this encourages equity and respect by focusing on the individual first rather than the disability or cultural background that is likely to cause social exclusion. For instance using the term 'student with disability' rather than 'disabled or special needs student' ensures more dignity. The use of 'child with disability', 'typical', 'intellectual disability', 'student with autism' is much rather preferred than 'handicapped', 'normal', 'mentally challenged' and autistic student' respectively. In the local context there has been an attempt to modify the terminology as we moved away from a charitable stance to the idea that every individual has a right to a quality education and deserves the same respect and opportunities as an equal human being (NCPD, 2007). Further changes in terminology has seen a shift from referring to students with 'Special Educational Needs' (SEN) to 'Students with Individual Educational Needs' and this was followed by the *National Minimum Curriculum* Working Group on Inclusive Education in 2000. The term Individual Educational Needs:

> avoids stigmatizing such students as special and help us regard them as part of the normal diversity among all students. In this way, it is hoped that we will start viewing all students as lying within a spectrum of common and individual needs that should be met as far as possible within regular education provision (Bartolo *et al.*, 2002, p. 1).

Policy and legislation concerning inclusion serve to challenge assumptions and misunderstandings, to define and clarify the underlying conceptual issues, and to adequately address issues of social injustice and equity in the education system, and indeed society itself. (Lloyd, 2006). The *European Agency for Development in Special Needs Education* (2003) sets out principles that reflect universal elements of policies in particular to students with Individual Educational Needs, which however can be applied to a whole range of diverse learners.

These principles include: *A framework of law and policy that supports inclusion* involving legislation stating clearly the goal of inclusion and leading to the provision of facilities in order to enhance development towards inclusion. At a local level there are a number of legislations and policy documents in this regard. The *National Minimum Curriculum* (Ministry of Education, 1999) is supported by the legislation subsidiary to the *Education Act* (amended 2006) and recognizes Inclusive Education as being one of the basic principles in the local educational context. This applies to all students including those whose first language is not the native spoken language, in order that they are not excluded from the mainstream educational provision. Another policy statement was issued by the *Ministry of Education* through the *Ministerial Committee on Inclusive Education* (MCIE, 2000) namely, *Inclusive Education Policy* and this involves the procedure adopted for the Individual Education Programme (IEP) for students with a statement of needs. This was in line with another legislation – the *Equal Opportunities (Persons with disability) Act* 2000 referring to education as unlawful for an educational authority to discriminate against an acceptance of admission of a student on the ground of his/her disability, by refusing application, denying him/her access or limiting his/her access from an educational institution.

With regard to the Policy implementation, Head of Schools have an essential role in translating the inclusion policies in practice in their respective institutions. This is also highlighted in the document *Creating Inclusive Schools* (Ministry of Education, 2002) which provides guidelines for implementation of the *National Curriculum Policy on Inclusive Education* and specifically on this states that:

> Both within the Education Division and within Maltese society in general, there are still confused notions about who is ultimately responsible for the implementation of specialised educational provisions in an inclusive setting. Since the concept of a child receiving one-to-one support from an adult has become synonymous with "inclusion", the provision of a facilitator ... has given the false impression that an inclusion programme is taking place ... For all the above to happen, *there is a need for the whole school together with its school council to make a written commitment to and assure formal responsibility for fostering the school's Inclusive Education programme.* This concern should be reflected in the school development plan as well as the school ethos (Ministry of Education, 2002, p. 33-34).

Another principle would be *resourcing arrangements that promote inclusion* in terms of funding for inclusive practices to be realized in line with an explicit policy. Ideally, educational institutions will have flexibility to carry out resourcing arrangements which appear to be effective in promoting inclusion according to identified needs and requirements of the particular institution. Appropriate and flexible forms of support are provided to teachers who work with students with diverse learning needs. Learning Support Assistants who are employed without having specific training on disability are given training of up to a Certificate level from the *Directorate for Educational Services* in addressing individual educational needs or graduate with a Diploma Level from the *University of Malta*. This is important as this teacher support system needs to be responsive to the levels of individual needs presented in the schools. In the local context, whilst closure of Special Schools was not proposed, however a large movement towards mainstreaming has been going on for the past decades. In fact only four Special Schools are still in operation, providing an education to the small percentage (0.36%) of students having more severe difficulties often based on the parents' choice.

However, in line with the *European Agency* guidelines (2003) one way of resourcing arrangements to promote inclusion locally has happened by launching a reform in February, 2010 whereby Special Schools have been transformed into Resource Centers. This reform is a response to the recommendations carried forward by the *Inclusive and Special Education Review* (2005). This reform suggests a shift from the present scenario. "For example, students who attend a special school remain in the same school right through their school life, they will now as a result of the reform, be able to experience the different phases of school life as their peers do in mainstream education" (Ministry of Education, Culture, Youth and Sport, 2009). These Resource Centers have now become as part of the network of Colleges which all schools in Malta are based upon. Networking of schools is based on solidarity and cooperation and these are instruments for professional development and school development (Bezzina, 2006). Networks are described in the document *For All Children to Succeed* as:

> Purposeful social entities characterized by a commitment to quality, rigour, and a focus on standards and student learning. They are also an effective means of supporting innovation in times of change. In education, networks promote the dissemination and development of teachers, support capacity building in schools, mediate between centralized and decentralized structures, and assist in the process of restructuring and re culturing educational organizations and systems (Hopkins, 2005 as cited in *For All children to succeed*, p. 37; Bezzina, 2006).

Through this networking, Resource Centres and mainstream schools will be participating in inter-school collaboration, giving support and receiving it according to students' needs as well as sharing of expertise, knowledge and teaching strategies. It promotes effective arrangements for monitoring, evaluation and accountability in terms of promoting collaboration between schools, policy makers and parents. The support of Learning Support Assistants and organizations such as *Foundation for Educational Services* also offer support to parents after school hours in meeting the individual educational needs of children (Bartolo & Borg, 2008). These kinds of arrangements need to be accessible to everyone especially within a decentralized system. The policy initiatives of the *National Minimum Curriculum* as well as devolution of authority in schools encourages this decentralization form of governance and consequently empowers members of staff in educational decision making by giving responsibility and authority to schools (Bezzina, 2000; 2004).

Policy and Curricular Considerations

When developing policy, curricular issues must be given its due consideration. It is important to ensure that equal opportunities priorities are understood by those involved in the planning of the school curriculum and to analyze how equal opportunities considerations are underpinning the planning of the whole curriculum.

Curricular consideration at policy level aims at students with very low levels of attainment in the margins of Resource Centres to access and receive the same, albeit modified curricular entitlement as their classmates. This is an endeavour that necessitates a range of compensatory strategies and measures in order to support curricular access. In order to achieve this, as part of the *Inclusive Curriculum Project*, 15 syllabus supplements were published (Ministry of Education, Youth & Employment, 2007) aimed at providing an opportunity for all students and teachers to share a common approach. The Project takes a unique approach to inclusion because it is not concerned with student placement. Rather it stresses the importance of providing the best opportunities for learning. In doing so, the goal of raising standards of student achievement in schools can be realized. Consequently, a new paradigm in teaching and learning for students with Individual Educational Needs that is linked to student's abilities and attainment is introduced.

The fundamental core of the Maltese educational system is to provide quality education for all and access to equal opportunities need to be ensured regardless of their personal circumstances and experiences that are bound to exist within the community of learners. It is a national commitment that all teachers and other stakeholders work together to prioritise the needs of the learner, thus, translating the inclusive education policy into reality. The ethos of inclusion embraces the idea that the learner is at the centre, and consistently this entails individual planning to ensure quality education to meet the diverse needs of students.

The *Inclusive Curriculum Project* helps educators to reflect on the creation of a stimulating learning environment in which ALL students have the opportunity to reach their full potential. All teachers should be enthused by the learning potential of their students and appreciate how to unlock each individual's exceptional personality. Teachers in schools are encouraged to reflect on the consequences of an inclusive curriculum. All students should be given the privilege to enjoy their lessons and develop a healthy sense of curiosity of the world about them. The Project will provide a repertoire of teaching activities and ideas intended for all ages and abilities. This is the challenging starting point for equality of opportunity in raising standards in education for all.

The *Inclusive Curriculum Project* covers subjects which are taught at Primary and Secondary schools in Malta. The purpose of these Supplement Texts is to support the planning, development and implementation of the subject syllabi for students with Individual Educational Needs. It also draws on effective practice across a range of schools and can be used in State, Church and Independent Schools as these are regulated by the National Minimum Curriculum. It also provides support to the range of services that work with the schools.

A subject Supplement Text for example Mathematics identifies the mainstream subject syllabus and modifications required for students with Individual Educational Needs. These were discussed and agreed upon by curricular specialists in both mainstream and special education. Each Supplement also includes *Attainment Level Descriptions* which can be used by teachers to decide which description best fits a student's performance. The *Attainment Level Descriptions* can also be used to annually inform school developmental planning and evaluate where resources need to be placed in future years to raise the quality of education provision. As a consequence this should increase the levels of opportunity and raise student attainment (Ministry of Education, Youth & Employment, 2007).

An avoidable approach is to present a policy which corroborates rhetoric language and has underlying assumptions which fail to address the practical aspect of delivering access to the curriculum and equal opportunities in education. In this regard the *Inclusive Curriculum Project* seeks to ensure that deliverance of curriculum for all is possible (Ministry of Education, Youth & Employment, 2007).

Who can create educational change? Policy or teacher practice?

> Educational change depends on what teachers do and think – it's as simple and as complex as that... (Fullan, 2001, p. 115).

The intention of creating inclusive communities even in our classroom is undeniably a laudable and vital aim. For this reason policy rooted in legislation in favour of inclusion is essentially a prerequisite. This policy ideally includes clear statements on inclusive education, abandonment of special educational legislation as well as empowerment of the position of parents (Pijl & Frissen, 2009). Policy statements are ideally free from 'conditional statements' (Slee & Allan, 2001) including phrases such as 'most appropriate setting' as this enlists as a form of exclusion.

Strong political and governmental commitment is critical in creating inclusive communities and concerted efforts need to be made at national level even in the form of clear policies to promote mainstream approaches. Policymakers can be tempted to use their power to change daily practice directly in schools by drawing up additional guidelines and regulations. This does not generally lead to a change in teachers' attitude, self-confidence, knowledge and skills. Oppositely, when forced upon the school, policy is likely to initiate disconnection and enhance segregation (Allen, 2006).

Policymakers cannot make education inclusive on their own, but they can support this. The best support is by clearly stating what is expected from schools without prescribing how it should be done. They can support by removing all obstacles in regulations and funding, by stimulating forms of additional training for teachers and by avoiding as much as possible funding systems requiring formal labelling procedures (Pijl & Dyson, 1998). Studies confirm that policy-makers could not have full control over teachers' teaching behaviours (Wong, 2001). Policy makers could be underestimating the complexity of change being required from teachers and staff at a micro level. Also it needs to be ensured that for change to be implemented teachers are not neglected in terms of support in knowledge and skills related to the demands of the new changes.

Support is the crux of the debate as teachers are those who mediate policy through their activities in and out of classroom and through their participation in the realization of curriculum (Clough, 1999). Teachers need to be supplied with the tools to face challenges that occur in the classroom in the quest for providing the quality education to all students. A positive attitude is also an asset as it can greatly weigh on the achievement of successful inclusion. These attitudes can be influenced by the availability of resources, knowledge and skills of teachers and level of exposure to pupils with difficulties (Avramidis *et al.,* 2000; Croll & Moses, 2000). It is a reality however that no matter how much inclusion is encouraged it is not always possible to account for the attitudes of staff or to understand the underlying factors and negative attitudes. Policymakers can ask teachers to take full responsibility for all students in their class and make 'escape' routes (i.e. the possibility of referring students to specialists or schools taking over responsibility) less attractive, but it is essential that teachers know they are not on their own.

One possible route to take in bringing about change is using a teacher-centered action approach to encourage educational transformation. Teachers can identify what they consider to be important issues that need to be examined, carry out research, present their findings between them and implement and evaluate changes proposed. This approach acknowledges teachers' contribution and the likelihood to accept and implement better practice are increased. This would also create more opportunities for teachers to be involved in the decision making process. Practice together with research findings could possibly lead to revision of policies at departmental or national levels and this would provide teachers with enough confidence to be active in professional development.

Creating educational change is a time consuming and complex process. This requires skills, new knowledge, commitment, strong beliefs as well as support from change facilitators (Hall & Hord, 2001; MacGilchrist *et al.,* 2004) Within the process of educational change, implementation is a critical step and without change in individual teachers, lasting change in education is unlikely to be successful (Fullan, 2001; Hall & Hord, 2001).

Thinking Point 1:
Are adaptations, special pedagogies, a curriculum for all, and assessment procedures the means to have access to education opportunities or do we need to reorganize and create a fundamental change in the provision of education in our mainstream schools in order to ensure equity and success for all?

Thinking point 2:
Do more policies automatically mean more inclusion for our diverse communities or is it a reaffirmation of continued exclusion of students?

Thinking point 3:
What factors contribute in the successful implementation of an inclusive educational policy to practice?

Thinking point 4:
Teachers and stakeholders do not engage often in reading new policies that decision makers put forward at a national level. Suggest initiatives, training and other events that can be organized in order for the content of the policies and legislations to be known to educators who need to implement these in their every day setting.

REFERENCES

Allen, J. (2006). The Repetition of Exclusion. *International Journal of Inclusive Education 10(2/3): 121–33.*

Avramidis, E., Bayliss, P., & Burden, R. (2000). A survey into mainstream teachers' attitudes towards the inclusion of children with special educational needs into the ordinary school in one local education authority. *Educational Psychology 20 (2), 191-211.*

Bartolo, P. A., Agius Ferrante, C., Azzopardi, A., Bason, L., Grech, L., & King, M. (2002). *Creating inclusive schools: Guidelines for the implementation of the National Minimum Curriculum policy on inclusive education.* Malta: Ministry of Education.

Bartolo, P.A., MolLous, A., Ale, P., Calleja, C., Cefai, C., Chetcuti, D., Hofsaess, T., Koinzer, P., Humphrey, N., Janikova, V., Vilkiene, V., & Wetso, G. (2007). *Responding to student diversity: Teacher's handbook. Malta:* University of Malta. (available online www.dtmp.org).

Bartolo, P.A., & Borg, G. (2008). The development of Inclusive Education in Malta. In Bunch, G. & Valeo, A. *Inclusive Education: To Do or Not To Do.* Ontario: Inclusion Press.

Bezzina, C. (2000) Educational leadership for twenty first century Malta: breaking the bonds of dependency. *The International journal of Educational Management 14,7, 299-307.*

Bezzina, C. (2004).Towards the learning community: a Maltese experience. *The International Journal of Educational Management, 18, 7, 446-454.*

Bezzina, C. (2006). Inclusive learning communities: The real challenges facing reform in Malta. *International Journal of Educational Management, 20, 6, 453-465.*

Clough, P. (1999). Exclusive tendencies: Concepts, consciousness and curriculum in the projection of inclusion. *International Journal of Inclusive Education, 3, 1, 63-73.*

Croll, P., & Moses, D. (2000). Ideologies and utopias: educational professionals' view of inclusion. *European Journal of Special Educational Needs, 15 (1), 1-12.*

Education Act. (2006). Available from http://www.education.gov.mt/ministry/ doc/pdf/acts/edu_laws_2006/Chapt327.pdf

Equal Opportunities (Persons with Disability) Act (2000). Available from www.knpd.org

Florian, L. (2008). Special or Inclusive Education: future trends. *British Journal of Special Education, 35, 4.*

Fullan, M. (2001). (3rd Ed). *The New Meaning of Educational Change.* London: Routledge Falmer.

Hall, G.E., & Hord, S.M. (2001). *Implementing Change: Patterns, Principles and Potholes.* Massachusetts: Allyn and Bacon.

Lloyd, C. (2006). Removing barriers to achievement: A strategy for inclusion or exclusion? *International Journal of Inclusive Education,12, 2, 221-236.*

MacGilchrist, B.; Myers, K.; and Reed, J. (2004). T*he Intelligent School.* London: SAGE Publications.

MCIE (2000). *Inclusive education: Policy regarding students with a disability.* Malta: Ministry of Education.

Ministry of Education (1999). *Creating the future together: National Minimum Curriculum.* Malta: Klabb Kotba Maltin.

Ministry of Education (2002). *Creating inclusive schools: Guidelines for the Implementation of the national Curriculum Policy on Inclusive Education.*

Ministry of Education, Youth & Employment (2005). *Inclusive and Special Education Review Report 2005.* Available from http://www.education.gov.mt/ministry/doc/pdf/inclusive_edu.pdf

Ministry of Education, Youth and employment. (2007) *Syllabus supplement.* Malta: MOED. Available from www.inclusivecurriculum.com

Ministry of Education, Culture, Youth and Sport – Student Services Department. (2009). *Special Schools Reform.* Available from http://www.education.gov.mt/ministry/doc/pdf/special_schools_reform/Special _Schools_Reform_ENG.pdf

National Minimum Curriculum – Working group on Inclusive Education, Report (June 2000). In Giordimaina, J. (Ed.). *National curriculum on its Way: A Conference on the Implementation of the National Curriculum*, Malta 9th-11th June 2000. Malta: Ministry of Education.

NCPD (2007) *Rights, not charity: Guidelines towards an inclusive society and a positive difference in the lives of Maltese and Gozitan disabled people.* KNPD: St Venera.

OECD (2007). *No More Failures: Ten Steps to Equity in Education.* OECD Publishing.

OECD (2008). *Reviews of National Policies for Education*: South Africa 2008. OECD Publishing.

Pijl, S.J. and Dyson, A. (1998). Funding Special Education: A Three-Country Study of Demand-Oriented Models, *Comparative Education 34(3): 261–79.*

Pijl, S.J., & Frissen, P.H.A. (2009). What Policymakers Can Do to Make Education Inclusive. *Educational Management Administration Leadership, 37; 366.*

Rix, J., Simmons, K., Nind, M. & Sheehy, K. (2005). *Policy and Power in Inclusive Education.* Open University, Routledge Falmer.

Slee, R., & Allan, J. (2001). Excluding the included: a reconsideration of inclusive education. *International Studies in Sociology of Education, 11:2, 173-192.*

UNESCO (2003). *Open file on Inclusive education – support materials for managers and administrators.* Retrieved February 9th, 2010 from http://unesdoc.unesco.org/images/0013/001321/132164e.pdf

Xuereb, P. (Ed) (2005). *Anti discrimination, inclusion and equality in Malta.* Civil Society Project Report. Malta: University of Malta.

THE ROLE OF PARENTS IN INCLUSIVE EDUCATION

ABSTRACT

Louisa and Philip, who are the parents of Ben Grech, a young person with Down Syndrome, share the experience of their son's journey through inclusive education, from pre-school up to post-secondary level. It covers personal reflections on the local developments in society and in particular in the education sector. They talk about the challenges they and many others have faced and are still facing and voice their apprehensions for the future, where a lack of clear vision and policy is apparent. Louisa and Philip promote a more pro-active role for parents in the education and development of their children.

Injustice anywhere is a threat to justice Everywhere
Martin Luther King, Jr.

A community that excludes even one of its members is no community at all.
Dan Wilkins, Poet and Motivational Speaker

Introduction

When our fourth child was born with Down syndrome in 1992, we entered the world of disability with little or no knowledge of what this would entail and what this would mean to us. Initially the greatest obstacle to overcome in the first few weeks and months was to come to terms with the fact that our son had an intellectual disability and we had to learn to cope with the barrage of feelings and thoughts that assailed us. Would we be able to relate to him – to share the things that mean the most to us? What would this mean to his brothers? After the first weeks and so much emotional tumult we had realised that we wanted our son to grow up in a safe and loving environment and be given all the opportunities to grow, learn, develop and enjoy life to the full. We knew that we would try our utmost to provide him with all the possibilities to achieve this.

The next obstacle that we knew we would have to face was the reaction of family members, friends, neighbours and work colleagues when we passed on the news that our son had Down syndrome. As one can imagine the reactions were varied and perhaps provided the first taster of what life would present us with. We saw acceptance, encouragement, hope and positive attitudes, but there was also denial, fear and disbelief. We latched on to the positive and decided to move on. Eighteen years down the line we know that our son's disability has conscripted us to become parent advocates for the rights of persons with disability.

Parent Advocacy

We know that parents of children with a disability find a multitude of barriers when it comes to access opportunities for their offspring. Most of the times these barriers are not of the parents' making, neither are they caused by the child's disability, but these are barriers originating from the perception of society with regards to the capabilities, the worth and the rights of persons with a disability. These perceptions highlight most dramatically the irresponsibility of society in general and of governments in particular. Perhaps one has to keep in mind this axiom that it is enough to have failed one person to have failed them all.

This irresponsibility can perhaps be seen in many areas that affect the life of persons with disability and these areas are all connected to accessibility – physical, sensorial and intellectual. This in turn shapes life in the community, education, health, communication, transport, employment, relationships and housing. The list is endless and whole volumes could be written about the obstacles that persons with disability are still facing locally.

However, on a more positive note, we need to say that people in general have become more aware of the rights of persons with disability, and effort is being made to make it possible for them to live meaningful lives. Most children with disabilities are attending mainstream schools and are being accepted by their peers and the parents of their peers. Persons with disability are more visible in the community and they are raising awareness about their rights to education, employment and supported living. We have schemes that help persons with disability to find employment which they do even if only until the scheme lasts (due to its dependency on funding from some EU-programme) and then they are back on the unemployment register. These last few years have also seen an effort to move away from institutional residences to the opening of several community-based small-scale housing projects. However, in spite of all this, people generally still look upon persons with disability as requiring and dependent on charity rather than acknowledging that they have rights that need to be respected and recognised.

Legislation: The Answer to all Woes?

At the start of the millennium, the Maltese Parliament passed the *Equal Opportunities Act (Persons with Disability) 2000* which was unanimously approved. The Maltese Government also signed the *Convention on the Rights of Persons with Disability* and the *Optional Protocol* at the end of March 2007. This *Equal Opportunities Act* together with the *UN Convention* take on board the rights of persons with disability, but there also needs to be the commitment to adopt policies with tangible measures to safeguard these rights and to work wholeheartedly to ensure that these rights are enjoyed by one and all.

Article 3 of the *UN Convention on the Rights of Persons with Disabilities* March 2007 states:[1]

> The principles of the present *Convention* shall be:
> (a) Respect for inherent dignity, individual autonomy including the freedom to make one's own choices, and independence of persons;
> (b) Non-discrimination;
> (c) Full and effective participation and inclusion in society;
> (d) Respect for difference and acceptance of persons with disabilities as part of human diversity and humanity;
> (e) Equality of opportunity;

---

[1] http://www.un.org/disabilities/documents/convention/convoptprot-e.pdf

(f)   Accessibility;
(g)   Equality between men and women;
(h)   Respect for the evolving capacities of children with disabilities and respect for the right of children with disabilities to preserve their identities.

These are the rights that persons with disability seek to enjoy fully, however there are laws in the Maltese legislature that still discriminate against persons with disability and which have to be revised to come in line with the *UN Convention*. Disappointingly, at the beginning of 2010 the Maltese Government had however not yet ratified the *Convention* or the *Optional Protocol* which leaves a vacuum in some realms.

Article 58 of the *Education Act* as amended in 2007, Article 58 stipulates:

> 58. (1) The Minister shall ensure that the national policy on inclusive education is being applied in all schools and that there are available the resources, tools and facilities required so that this may be given as effectively as possible.[2]

Whilst Article 45 states:

> 45. (1) Without prejudice to the provisions of article 58, it shall be the duty of the State to provide resource centres, whose specialised role will include provision for children with individual educational needs who would benefit more from being in such centres than in mainstream schools, for such time as may be appropriate depending on their needs.[3]

This is a contradiction in terms and has not really helped the cause of inclusive education. Who is to decide which children would benefit more from special schooling? Will it be the parents or the State? And will the parents hear both sides of the coin when and if they come to make the decision? The danger will always exist that those children who prove to be a challenge to the educational system will find themselves shoved away from regular schooling and into the resource centres. Resource Centres, however well they are equipped and maintained, can never improve the children's socialisation with their peers who are ultimately the principal educators for children with Individual Educational Needs.

As the parents of a young man with Down syndrome who has been through primary and secondary mainstream education, and who is now also in post-secondary education following the *Pathway to Independent Living Course* at MCAST[4], we can emphatically say that we are strong believers in inclusive education. The *Pathway to Independent Living Programme* is designed to provide an opportunity to school leavers in possession of the School Leaving Certificate to follow a structured programme of study in the area which is closer to student needs. The two year programme is provided for students with mild to moderate disabilities/ learning difficulties. It is intended to support students acquire skills

---

[2] *Education Act* (Ch. 327, Part V, Colleges of State Schools).
[3] *Ibid.*, Part IV Duty of the State to provide education.
[4] MCAST is the *Malta College for Arts, Science and Technology* (a vocational college).

required to gain and maintain employment. Students pass through a selection process which includes an interview and/or aptitude test. Students should have basic skills in Literacy and Numeracy, be able to tolerate classroom environment and be willing to take up employment. Students are given ample opportunities to experience hands-on learning in all subjects (cf. MCAST Prospectus, 2009/2010, p. 12).

We have seen our son go through the system, and with all its difficulties, challenges and short-comings, we have seen him develop and grow into an independent young man. We see a person who socializes, gets on well with other people, is literate and computer literate, numerate, takes part in various sports and has acquired many skills which will serve him well in his adult life.

We have been actively involved in all stages and in all aspects of his education. In his primary and secondary education we have attended the yearly MAPS[5] and IEP[6] sessions, discussed with educators what we wished for our son, what he was capable of doing, what his challenges were. We worked together with the teacher and the LSA[7] in realizing the goals set for him. We helped at school with providing resources that could help him out, we consolidated the work at home, we tried to generalize concepts to broaden his education and we cooperated with the school when they faced difficulties with his behaviour.

His experiences in primary and secondary school, his interaction with his peers, were beneficial to his growth, to his social skills and to his independence. In primary education he was able to participate more effectively in the classroom. In secondary education, especially in the latter years, his experience of a classroom setting were less frequent although he was never alone but with a group of other students who had difficulties in coping with the vast syllabus that was part of the curriculum. Was the system failing him? Perhaps, but the fact that he could still socialize, still take part in certain subjects like P.E. and PSD[8] with the whole class, take part in any extracurricular activity taking place, was for him an education in itself.

Throughout his years in secondary education, we tried to encourage the school to look at his capabilities and we worked well with the school in that they provided him with a lot of opportunities to learn new skills. He learnt to cook; he worked with the sports masters to set up equipment during the lessons for other classes; he learnt to catch the bus from home to Valletta alone and back again, that is a 30-40 minutes bus ride; to use a mobile phone; to understand what amount of money he required to get certain goods; in other words, he was gaining independence.

Making sure that he had access to post-secondary education was a struggle. We were faced with a stated policy of *numerus clausus* when we went to the initial meeting for parents and many parents were apprehensive and discouraged when they realised that the idea of the College was to take on just a limited number of students. Alone and with others we challenged the system and got assurances of change both from the Minister of Education, Hon. Dolores Cristina, and the

---

[5] MAPS: Multi-Action Planning System
[6] IEP: Individualised Educational Programme
[7] LSA: Learning Support Assistant; generally a University of Malta
          Diploma level - class teachers' aide
[8] PSD: Personal and Social Development

Principal of MCAST, Prof. Maurice Grech. That policy effectively changed – another indicator of the effectiveness of parent activism. In fact, to the best of our knowledge, all or most of the students who applied did get into the course but this only after a written and oral examination, which we were informed was run to discover their capabilities and suitability and not to assess their competencies.

It is to be commended that the two-year *Pathway to Independent Living Course* has moved from an exclusive to an inclusive setting and is now on the main campus at Kordin (south of Malta, immersed in a very busy community). This will really benefit all the students and it would be commendable if more activities were to be held jointly with other courses at MCAST. We realise also that this course is still establishing itself and there is a lot that still needs to be done. Parents still need to be involved in the education of their teenage sons and daughters, so that they can consolidate the learning. We believe that the College still has to learn how to maximise on this resource that is the parents of their students. The process of MAPS and IEP sessions[9] has yet to begin at time of writing, well into the second semester.

Parent's Understanding of Inclusive Education

The title of this Chapter is 'the role of parents in inclusive education'. Perhaps before we can talk about the role of the parents, we need to understand how parents conceptualise inclusive education. From our personal experience and our discussions with other parents, we can perhaps say that there are many varied experiences when it comes to inclusive education. There are parents who like us believe that inclusive education should be for all children with a disability and that provisions need to be in place, and training given to school administrators, teachers and LSAs to be able to provide the best possible practice of inclusive education.

Other parents are just ready to accept the system in the school attended by their child as it is, either because they do not really know better or because they fear that any demands from their side will result in repercussions on their child. Some parents have tried placing their children in what they believe to be inclusive education but the system has failed their child and they have moved away from it and gone back to special education, only to find that their child will not necessarily have gained from this move either. These belief permutations are endless and each situation has to be considered on its own merit to be able to understand where the inclusive education process has benefited or failed the child with a disability. Inclusive education is a right also for other children with individual needs that might not necessarily be tied to disability but rather to social, cultural and emotional challenges that they might be experiencing. Such challenges are far more pervasive and diverse than disability.

Perhaps we should try to define what we think inclusive education is all about, what parents expect it to be. The first word that comes to mind is 'belonging',

---

[9] At the time of writing MAPS and IEP sessions with the parents had not been held. The educators responsible for the *Pathway Programme* monitored the students in the first few weeks and based on their observations, made a list of the goals and objectives they believed the student still needed to achieve. There was no consultation with the parents and these objectives had still not reached them when five months of the course were nearly up.

'belonging' to a school, to a classroom. Although provisions have to be in place to cater for the individual needs, the child together with his/her peers is accepted as one of the students and is made to feel an integral part of the class and involved in all that happens in the classroom and in the school.

However, we need to ask another important question, as parents, whether 'inclusion is really happening?' We need to ask this question because we keep hearing over and over again from other parents that the system is failing or not working justly.

- Why are some children still being sent to the back of the class and are considered the sole responsibility of the LSA? Why are they are not involved at all in the class? Whatever their capabilities they should be involved in the lesson/class with the other children. If differentiation or adaptations are necessary then teacher and LSA should liaise to provide the necessary support to see that the child learns alongside his/her peers.
- Why are children taken out of class to spend time in resource rooms – special areas that are set aside for children with disabilities or challenging behaviour, some beautifully equipped and decorated but devoid of peer interaction and stimulus - and the students are therefore isolated for long periods of time away from the classroom?
- Why are children with disabilities attending other institutions, special schools or private entities providing services or programmes for persons with disability that take them away from the school during school hours? This practice works against inclusion as the children will adopt a different schedule and experiences from their peers and will thus never be considered an integral part of the class community.

This is not 'inclusive' education and parents, if they are aware that this is happening, should not accept the situation as is, but should speak up and encourage the school staff to find creative ways and means of getting their child involved with the rest of the class.

To have an inclusive classroom, teacher and LSA need to work as a team, discussing and planning resources and activities that will involve all the children irrespective of their abilities. Use of visuals, manipulating and exploring objects, hands-on activities, group or paired work and other creative methods can all be used to get all the children in the classroom on board, maintaining their interest and increasing their level of participation. Differentiation and adaptations all need to be planned beforehand so that all children are included.

Parents are also an excellent resource and can be roped in to help consolidate and generalise the learning done in school. It is important that there is communication and dialogue between all parties concerned, as this will benefit the child. Parents are an invaluable part of the educational team and if they are not fully included both the school and the pupil will be disadvantaged.

We know that this can work, not only because we have seen it in practice with our son, but because for some years I (the mother) also worked as a teacher and the school encouraged this kind of collaboration. It was effective; all the children learnt and moved forward, always according to their capabilities. Our son too was able to participate and contribute to the lesson, although we believe that perhaps the most important thing for him was that he was participating in the activities and life of the school just as his classmates were. It gave him a sense of belonging, of being one of the students, and not somebody who was just being tolerated in the classroom.

The differentiation and adaptations have to go beyond the lesson. It has to be reflected in the class work and in the homework given to the child. If we want the children to feel that they are achieving, then the tasks must be appropriate and at the level of his/her understanding. The dialogue between parents and school has to be consistent and, especially if the child is receiving services from an outside entity, all parties need to be informed of the methods used, so that there is continuity and achievement. Parents can report back on the success or the difficulties that the child encountered in carrying out the activity, and this feedback can help to timely reflect on whether the task or the objective was too ambitious, too easy or just right.

Differentiation and adaptations definitely need to be reflected also in examination papers. Children with a statement of needs should not have to sit for the one and only exam paper issued by the Department of Education. The exam paper has to be designed to show what students with individual needs have learnt and achieved as at present it in no way addresses the skills and the progress they have achieved. These children graduate from inclusive secondary school at present with a school leaving certificate that lists none of their abilities. However, in this respect there is some movement towards building a portfolio with the achievements of these students and hopefully a certification of the skills they acquired.

Communicating

One thing that we found extremely helpful was the communication diary in which the LSA could give us a breakdown of our son's day, the activities and tasks he participated in, the way these were conducted and the way he responded to them. On our part as parents, we communicated what was happening at home and how he was approaching the tasks sent from school to ensure continuity. We would also inform each other if there was a break from his normal routine at home that could affect the way he behaved in school, if he had been unwell, or if he required medication. We would communicate anything that would help the teacher and the LSA make their job a little bit easier. When there were more pressing issues to be tackled, then there were meetings arranged or long telephone conversations to see how best to manage these issues. The expertise of the parents has to be taken on board at times like these because being the main carers of the child they are generally more knowledgeable about their child's health, behaviour, achievements and challenges.

Moving on to other experiences, I (the mother) vividly recall the time I got a phone call from the school advising me to pick my son up from school quite early in the day because his LSA was unwell and had not turned up at school. My son must have been eight years old at the time. I turned up at the school and had to take my son back home. I cannot begin to describe the emotions that assailed me – the anger at the system, the hurt of knowing that my child was not really one of the class, that he was being singled out and not treated in the same way as the other children – and I cried my heart out. I remember telling the school staff that the family goes through so much and to cap it all there is this discrimination that continues to create difficulties and hurts. Unfortunately, ten years down the line, this practice still goes on and parents are still so hurt and confused with this policy. The children end up spending too much time at home especially if their LSA has health problems. When will this discrimination stop?

Parents find themselves in the precarious situation that they cannot both work to cope with the financial burden that disability in the family accentuates. This hurt is further compounded by the directives issued during industrial action by teachers. It is shameful that these directives target the children and most especially the children with individual educational needs. Does the Maltese Union of Teachers need to show its strength by targeting the very persons it should be duty bound to protect and safeguard? Does it realise, and does anybody else realise, for that matter, that the rights of the child to be:

> given opportunities and facilities, by law and by other means, to enable him to develop physically, mentally, morally, spiritually and socially in a healthy and normal manner and in conditions of freedom and dignity[10]

....are being trampled upon?

Finally

Parents should unite and have the courage to stand up to this bullying from the 'service providers' and not allow this situation to perpetuate. The State should have the political will to implement the rights of all its citizens, especially the most vulnerable.
- The rights of children should be safeguarded over the rights of workers.
- Parents should be actively engaged in the education of their children;
- All should recognise that the child has rights that need to be acknowledged and respected;
- Parents should unite with other stakeholders and work in harmony towards establishing a truly inclusive society.

What is difficult is standing up and taking action!
Balzac, French novelist & playwright

Thinking Point 1:
Do you agree that society needs to develop within itself an expectation of 'a return on its investment' in inclusive education?
Thinking Point 2:
Do you agree that parents need to assert their rights on the education of their children and collectively influence the providers of inclusive education?

---

[10] Declaration of the Rights of the Child 1959 http://www.cirp.org/library/ethics/UN-declaration/

PROGRESS IN THE GENERAL CURRICULUM
THROUGH UNIVERSAL DESIGN FOR LEARNING

ABSTRACT

UDL offers students the opportunity to be themselves, to learn according to their abilities and learning patterns thus facilitating their progress in the general curriculum. I want to convey the importance of understanding and implementing UDL. I try to explore: What is UDL? Where are it's roots and foundations? How is UDL linked with inclusive education and the creation of a community of learners? I present the three principles of UDL as outlined by CAST and provide a rich list of resources for educators. The Maltese educational situation is also contextualised and the chapter ends with a vignette describing a class of students with diverse needs for whom the educator needs to plan for by using UDL.

Introduction: Universal Design for Learning

> 'Regular schools...are the most effective means of combating discriminatory attitudes' (Salamanca Statement, 1994) and creating 'a strong, cohesive classroom community is increasingly recognised as the foundation of successful classrooms. All students must feel safe, respected, and valued in order to learn new skills. Fear discomfort and anxiety are fundamentally incompatible with the learning process, and make teaching and learning difficult. Successful classes are those in which students feel supported in their learning, willing to take risks, challenged to become fully human with one another, and open to new possibilities (Shapon-Shevin, 1999, p. xi).

'Streaming', 'setting', 'learning zones', 'resource centres' are segregating alternatives at times offered to educators as providing the best educational options. To my understanding they are most certainly not the best options. Prof Susan Hallam, *Institute of Education, University of London*, upheld that not all students benefit from streaming and setting. Students with greater academic difficulties do better in mixed ability classes and worse in streamed and set classes (Hallam, 2002). Through their research Vianello & Lanfranchi (2009) suggest that Italian children with intellectual impairment, due to genetic syndromes (students with Down syndrome, Williams syndrome, Prader Willie Syndrome, Cornelia de Lange syndrome and Frangile X syndrome) seem to develop cognitively more than those from other countries. Italian students seem to overcome, to a certain extent, the barriers of their genetic 'limitations' and develop what Vianello & Lanfranchi call 'surplus'. Incidences of students with intellectual impairment with such;

'surplus' in Italy are more frequent than those found in international literature and this may be due to the positive effects of the inclusion in mainstreaming classrooms of most pupils with intellectual disabilities (Vianello & Lanfranchi, 2009, p. 41).

Vianello & Maoelli (2001) citing an earlier work by Vianello (1990) were categorical in stating that teachers with a direct and engaging experience with students with disability confirm that they would have encountered less difficulties than an inexperienced teacher. The catch words, in my opinion, are 'engaging experience', that is, an experience by educators who took it onto themselves to make inclusion happen.

Universal Design for Learning

During these last years we have seen that Differentiated Learning and the creation of Individual Educational Programmes have facilitated the teaching of students. However,

> Universal design for learning (UDL) is a framework for designing curricula that enable all individuals to gain knowledge, skills, and enthusiasm for learning. UDL provides rich supports for learning and reduces barriers to the curriculum while maintaining high achievement standards for all
> (CAST (a) http://www.cast.org/about/index.html).

"UDL provides a blueprint for creating flexible goals, methods, materials, and assessments that accommodate learner differences" (CAST(b) http://www.cast.org/about/index.html) "ensuring that all students have access to academic content information and provide evidence of their learning through more than one means" (Thurnbull, Turnbull & Wehmeyer, 2010, p. 41). Through UDL all students, including students with disabilities "can have access to the general curriculum via curriculum modifications achieved through technology and instruction (i.e. pedagogy)" (Thurnbull *et al.,* 2010, p. 41). UDL is the teachers' answer to "How can we teach a class of students with diverse needs?" (http://www.cast.org/about/index.html).

UDL: Roots in Architecture

The concept of Universal Design has its roots in architecture and can be traced back to the early 50's when there was an increasing awareness that building environments needed to be accessible for all, especially for persons with a physical disability (Moore, 2007). This could have emerged following the World War Two due to an increase in persons with acquired physical impairments. Stephanie Moore in her book review of Rose, Meyer, Strangman and Rappolt (2002) gives a very concise and interesting background to the concept of Universal Design. She describes the development of the concept and how, in the 70's, U.S architect Michael Bednar, emphasised that everybody's functional capabilities are enhanced through barrier free structures accommodating a 'wide range' of users; persons with physical impairment and persons throughout their life which, Mace *et al.,* (1999), cited in Moore, (2007) calls 'life span design'. What was first intended as the creation of environments to facilitate mobility for persons with physical impairment, the 'wide range of users' who benefited from this was far reaching as many non-disabled persons preferred using smooth paths to stairs. The quest for barrier-free environment gained political strength with it's adoption by the *Disability Movement*. The term 'Universal Design' was coined by Ron Mace in 1987 to differentiate from accessible design. Mace (cited in Moore, 2007) states that:

> it's not a new science, a style, or unique in any way. It requires only an awareness of need and market and a commonsense approach to making everything we design and produce usable by everyone to the greatest extent possible (p. 522).

These concepts have been given legal status in many countries, including Malta with the *Equal Opportunities (Persons with Disability) Act 2000.* However, as Moore (2007) points out 'education has been somewhat behind the curve in this area'. Malta does not have a legal framework which safeguards the inclusion of students with learning difficulties.

UDL: CAST Centre for Applied Special Technology.

David Rose (Co-director of the Massachusetts based Centre for Applied Special Technology) during the first workshop of the *National Centre for Assessing the General Curriculum on Universal Design* (October 12th, 2000) stated that Universal Design for learning 'is an evolving approach that draws on new brain research and next stage technologies' (Rose, 2000). (See also video on Brain Research http://bookbuilder.cast.org/udl_videos.php).

Rose, Meyer et. al. (2002) sustain that "...barriers to learning are not, in fact, inherent in the capacities of learners, but instead arise in learners' interactions with inflexible educational materials and methods" (http://www.cast.org/teachingeverystudent/ideas/tes/preface.cfm).

UDL: Inclusive Education and the Community of Learners

When learners fail we need to look at the curriculum and the way teaching has been conducted and not blame the student (Rose & Meyer, 2000 cited in Meo, 2008). UDL is inherent in the definition of inclusive education seen as an educational process that welcomes all students from different race, socio-economic background, religions, abilities and disabilities and learning patterns. Inclusion traditionally has it's *raison d'etre* in heterogeneous groups only. It is an educational system which is flexible and which creates a community of learners in:

> classrooms that not only include children who are diverse in many ways, but also make them welcome, appreciated and valued members of the classroom environment.... community building' needs to be 'a high priority (Sapon-Shevin, 1999, p. xi).

With UDL, all students benefit, from having more flexible learning environments (Meo, 2008) including those with no identified learning difficulty. State of the art educational practices are founded on and guided by solid values and in such situations "no challenge that students and their families, schools, and teaching staff face will be too daunting" (Turnbull *et al.,* 2010, p. 5). Value guided principles are also at the root of Sapon Shevin's teaching of a new 'C.I.V.I.C.S. curriculum' "that would help us shape classrooms, schools and a society that value community. Learning to be a part of that community is an essential, perhaps the essential, goal we should set for our students and ourselves" (Sapon-Shaven, 1999, p. 1).

Universal Design for Learning facilitates the creation of this community of learners progressing together, in solidarity, without fear, stress and anxiety, in the general curriculum. 'Universal Design and inclusion' are seen as "high quality *special* education services" (Thurnbull *et al.,* 2010, p. 34) (I have italized the term 'special' since I consider this word superfluous when one talks about inclusive education). The catch phrase when discussing Universal Design is 'progress in the general curriculum'. Having said that, Universal Design for Learning needs to be sustained by an inclusive philosophy all around, where, just as the architect thinks of accessibility, when still at the drawing board stage and not when the design is ready, making access for all an integral part of the design and not an addendum, educators need to think of all their students and ways of addressing their diversity at the point of curriculum development rather than "as an afterthought or retrofit thus maintaining high expectations for all" (Meo, 2008, p. 22).

UDL is based on recent research drawn from cognitive-neuroscience and cognitive psychology and learning theories of Vygotsky and Bloom. Cognitive-neuro-science has shown that every individual's brain "processes information differently. The way we learn is as individual as DNA or fingerprints" (CAST (b) http://www.cast.org/about/index.html). Vygotsky's concept of 'shaffolding' is a key concept of a UDL curriculum:

> the idea that supports or 'scaffolds' are not permanent but rather are gradually removed as an individual becomes an expert learner, the way training wheels are unnecessary once a person has successfully mastered riding a bike
> (http://www.udlcenter.org/aboutudl/udlguidelines/introduction).

Brain Networks

In its research, CAST has identified three primary brain networks and the roles they play in learning (CAST (a)). These are:

1. Recognition networks:
   The way we gather facts, identify and categorize what we see, hear, and read. How we identify letters, words or an author's style are recognition tasks — the "what" of learning. This consists of the content, the knowledge, of what we learn and what the teacher teaches.
2. Strategic networks:
   The way we plan and perform tasks, organize and express our ideas. Writing an essay or solving a math problem are strategic tasks — the "how" of learning. These involve our essential skills, the strategies and processes we use.

3. Affective networks:
    These consider ways students are engaged and motivated, challenged, excited, or interested. These are the affective dimensions — the 'why' of learning and how we are engaged in learning, discovering where our passion lies and that of mour students.

Principles of UDL

CAST maintains that 'Universal Design for Learning is an educational approach with three primary principles based on Rose & Meyer (2006): "A means of identifying and removing barriers in the curriculum while building scaffoldings, supports and alternatives that meet the learning needs of a wide range of students" (www.cast.org; Meo, 2008, p. 22; Thurnbull & Thurnbull, 2004; Wehmeyer, 2006; Meo, 2008; Thurnbull et al., 2010 discuss these three principles in some detail. Firstly, "Multiple or flexible representations of information and concepts (the 'what' of learning)" (Meo, 2008, p. 22). Information and knowledge is presented in various ways. This is linked with the recognition networks. "Students perceive and comprehend information presented to them in different ways" (www.cast.org). For example, students with sensory impairments (visual or auditory), specific learning difficulties (dyslexia, dyspraxia), cognitive impairment at different levels, physical impairment, emotional and behavioural difficulties and language and cultural difficulties. However, all these students need different ways of having the teaching/learning material presented to them.
    Presenting material in digital and electronic formats provide great flexibility and can be transformed into:
- Text-to-speech (options in programmes): *Microsoft Word*, *Adobe Acrobat Reader*, *Kidspiration* and *Inspiration* offer text-to-speech options;
- Text with magnification, image contrasting;
- Text to speech with synchronized text highlighting (for example *Kurzweill 3000* for students with dyslexia, attention difficulties and cognitive impairment);
- Text to speech (e.g. *Kurzweill 1000*, for students with visual impairment);
- Electronic Braille;
- Digital talk books;
- Text descriptions of images;
- Simple main text and removal of clutter.

The above provide multiple representations. On presenting *Kurzweill 3000* to Peter, a twelve year old boy with a profile of dyslexia, he spontaneously exclaimed and asked with great joy 'I can now read Harry Potter!?' 'Yes', I quickly replied. 'Then I can talk with the others', he sighed. This became a 'scaffolding' which not only gave him a leg-up, provided him with scaffolding, to access a book but a leg-up which catapulted him amongst his peers where he wanted so much to feel that he too belonged. *Kurzweill* gave Peter access to all his school books and he did not have to rely on his parents to read to him material which was appropriate for his age and studies.
    Secondly, "Multiple or flexible options in expression and performance (the 'how' of learning)' (Meo, 2008, p. 22). Students differ in the way they approach learning, and the learning environment and the way they express what they have

learned, what they know (http://www.udlcenter.org/aboutudl/udlguidelines/introduction).

Learners are allowed and encouraged to use multiple modes to demonstrate what they know and what they can do in the form of "artwork photography, drama, music, animation, and video that enable students to express their ideas and their knowledge" (Wehmeyer, 2006). Students and educators may also use different types of graphic organizers which have been found to be very effective teaching strategies (CAST (c)).

The avenues are never-ending with the ever increasing expansion of technology. Assessment procedures also need to reflect these changes. Why cannot a student with dyslexia sit for a language examination using a spell check or actually sitting for the examination orally?

> There is no one means of expression that will be optimal for all students: it is therefore essential to provide various options (http://www.udlcenter.org/aboutudl/udlguidelines/introduction).

Finally, Multiple flexible ways to engage learners in the curriculum (the 'why' of learning; (Rose & Meyer, 2002 cited in Meo, 2008, p. 22). Wehmeyer,(2006) talks about tapping into the 'learners' interests, offer appropriate challenges, and increase motivation' through the use of multimedia representation. "Some students are engaged by spontaneity and novelty" (http://www.udlcenter.org/aboutudl/udlguidelines/introduction) while others will be frightened of this and want routine and structure. Once again multiple options are needed to engage and motivate all. Even some University students find it frightening if they do not have the exact pages to study from!

The educator needs to have detailed information about all the students they will be teaching in order to create and prepare a Universal Design for Learning for all their students, whether they have a statement of needs or not. Before the year is over educators should be given the space to meet with other educators who know the students for a smooth and detailed handover of each and every student. What are their leaning profiles? What are their learning patterns? What have we managed to teach them? For those students, with learning difficulties, the school could also use person-centred planning approaches with parental involvement, like MAPS, Mc Gill Action Planning System, (O'Brien & O'Brien, 2000; Turnbull, Turnbull, Shank, Smith & Leal, 2002) followed by an Individual Educational Programme (Turnbull *et al.*, 2002; 2010). The MAPS session, attended by the student's present and future educators, parents, siblings and peers, together with other professionals, the parents might want to invite, should be held before the summer recess giving the educators ample time to get to know their students. MAPS are particularly effective in times of transition. Unfortunately, our students (especially at primary level) are in this state of transition almost every year since our educational system fosters a change in teacher every year, i.e., teachers remain with the same students for one academic year only and by the time they get to know the students the year is up and a new group of students is presented to them. That is why it is important to hold MAP (McGill Action Plan) sessions every year. The IEP (Individual Educational Programme) planning session could be held some time after the beginning of the year giving the educator/s time to get to know the child. The IEP should maximize the student's involvement in the general curriculum together with any other educational needs the student might have (Turnbull *et al.,* 2010). Giangreco & Doyle (2009) provide a 'Student Information Form' which could help educators organize information about what strategies have been previously identified and implemented and clearly register which strategies worked and which did not. The majority of Maltese secondary school educators want more information about the students before the year begins (Tanti Burlo' *et al.,* 2009). Giangreco (1996) makes it quite clear that we need to be careful not to set discipline specific goals at school but to implement those goals which would facilitate access to the general curriculum. UDL learning goals focus on the end product and not on the process to achieve the end result. For example a student with cerebral palsy and difficulty in holding a pencil could be encouraged to use the computer and not dedicate a lot of time and energy in exercises hoping that he would one day write.

Literature and research on UDL is still evolving, although it draws on and extends some aspects of well known and researched strategies like differentiated instruction and cooperative learning (Meo, 2008).

> Universal design for learning overlaps considerably with differentiated instruction, particularly with regard to material and instructional choice. The additional contributions of UDL are its emphasis on initial design considerations' and digital technology' (van Garderen & Whittaker, 2006, p. 13).

Meo (2008) states that UDL "teachers support learning rather than impart knowledge, and students construct knowledge rather than passively receive it" (p.23). Another important issue is that UDL engages all students to progress in the general curriculum. Meo goes on to explain how bringing UDL into the classroom is indeed a difficult task if one has no clear defined curriculum goals, use traditional teaching methods and materials and inflexible methods of assessment. In the on-going study on Maltese secondary school educators preliminary results indicate that the great majority of educators use frontal teaching approach, are not aware of UDL, do not use peer tutoring, have little idea of graphic organizations (e.g. Mind Maps) and over 30% do not use IEP's at all but are said to use differentiated learning and cooperative learning. However, I have my doubts especially with regard to the former especially since most educators in that study state that they would prefer to teach highly selective streamed or set schools. They also identify the causes of the difficulties they encounter in teaching as being due to 'de-motivated', 'unmotivated', 'difficult to control' students, 'students with different abilities', 'students with social and family problems' and this is compounded by a syllabus which is 'too vast and difficult' (Tanti Burlo' *et al.,* 2009).

Many educators have been trained in designing IEP's and differentiated instruction (individualized adaptations) but how many of these IEP's are linked with the general curriculum? Having students in age-appropriate classrooms help, however, many LSA claim that they regularly remove the student from the classroom in order to follow and implement the student's IEP. It would be interesting to research the level of correspondence between IEPs and the general curriculum. Many students, with disabilities, are taken out of school to attend other centres and also Resource Centres (former Special Schools). This practice seems to be, unfortunately, on the increase.

Planning for All Learners

Meo (2008) describes the implementation of UDL using PAL (Planning for All Learners) which is made up of a four step process for designing and implementing a curriculum that improves learning outcomes for all students. First of all a PAL team needs to be set up. This is usually made up of the general and special education teacher and any other specialist, as needed (Meo, 2008). In Malta this could be made up of the class/subject teacher, the LSA/subject LSA and the school's INCO (Inclusion coordinator) responsible for the inclusion of children with a statement of needs, or the responsible person for 'access to the curriculum'. This last figure is used in one of our inclusive schools which has also developed the subject LSA at secondary school level. In my opinion, and from my experience, this latter structure is more conducive for developing UDL.

Another important question we should be asking ourselves is:

> Is what is being taught "meaningful" for the student? Will what is being taught 'improve this student's life, help him or her obtain a job, develop meaningful friendships, or increase access to meaningful activities? .... We must make sure that in our effort to create access to the core curriculum, we do it in a manner that makes the most sense for the individual and supports quality of life issues' (Downing, 2006, p. 328).

As explained further on Universal Design for Learning, cooperative learning, teaching mixed ability groups, graphic organizations are new concepts and relatively unknown teaching techniques for Maltese educators (Tanti Burlò, 2009). Training has focused more on IEP for children with a statement of needs and we should now shift the focus of training for educators on the development of the above mentioned teaching strategies.

A study conducted by Spooner, Baker, Harris, Delzell & Browder (2007) indicated that a mere one hour lecture on UDL focusing on the three components of UDL (i.e. representation, expression, and engagement) developed by CAST helped teachers make the curriculum more accessible for students with disabilities by modifying their lesson plans. However, I believe that we need to develop teaching strategies and techniques like cooperative teaching and learning under the umbrella of UDL for a radical change to occur in our educational system for true inclusive education to develop further. A research project could be set up to evaluate training strategies in UDL within an extremely selective and traditional educational system.

Concluding Remarks

UDL seems to focus on the classroom situation and I would therefore like to end this Chapter by introducing yet another concept taken from architecture. This is relatively unknown and has been introduced to me by David Wetherow.

> ...a Pattern Language and has been developed by Christopher Alexander. Alexander and his team noticed that there are certain patterns in the design of towns, neighbourhoods and buildings that generate experiences of dissonance and splinter community (on the one

hand) or generate experiences of harmony and ... community (on the other)' (David Wetherow, PSYCH-DD@LISTSERV.NODAK.EDU *personal correspondence* 15.2.2010).

Wetherow is 'personally deeply involved in discovering/exploring/ developing a pattern language for community and inclusion'(ibid). I am totally in agreement with him when he states that: "In the field of education, a cluster of patterns known as Cooperative Learning would help to provide a supportive context for the cluster of elements that comprise 'universal design for learning". I would also add, what I like to call the essential ingredients for successful inclusive education, namely; Quality of Life Issues, Person Centred Planning (MAPS), Social Model of Disability, Transdisciplinary School Based Team with parents as partners, planning/collaboration, Collaborative Teaching, Universal Design of Learning, IEPs, collaborative learning, celebrating differences, Peer Preparation, Peer Programs, sharing of abilities, Transition Programs and evaluation on the level of inclusion (Tanti Burlò, 2007).

Our next step on this journey towards inclusion is the identification and putting into place these 'pattern language' within the whole school and educational system. This could be done through the implementation of UDL and Cooperative learning together with the other essential ingredients for inclusive education listed above. Universal does not mean 'one size fit's all'. It means that every student has access to the general curriculum and all students are supported to find their 'passion and talents' (Robinson, 2009).

Thinking Point 1:
Next year you will be teaching a class of students with diverse needs. Remember, we all process information differently. You will be supported by an LSA and a transdisciplinary school based support team. You have attended MAP sessions for four students: Sarah who has a profile of severe dyslexia and has difficulty in reading and expressing herself in writing, Maria who has a profile of Attention Deficit (she is very quiet but aloof), Michael who has physical and multiple disabilities including intellectual impairment and John who has a profile of Attention Deficit and has difficulty keeping still and attending to his academic task. How would you start thinking about creating a UDL for any of the subjects you teach following the three primary principles of UDL:
1. Multiple or flexible representations of information and concepts: What information and how will you present that information?
2. Multiple or flexible options in expression and performance: How will the students approach their learning? How will they demonstrate what you have managed to teach them?
3. Multiple and/or flexible ways you would engage the students to learn. What would motivate them?
Thinking Point 2:
From the sites listed further down, how would they encourage you to evaluate your teaching techniques so that all your students will be challenged, valued, motivated to engage, progress safely and meaningfully in the general curriculum?

RESOURCES

Tutorials on-line on UDL:
CAST is totally committed to disseminating knowledge on UDL and offers the following on-line tutorials. Students and educators could set up working groups and go through these modules implementing UDL during their teaching practice and in their classrooms.

Module 1:   Introduction to UDL (CASTd)
            http://udlonline.cast.org/page/module1/l3/
Module 2:   Applying the UDL Framework to Lesson Development (CASTe)
            http://udlonline.cast.org/page/module2/l3/

WEBSITES

www.naturalreader.com
www.wordq.com
www.speakq.com
www.nuance.com
www.flashcardmachine.com
www.flashcardexchange.com
www.proprofs.com/flashcards
www.studystack.com/FlashCardLinks.jsp
www.widget.com
www.infovisual.info
www.pdictionary.com
www.visuwords.com
www.http://nimas.cast.org/
www.nectac.org/topics/atech/udl.asp#Recources
www.http://quizlet.com
www.scholastic.com/kids/homework/flashcards.htm
www.studystack.com
www.osepideasthatwork.org/UDL/index.asp
www.visuwords.com/?word=group
www.pachyderm.cdl.edu/elixr-stories/active-learning-chemistry/
www.youtube.com/watch?v=yETe92mwoUE
www.youtube.com/watch?v=vH5O1eCdHIY
www.youtube.com/watch?v=rH1CxE3yO8s&NR=1
www.youtube.com/watch?v=jCVJNKxLyts&NR=1
www.pachyderm.cdl.edu/elixr-stories/udl-music/

REFERENCES

Acrey C., Johnstone C., Milligan C., (2005). Using Universal Design to Unlock the Potential for Academic Achievement of At-Risk Learners. *TEACHING Exceptional Children, Vol. 38, No.2, 22-31.*
CAST(a). Centre for Applied Special technology. Retrieved on February 14th, 2010 from www.cast.org

CAST(b). Centre for Applied Special technology Retrieved on February 20th, 2010 from www.cast.org/research/udl/index.html

CAST(c). Centre for Applied Special technology. Retrieved on February 28th, 2010 www.cast.org/publications/ncac/ncac_goudl.html.

CAST(d). Centre for Applied Special technology. Module 1: Introduction to UDL. udlonline.cast.org/page/module1/l3/

CAST(e). Centre for Applied Special technology. Module 2: Applying the UDL Framework to Lesson Development. udlonline.cast.org/page/module2/l3/

Downing, J. (2006). On Peer Support, Universal Design, and Access to the Core Curriculum for Students With Severe Disabilities: A Personnel Preparation Perspective. *Research & Practice for Persons with Severe Disabilities, Vol. 31, Nc. 4, 327-330.*

Doyle, M.B., Giangreco, M. (2009). Making Presentation Software Accessible to High School Students with Intellectual Disabilities. *Teaching Exceptional Children Vol. 41. No. 3, 24-31.*

Education Act (Amendment) Act, (2006) Retrieved on February 22, 2010 from: www.education.gov.mt/ministry/doc/pdf/acts/edu_laws/amendment_to_2003/ Act_ XIIIE.pdf

Equal Opportunities (Persons with Disability) Act 2000. www.knpd.org

Giangreco, M.F. (1996). VISTA, *Vermont interdependent services team approach.* US: Paul Brookes.

Hallam, S. (2002). *Ability grouping in schools: a literature review.* Institute of Education, University of London.

Ministry of Education, Youth, Employment (2002). Creating Inclusive Schools: Guidelines for Implementation of the National Curriculum Policy on Inclusive Education (2002) Retrieved on February 22nd, 2010 from: www.education.gov.mt/ministry/doc/inclusive_schools.htm

Ministry of Education, Youth, Employment. (2005). *For All Children to Succeed: A new network organisation for quality education in Malta.* Retrieved on February 22nd, 2010 from: www.education.gov.mt/ministry/doc/pdf/for_all_children_to_succeed.pdf

Ministry of Education, Youth, Employment (2005). *Inclusive and Special Education Review.* Retrieved on February 22nd, 2010 from www.education.gov.mt/ministry/doc/pdf/inclusive_edu.pdf

Ministry of Education, Youth, Employment. (2007). Job descriptions handbook for grades and positions within the directorate for quality and standards and the directorate for educational services.

Ministry of Education. (2009). *Special schools reform.*

McGuire J., Scott S., Shaw A., (2006). Universal design and its applications in educational environments. *Remedial and Special Education. Vol. 27. No.3.166-175.*

Meyer, A. & Rose, D.H. (2000). Universal design for individual differences. *Educational Leadership, 58, 39-43.*

Meyer, A. & Rose, D.H. (2005). The future is in the margins: The role of technology and disability in educational reform (p. 13-35). In Rose D.H., Meyer A., & C. Hitchcock C., (Eds), *The universally designed classroom: Accessible curriculum and digital technologies.* Cambridge, M.A: Harvard Education Press.

Meo, G., (2008). Curriculum Planning for All Learners: Applying Universal Design for Learning (UDL) to a High School Reading Comprehension Program. *Preventing School Failure. Vol.52. No 2..21-28.* Heldref Publications.

Moore, S.L. (2007). Book Review: Rose & Meyer (2002), Teaching Every Student in the Digital Age: Universal Design for Learning. *Education Technology Research Development. 55:521–525. Springer Science and Business Media.*

National Centre for Accessing the General Curriculum (2001). New brain and next stage technologies draw fifteen educational associations to a Universal Design workshop. *The Council for teaching exceptional children. Jan/Feb 2001 p. 92-93.*

O'Brien J., O'Brien C., (2000). *A little book about person centred planning.* US: Inclusion Press.

Rose D., (2000). Workshop: National Centre for assessing the general curriculum on Universal design. www.bookbuilder.cast.org/udl_videos.php

Rose, D., Meyer, A., & Hitchcock, C. [Eds.). (2005). *The universally designed classroom.* Cambridge, MA: Harvard Education Press.

Rose, D., Meyer A., Strangman, N.M., & Rappolt, G. (2002).Teaching Every Student in the Digital Age: Universal Design for Learning. ASCD http://www.cast.org/teachingeverystudent/ideas/tes/preface.cfm

Salamanca Statement and Framework for Action on Special Needs Education (1994) Retrieved on February 22, 2010 from: www.unesco.org/education/pdf/SALAMA_E.PDF

Sapon-Shaven, M. (1999). *Because we can change the world. A practical guide to building cooperative, inclusive classroom communities. US:* Allyn and Bacon.

Spooner, F., Baker J., Harris A., Delzell L. & Browder D. (2007). Effects of Training in Universal Design for Learning on Lesson Plan Development. *Remedial and special education Vol28 No.2. p. 108-116.*

Tanti Burlo' E., (2007). *Ethics and Disability, Services in Malta* in *Towards a new humanism,* Italy: Mediterraneo senza handicap onlus.

Tanti Burlo', E., Camilleri, L. and Zucca, D. (2009). *When Educating becomes difficult. Are Inclusive schools the answer?* National Conference in Inclusive Education Programme for inclusive education. University of Malta. Work in progress.

Turnbull, R., Turnbull, A., Shank, M., Smith, S., & Leal D. (2002). (3rd Ed.). *Exceptional lives.* US: Pearson Education Inc..

Turnbull, R. & Turnbull, A., (2004). (4th Ed.). *Exceptional lives.* US: Pearson Education Inc..

Turnbull R., Turnbull A. & Wehmeyer, M.L. (2010). (6th Ed.). *Exceptional lives. US:* Pearson Education Inc..

Universal Design Centre. Retrieved February 21st, 2010, from www.udlcenter.org/aboutudl/udlguidelines/introduction

van Garderen, D., & Whittaker, C.,(2006). Planning Differentiated, Multicultural Instruction for Secondary Inclusive Classrooms. *Teaching Exceptional Children, Vol. 38, No. 3, 12-20.*

Vianello, R., (1990). *L'adolescente con handicap mentale e la sua integrazione scolastica.* Padova: Liviana.

Vianello, R., & Lanfranchi, S. (2009). Genetic syndromes causing mental retardation: Deficit surplus in school performance and social adaptability compared to cognitive capacity. *Life Span and Disability, 12 (1), 41-52.*

Vianello, R., & Maoelli E., (2001). Integrazione a scuola: le opinioni degli insegnanti, dei genitori e dei compagni di classe. *Integrazione a scuola,* GID *Anno 1, (2), 29-43.*

Vygotsky, L.S. (1978). *Mind and society: The development of higher mental processes.* Cambridge, MA: Harvard University Press.

Wehmeyer, M.L., (2006). Universal Design for Learning, Access to the General Education Curriculum and Students With Mild Mental Retardation. *Exceptionality, 14(4), 225–235*

Wetherow, D., PSYCH-DD@LISTSERV.NODAK.EDU., (email correspondence 15.2.2010)

A VISION OF EARLY INTERVENTION AND INCLUSION

ABSTRACT

This Chapter reports some of the insights into current practice and the implementation of both early intervention and inclusive education in Malta. Early intervention is seen as one of the variables that lead to the successful education of disabled students within mainstream schools. I see early intervention and its implementation as creating environments, which facilitate positive relationships and high expectations. The backbone of this programme is based on *The Portage Guide to Early Intervention*. The principles of the model are based on the concept that parents are partners and the need to recognise the expertise they possess - which no professional can provide. All support is given within all environments helping to create an inclusive community and a network of solidarity. Intervention is based on the child's strengths, abilities and interests. In the school being reported on, teaching and learning is organized to meet a diversity of talents and learning entitlements. In order to support this Chapter, narratives from parents will be included. Most professionals in the field of inclusive education will recognise that two of the most influential systems in an individual's development are the family and the school, however, is enough being done to bring these two systems together?

Introduction

Early intervention is a service offered to families having an infant or child thought to be at risk of developing in an atypical way. Early intervention is an evolving discipline with unlimited potential for growth. It is an expansive field comprised of a host of medical, therapeutic and educational professionals who join together in a collaborative effort to deliver the most effective programmes for infants and young children who are at risk. The families take on a very decisive.

Disability

Having a disabled baby or child is not the same experience as having a typically developing infant. As soon as the child has been diagnosed and given a label the infant's status changes to a child having an impairment, being trouble, seen as a problem and disabled (Booth, 1978), as does the family's.

> On the way back home as I was driving I was thinking what they had told me down at the hospital and convinced myself that I was her mother. So from that moment on, I had built up my courage and gave her the best care I could give her (Mrs. Sammut).

The label does not help or explain in any way how these infants are loved, valued and treated by their respective families in their day-to-day chores. From the individual/medical model's perspective, impairment is inevitably a serious harm and a significant infringement on the autonomy of the future of the child (Shakespeare, 1999). Within the social model thinking disability has more to do with how individuals and society relate to disabled people and their families. Naturally each child is an individual with their own strengths and needs, their own likes and dislikes, and their own abilities and entitlements.

> When Ted was born in 1992, it was not immediately apparent that he had Down syndrome and it was only when he got to the nursery that the nurses/midwives noted his features and spoke to the paediatrician. An added complication was that they knew from the case notes in the file that we had only just recently lost a daughter, the only daughter, to a traffic accident, and they were very apprehensive about telling us what they were suspecting. In fact they took Ted the day after he was born for some blood tests, which was not normal in my books and this is from him being my fourth child. We eventually learnt that he had Down syndrome and through the advice of a neighbour got in touch with a person who was to become our lifeline and help us to work with our son so that he could develop and grow as much as he possibly could (Mrs. Borg).

The needs of disabled infants and toddlers and their families create many challenges for the service provider. Recommended practice mandates that early infant education programmes be family-centered, comprehensive, and community-based and coordinated. Although presently in Malta we are struggling to provide such programmes, there are indeed exceptions that could provide a model for the Island. In Malta the early intervention programmes consist simply of limited services that are based on the medical model. Services are limited in type, frequency and location of their delivery. Additionally, the Agencies providing the services have different goals, orientations, funding sources and continuing eligibility requirements that further limit the availability of services.

> We first started speech therapy at 18 months of age. Mandy was always very fidgety and inattentive. During the sessions she was always trying to explore the therapist's office and was finding it difficult to focus. At that time her attention span was close to zero hence the therapist simply could not get through to her. After 8 weeks of getting nowhere I simply gave it up and decided to go back to the neurologist determined to do something better for my child (Mrs. Agius).

One model that has proved robust and is being implemented on the Island is *The Portage Home Teaching Model*. Dinnebeil, Hale, & Rule (1999) found several factors that influence service delivery for infants and toddlers. These included the early intervention program climate and philosophy, the management and delivery of services (e.g., staffing, scheduling of programs, and variety of service options available), the ways early intervention services are accessed, the teaming approach used, and the values of the service delivery system.

The Portage Model

The Portage Model was developed in the United States of America in the seventies. It is an early intervention progamme that offers a wide array of highly structured, individualized activities designed to facilitate a young child's development. *Portage* places emphasis on carrying out intervention in a natural and significant learning environment for the child and the family. *The Portage Model* is based on an integrated service delivery and according to this model parental involvement is critical to successful intervention. Parental involvement serves as a reminder to the professionals that parents play a crucial role in their child's education. Literature indicates that the education of disabled children is more effective when parents take an active role in their child's education (Giangreco, 2001).

The Portage Model is a strong model due to the fact that its' foundation is the parents and the family. Apart from that it is transdisciplinary, family focused and supports the needs of the family. This Model and all those who are working with it are advocates for the rights of parents and work towards parental empowerment and autonomy. Though parenting, parenting skills and developmental patterns vary across cultures, the nutrient role of the parents and family is a constant for all children disabled or not. *Portage* rejects categorizing children and demonstrates this by treating each child as unique with their own strengths, needs and entitlements. Families are also viewed as individual in their strengths and needs. There is a general consensus that families of disabled children should be actively involved in their child's intervention and education. The interventionist seeks a workable, mutually satisfying partnership with the family.

> We worked very hard and long with Ted and spent a lot of time with him. He was also often sick and had to be taken care of and sometimes even hospitalized. It was a challenge raising him. There were very precious moments but also some heartbreaking ones as well, especially when it seemed that others were not ready to accept him and learn how to get along with him. As he reached the important milestones in life we felt very proud of him, of the effort he had made and the achievements he had achieved. His extrovert character has helped him a lot and will continue to help him in life (Mrs. Borg).

Mahler, Pine and Bergman (1975) have emphasized the embeddedness of early development in care-giving relationships. *The Portage Model* is designed so that families participate from the beginning, and is comprehensive to include the child's home life, school activities, after-school recreation and support services such as speech, physical and occupational therapy.

> I used to spend an hour with her everyday just to teach her and help her to become more independent. With my help and that of our early interventionist, Molly recognised about 50 flashcards now that she is 11months old (Mrs. Sammut).

Portage also takes into account the family's cultural background, available resources, demands on time and energy, educational level, their attitudes, values and interests. Bringing intervention procedures inline with both family and school activities requires using a judicious mix of formal and incidental teaching techniques.

> Intervention in my case has given me the much required direction. As a parent it has made me feel useful and capable of helping my child get through her difficulty (Mrs. Zammit).

Play and Portage

Play is a child's most natural activity and research has shown that play encourages cognitive development, thinking skills, social-emotional development, communication and language abilities and movement proficiency. Play is an important indicator of children's language and symbol systems, and the meanings children give to persons, places and events. Play is also an index of children's imagination, curiosity, motivation, preferences, interests and persistence. Through child-led play, the child's interests and abilities a structured teaching programme is designed and implemented.

> Play is also a very important part of early intervention. We spend around 45min on play every day. This includes drawing & colouring in, puzzles, turn taking games and reading... Exposing the child to these daily games has helped Mandy to learn the alphabet, have better hand coordination & turn taking while practicing listening and eye contact amongst other things.... Reading is also one thing we are encouraged to at home. Mandy is surrounded by picture books and we try to make reading a fun activity every time by acting out the story. Nowadays, Mandy carries her books everywhere.... they are simply her favourite toy (Mrs. Agius).

These play skills in turn are all building blocks for life. Disabled infants and children are known to have little interest in play and have limited play skills.

> Molly was much more confident with her school friends now, she also loved her teachers especially Ms. Polly. She was getting better at doing jigsaw puzzles and colouring. Sometimes we would laugh as she used to pick some habits from her school friends (Mrs. Sammut).

Total Communication

Total communication is implemented as a major component within the infant or child's structured teaching programme. Total communication is a language programme that teaches the written word, key word signing, spoken word and communication skills simultaneously.

This structured language programme supports the *Portage Project's* (2003) language milestones. Flashcards are taught in a structured format combined with play, which helps the child to generalise, and practice their pre- lingual skills (sitting, eye contact, joint attention, pointing and imitation together with an ever-increasing vocabulary.

> Once we started flash cards at home we could from an early stage already see Mandy settling down, we were seeing improvement in eye contact and the sitting tolerance during the session was noticed to increase in attention almost instantly. In less than 3 months Mandy was able to identify the words and point at the right word when shown 2 flashcards. At that stage we were happy to know that at least she would know what an object's name is (Mrs. Agius).

The *Flash Card Language Programme* enables parents and children to maximise communication and learning. Language is a tool for thinking and as educators it is vital that we in put language from the inset of the programme. If we fail to do so we have failed the child and the family.

> To me lots or repetition and is are is key when using this system (Mrs. Borg).

Collaborative Teamwork

Both in the field of early intervention and in inclusive schools the most likely individuals to be members of the team are the parents, educators, teacher and facilitator team, student and peers, (Stainback and Stainback, 1992). They are also the people who will be directly involved in the daily living, teaching, education, and supporting of the disabled student.

> I started Portage early intervention with Mandy at age 20months, whilst keeping speech therapy and OT which we still attend to today. The first lesson with the educator was extremely frustrating. Mandy was opposing the educator with a horrid tantrum, which kept going throughout the whole session. Even though I could tell that Mandy was very upset with whole setup of the session consisting of flashcards and play I remember vividly the educator stepping out of my house and me telling my husband that this is it, I finally found the way to help my child. Maybe it was maternal instinct but from that day onwards I never looked back (Mrs. Agius).

Placement of the disabled student really does matter and everything we do, as educators need to become portable. Supports for the disabled student need to be in place, only as special as necessary and strategic. The most critical strategy for creating successful learning experiences for all children, regardless of disability, is teamwork. Collaborative teamwork is when all members of the team have common goals and a shared understanding (Garner, 2001). Family involvement is a must and families must be helped to understand the instructional content of each subject, in order to contribute effectively in their child's life.

Most importantly these daily sessions have helped me find a way to communicate and feel close to my child. When rarely I have to miss a session even though I might have spent a whole day with my child it does feel like I have missed something. During the session I feel that Mandy is there for me as I am there for her, this is our way of spending quality time together, as many times autistic kids are often noticed playing alone and ignoring what is happening around them. Recently the school offered to take over the flashcards and I immediately refused! I would never give up our daily sessions and if presented with the same situation I would without any doubt go for Early Learning Intervention once again (Mrs. Agius).

Parents and professionals are constantly bringing new meaning to what constitutes an appropriate and effective inclusive education and what facilitates effective partnerships among professionals, families and others involved in the education of disabled students. Collaborative teamwork is hardly a new idea. It has been put forward as a strategy that could improve education for disabled students (Whitehouse, 1951 cited in Stainback & Stainback, 1992). Team members are constantly struggling with redefining roles, relationships and responsibilities in order to collaborate more effectively in inclusive school environments. The nature of the relationships between teachers and class facilitators (or Learning Support Assistants - LSA) is constantly changing. In schools, the instructional strategies associated with each discipline are among the most significant contributions team members make in the collaborative teamwork process. In teaching teams, each member works to achieve the common goals within a transdisciplinary framework (Lyon & Lyon, 1980). Members of the team both depend on and support other people to achieve the agreed upon goals (Villa, 1996).

Inclusion

Inclusion is about social justice and having insight into disability equality and human rights issues that underpin the social model of disability (Oliver, 1999). Inclusion is about ones own ability to refrain from trying to place people we view differently into pigeon holes and making ourselves comfortable with the idea it is about service provision 'for the good of the student'! Inclusion is about acknowledging people are *people first* and everyone's an individual, not a label. It is about treating persons equally rather than the same. There is no one approach to inclusive education. Being inclusion orientated is a different experience in every school due to the cultural context and one's social construction of disability. Inclusion is a process and not a fixed point to be reached. We need to explore how inclusion can be developed further within one's own context so that it becomes a strategic framework both in education and within the community. We need to look toward the families to gain the best models of inclusion. This is where the experience is one of unconditional acceptance, (Turnbull *et al.*, 1994; Orelove, 2004).

During the past twenty years the Maltese educational system has pledged a commitment to inclusive education. An inclusive educational policy was introduced in 1995 (MIE, 1995), and as a result, disabled students were given a legal statement of needs and were placed in mainstream schools with identified support. The *National Minimum Curriculum* (NMC), published in 1999 stressed its commitment to inclusive education:

> Each school is endowed with a vast repertoire of skills, experiences and needs. This diversity, allied with the individual and social difference evident in the student population, enables and requires pedagogy based on respect and the celebration of difference...it is a well-established fact that not all students develop at the same rate. Students should be allowed time and be given the necessary support for their personal development (NMC, 1999, p. 31).

Inclusive education is based on the commitment of society as a whole to adopt and to implement inclusive educational strategies and policies, as well as respecting and celebrating diversity. Inclusion in reality on this Island (Malta) is experienced very differently in schools, really and truly depending on the School Management Team's beliefs. Maltese schools now embrace inclusive settings. This entails placing disabled children in their local schools, or the school of their parents' choice alongside their peers from the age of three years.

> Ted started school when he was three. He went to a nursery, which was in an inclusive setting. He was very happy there and he learnt a lot. When he was five we applied for him to start school where his brothers were, in a church school, but this particular school did not really have an idea how to deal with children like Sam so we decided that it would be best if he remained in the nursery school for another year and we would then either send him to a government school near our house or try for a church school again. We started talks with the primary school in our village and they were very receptive but then the chance came for him to enter St. Benild's and we took it. He then proceeded to Stella Maris College and moved up with his peers every year (Mrs. Borg).

Most of these children have received and or are receiving the support of early intervention services and have a formal statement of educational entitlement. This entitlement is the provision of a class-based Learning Support Assistant (LSA) assigned to the child.

> Mandy recently started pre-grade, and has the provision for individual support. She knows all letters, numbers, shapes & solid shapes, colours, body parts and more... much more. Even though she might not be taking in the whole lesson I can put my mind at rest that whatever is being done at school has already been covered at home (Mrs. Agius).

Whilst Malta prescribes to inclusive education, the complex debate surrounding it seems to be inexhaustible. The concept of inclusive education needs to be viewed as a process located within the cultures, policies and practices of a whole school (Salamanca Statement, UNESCO, 1994). We need to reflect relentlessly to ensure that we acknowledge the fact that school culture is still selective, exclusionary, credential-oriented and standards-based (Ainscow, 1999; Slee, 2000). Education is a mainstream environment that should encapsulate the fundamental principle of 'schools for all':

> believes in the broadening of democratic boundaries, in the fostering of a participatory culture, in the defence of the basic rights of the children, in the constant struggle against all those factors that prevent the students' different abilities from being brought to fruition and in the safeguarding and strengthening of our country's achievements in the social and cultural fields (NMC, 1999, p. 47).

Whilst parents of disabled children are demanding that their child receives his education within mainstream schools, it is interesting to hear the views of parents of typically developing students. The research clearly shows that the other parents are positive about this experience and appreciate the support that having another adult in class brings.

> Having students with disabilities in the school is a very positive experience, both for the children and for us parents. Personally it impacted me as a parent understanding difference and intolerance. The new experience is definitely reaching far more of our students, supporting each student according to his needs (Mrs. Agius).

Stella Maris College

Stella Maris College is a boys' Church school for children between five and sixteen years of age. It has a population of just over a thousand children with around ninety boys in each year group. *Stella Maris College* has two LSA's in every classroom in the Junior School, except for three, and subject – pegged and class LSA as from the last year of primary school through to Form 5. Therefore, the School has created teacher-facilitator teams, where the teams stay on working together and the class moves on.

The College process of inclusion is a unique experience and whilst recognizing that there is no inclusion utopia, the college strives to be inclusive-oriented. Today all classes have teacher/class facilitator teams and collaborative teamwork is fostered and targeted for. Early identification, referral, assessment and provision policies are in place.

McGill Action Planning System (MAPS) and *Individual Educational Programme* (IEP) meetings are held for all students with an educational statement of needs, (An educational statement formalizes the support structures that the student is entitled to) where all the teachers, facilitators, students, supporting professionals and parents participate. Parents are respected and are in partnership with the teaching teams. The School follows a transdisciplinary philosophy (Giangreco, 2002; Giangreco, Cloninger & Iverson, 1998; Orkwia & McLane, 1998; Orelove, 1994).

The way teachers know our son is marvelous. They can explain his character, his strengths and needs in an incredible way. This all shows the interest that all the members of the team have in our children. The MAP session has helped me to increasingly put my mind at rest regarding my sons education (Mr. Attard).

IEP sessions are very helpful for us parents to know what is happening at school. This is good because there is communication between teachers, facilitators and parents (Mrs. Briffa).

Finally

It is therefore clear that the College has made a philosophical and a pragmatic commitment for an inclusive experience for all the boys. Inclusion has become a whole-school issue supporting an environment of collaboration and solidarity in diversity. Whilst support for statemented students is provided by teaching teams, the teacher takes full responsibility for the students learning. Meaningful and effective assessments are in place and are tailored to each student's in class support. Differentiated teaching is infiltrating classrooms and good practice is shared between teaching teams. Teaching teams are made up of class or subject teacher together with class or subject facilitator. Roles and responsibilities of the teachings teams are clearly defined. Transition meetings from kindergarten and each year following to Form 5 and on into post secondary have been implemented and are in place. The College works in partnership with parents and has an open door policy clearly encouraging open communication with parents.

The College puts at its centre young people and their needs. Young people are growing up in a rapidly changing society. To respond to these needs, we need a system of education that is flexible and adapted to different levels of development. All input from the various stakeholders in the school overwhelmingly indicates that this new approach is superior and more effective in all aspects. The College identified appropriate goals and continues to work towards the challenges of being truly supportive, flexible and adaptive to the individual needs of all students. Therefore, this concept should be implemented throughout the Maltese school system?

Thinking Point 1:
'Early intervention' supports inclusive practices and empowers parents to continue their vital role in their child's school journey. How do your own reflections, impact on your perceptions, experience and feelings concerning parental involvement?
Thinking Point 2:
The biggest barriers to inclusion are adults and the less than appropriate support systems. Support does matter and seeking a balance between teacher and LSA involvement in the disabled student's learning as well as the other children's is crucial to sound educational practice. Comment.

REFERENCES

Agius Ferrante, C. & Falzon, R. (2001). *Teacher-facilitators teams - a different experience.* Unpublished research Paper presented at Antalya.

Ainscow, M. (1999). *Understanding the development of inclusive schools.* London: Routledge/Falmer Press.

Arnold, L. (2006). *Disability and Impairment, what is the essential difference? Deconstructing the language of the social model.* Retrieved June 7th, 2010 from http://www.lancs.ac.uk/fass/events/disabilityconference_archive/2006/papers/arnold2006.pdf

Bartolo, P., Agius Ferrante, C., Azzopardi, A., Bason, L., Grech, L. & King, M.A. (2004). *Creating inclusive schools - guidelines for the implementation of the national minimum curriculum policy on inclusive education.* Sliema: Salesian Press.

Booth, T. (1978). From a normal baby to a handicapped child: unraveling the idea of subnormality in families of mentally handicapped children. *Sociology, 12, 203-221.*

Dinnebeil, L. A., Hale, L., & Rule, S. (1999). Early intervention program practices that support collaboration. *Topics in Early Childhood Special Education, 19, 225-235.*

Glenn, G. (2001). *Helping others through teamwork: A handbook for professionals with workbook.* CWLA Press (Child Welfare League of America).

Giangreco, M. (Ed.) (2002). *Quick guides to inclusion 3: Ideas for educating students with disabilities.* USA: Brookes Publishing Co.

Giangreco, M., Cloninger, C.J. & Iverson, V. S. (1998). *Choosing outcomes and accommodations for children (COACH): A guide to educational planning for students with disabilities.* USA: Brookes Publishing Co.

Giangreco, M.F., Cloninger, C.J., & Iverson, V.S. (1998). *(2nd Ed.). Choosing outcomes and accommodations for children (COACH): A guide to educational planning for students with disabilities.* Baltimore: Paul H. Brooks Publishing Co.

Jupp, K. (1992). *Everyone belongs: Mainstream education for children with severe learning difficulties.* London: Souvenir Press.

Lyon, S. & Lyon, G (1980). Team functioning and staff development: A role release approach to providing integrated educational services for severely handicapped students. *Journal of the Association for the Severely Handicapped, 5, 250-263.*

Mahler, M.S., Pine, F.,& Bergman, A. (1975). *The psychological birth of the human infant: Symbiosis and individuation.* New York: Basic Books.

Ministry of Education (1999). *National minimum curriculum.* Floriana: Ministry of Education.

Morris, J. (1991) *Pride against Prejudice: Transforming attitudes to disability.* London: The Women's Press.

Oliver, M. (1999). *Disabled people and the inclusive society or the times they really are changing.* Public lecture on behalf of Strathclyde Centre for disability research and Glasgow City Council

Orelove, F.P. (1994). Transdisciplinary teamwork. In Garner, H.G. & Orelove, F.P. (Eds.), *Teamwork in human services: Models and application across the life span (p. 37-59).* Boston: Butterworth-Heinemann.

Orelove, F.P. (Ed.) *et al..* (2004). *A transdisciplinary approach.* USA: Brookes Publishing Co.

Orkwis, R. & McLane, K. (1998, Fall). A curriculum every student can use: Design principles for student access. *ERIC/OSEP Topical Brief, 3-19.*

Pearpoint, J., Forest, M., & Snow, J. (1992). *The inclusion paper.* Canada: Inclusion Press.

Portage Project, (2003). Child Development Tool for Observation and Planning. Retrieved on 6th June, 2010 http://www.portageproject.org/npg/npg_3.HTM

Shakespeare, T. (1999). Losing the plot? Medical and activist discourses of contemporary genetics and disability. *Sociology of Health and Illness, 21 (5), 669 – 688.*

Slee, R. (2000). *Talking back to power: The politics of educational exclusion.* Paper presented at ISEC Conference.

Stainback, S. & Stainback, W. (1992). *Curriculum considerations in inclusive classrooms: Facilitating learning for all students,* Baltimore: Paul H. Brooks Publishing Co.

Sultana, R. G. & Baldacchino, G. (1994). *Maltese society – a sociological enquiry,* Msida: Mireva Publications.

Turnbull, R., Turnbull, A., Shank, M. & Smith, S. J. (2004). *Exceptional lives: Special education in today's schools.* New Jersey: Pearson Education, Inc..

United Nations Educational and Scientific Organization. (1994). *The Salamanca statement and framework for action on special needs education. World Conference on Special Needs Education.* Paris: UNESCO.

Villa, R.A., Thousand, J.S., Meyers, H., & Nevin, A.I. (1996). Teacher and administrator perceptions of heterogeneous education, *Exceptional children, 63, 29-45.*

THE ROLE OF AN LSA IN AN INCLUSIVE EDUCATION SETTING

ABSTRACT
Equality of access to education for all, and more specifically for students with disabilities, is the documented policy both of the United Nations (UNESCO, 2009) and of the European Union (Schools for the 21st Century, 2007). Notwithstanding this, inclusive education is still a contentious notion in contemporary education. The objective of this Chapter is to examine and lay out the reasons why inclusive education is effective. In this Chapter, I have analyzed two broad themes in inclusion, firstly, the actual and specific roles and responsibilities of the LSA and secondly, the key issues and challenges that surround them.

Introduction

Camilleri states that, "in Malta, one of the most remarkable developments has been the Maltese Ministry of Education's incremental phasing-in of an inclusive education policy in 1994" (as cited in Azzopardi, 2008, p. iii). Our schools are full of students with diverse experiences, thanks to "a number of changes across the years (which) have characterized our educational system (Sultana, 2001, as cited in Azzopardi, 2008, p. 1) and which have permitted children and youngsters with individual educational needs to be included in mainstream schools and society in general.

The National Minimum Curriculum states that:

> Equally interwoven in its aims and provisions is the celebration of diversity. The holistic spirit of the document not only includes every aspect of human development and every phase of it but it also embraces the diversity of learning styles as well as the whole range of abilities, backgrounds, specific learning difficulties, and special needs that are bound to exist among the community of learners. This is why the document spares no effort to make clear its vision of inclusion (Ministry of Education, 1999, p. 9).

The thought of inclusive education has been lurking in the background for many years before it actually started being implemented locally. Bank-Mikkelsen (1969) argued against a shielding approach to services for children with disabilities, and emphasized that they should enjoy an ordinary lifestyle. Nirje (1985) added that the realization of such outcomes needed to be based on schemes that were culturally normative whereby persons with a disability enjoyed the same rights, privileges, opportunities, and access to services and facilities as those who do not have a disability or impairment.

The *Education Department* and non-government sectors have evolved, reformed and restructured themselves in the past twenty years and this change has inevitably pushed inclusive education high on the agenda. The growth trajectory of inclusive education has brought great achievements for parents, students and the teaching community but has also highlighted the lacunae that there still exist. Further development towards full academic and social accessibility is still required (for example, the meritocratic oriented system in Malta is a barrier towards the full benefit of inclusion). Until recently, schools were like factories that produced students for the sole purpose of excelling in various public examinations. The adoption of inclusive education has somewhat changed our educational focus but our culture still requires students to be valued against the amount of certificates they manage to accumulate. Thanks to committed educators, parents and positive development in our system, we are gradually moving towards ensuring that all children learn together and specific attention is given to each student according to his/her needs.

Learning Support Assistant

One size does not fit all, and that is why "… inclusion relates to the provision of appropriate educational experiences to meet the needs of all students, including those who are exceptionally gifted or talented, and those who have high support needs" (Elkins & Ashman, 2008, p. 35). A Learning Support Assistant (LSA), according to me, is the focal point through which a classroom must be adjusted to receive all pupils in a regular environment. LSAs offer the exciting prospect of making a difference, both for individual success and for society's continuing development. An LSA in most schools is still mostly classroom based and works alongside the teachers, supporting pupils to capitalise out of their learning. The role of the LSA in supporting and promoting inclusive education entails a vast variety of duties wherein successful deployment is based on good communication between staff and relatives and a willingness to support each other, especially in the classroom. LSAs work most effectively when they know what is expected of them through the liaising with teachers and administration staff and actively contributing to all relevant meetings and courses. I have divided the duties and responsibilities of an LSA into three comprehensible categories; (a) within the classroom, (b) personal support to the student/s and (c) school related duties.

These duties and responsibilities include, but are not limited to the following;
(a)   Inside the classroom;
• Explain, clarify, interpret and adapt the lesson content when required;
• Develop differentiated texts and worksheets and provide alternative methods;
• Teach reading;
• Teach students how to make notes;
• Teach writing skills;
• Teach organizational skills;
• Work on differentiated activities with groups;
• Supervise and support practical tasks;
• Ensure that pupils record homework tasks;
• Act as an informal amanuensis;
• Help students develop information retrieval skills;

- Draw up and contribute to the planning and reviewing of IEPs;
- Ensure that specific resources and equipment are available;
- Support students in accessing the curriculum;
- Focus and redirect attention;
- Help build students' confidence and self-esteem;
- Participate in the observation, assessment and documentation process of the performance and behaviour;
- Contribute knowledge and understanding;
- Model and encourage appropriate social skills;
- Provide pastoral care; be sensitive to individual, physical, emotional, personal or social needs.

(b) Personal support
- Mobility support;
- Support students in unfamiliar surroundings e.g. outings, school visits and experiences in the community;
- Participate in hydrotherapy, multi-sensory, sensory integration in school and outside school;
- Toileting, cleaning and washing;
- Seeing to the mobility, posture and seating needs, including lifting pupils and pushing pupils in wheelchairs;
- Assistance during physical education, games, excursions and therapy sessions;
- Assist in the boarding and un-boarding of pupils on and off the transport vehicle.

(c) School related
- Encouraging participation in EU projects;
- Reinforce the school's aims, ethos, policies and behaviour code and actively work as a member of the staff team;
- Promote an inclusive community by collaborating with the school and other agencies and multi- and trans-disciplinary teams;
  (Department of Information – Malta).

Statementing

Pupils with special needs may be assessed by the Statementing Moderating Panel (SMP), a specialist panel that identifies the specific needs of each pupil and advises on the special provision required within the mainstream education system. The SMP is the State recognized body empowered to develop a statutory assessment of the support required in order to ensure a quality education for pupils with an impairment. The work carried out by the SMP is based on the Inclusive Education Policy regarding pupils with a disability (European Agency for Development in Special Needs Education, 2009).

The interpretations and implications of the *Statementing Moderating Panel's* recommendations of support that are required to facilitate the inclusion of students with individual and education needs in the mainstream are the following:

- *Full Time Support on a one-to-one basis*:
  The LSA should dedicate all of his/her time to support that particular student.
- *Full Time Support*:
  The LSA is present in the classroom throughout the whole day and can support more than one student in the same class provided that only one of the students is in need of full-time support.
- *Shared in the same class*:
  The LSA is present in the classroom throughout the whole day. This type of support is determined by the students' statement. The LSA can support a maximum of two students in the same class.
- *Shared Support*:
  The student does not require support throughout the whole day. The LSA may either be assigned responsibility of up to three students who are in the same class and/or support up to two students who require shared support but are not in the same class. In the latter case, equity is recommended.
- *Benefits from resources*:
  The *Panel* recommends that the learners' needs should be met by the class teacher with the cooperation of the LSA in class if available. The child would benefit from being in a class where there is an LSA.
  (Letter Circular [Ref: HRD/46/2009] from the Director of Human Resources Development to all heads of school, dated 26th May 2009.)

While keeping all the above in mind, I must stress the fact that although each and every student should be included, any situations or experiences that would constitute an unreasonable hardship are to be avoided.

> Sometimes courses of study involve elements in which a student cannot participate, and it is expected that he or she will be offered another activity or content that fits within overall course aims. As far as possible, where activities take place outside school, they should be chosen or designed to include the student (Elkins & Ashman, 2008, p. 40).

Key Issues and Challenges

In order to embrace social justice, educational systems are attempting to become the most inclusive possible. Educating all children together remains a modern-day challenge, since inclusion can only be implemented if all of its principles are taken into account. It is widely acknowledged that the essential conditions allowing for successful inclusion contribute to overall school improvement and high levels of success for all children, irrespective of their abilities.

There is increasing evidence that children with disabilities learn better and become more skilled when they attend mainstream schools (Salend, 2007). Often, it is the only realistic opportunity they will have to receive a social, complete and holistic education. Inclusion and the good educational practice that comes with it, offers hope to a nation that needs to ensure educational equity and participation for all. "Regular schools with this inclusive orientation are the most effective means of combating discriminatory attitudes, creating welcoming communities, building an inclusive society and achieving education for all..." (Article 2, Salamanca Statement). However, most teaching staff still find the concept of inclusive education quite challenging. For instance, the demands of multilevel teaching, of flexible curriculum differentiation, of teamwork within the same classroom, of interprofessional discussions outside the classroom, of additional responsibilities and accountability across an Individualized Educational Programme, and of learning to feel comfortable with diversity – all these will tax even the best trained, most competent and dedicated teachers.

In fact, an important challenge is the adequate and pertinent teacher training in dealing with a heterogeneous student population. Teaching in an inclusive community entails unique skills, which can only be acquired through particular and specific training programmes. Teachers also need to be supported by innovative curriculum material allowing for creative and multilevel teaching. By increasing resources, schools will be able to support learning and involvement and above all, remain relevant institutions for all students alike. Furthermore, collaboration with teachers and school administrators is crucial

Another issue which resurfaces every year is the student population in our classrooms. Due to various factors, the number of pupils in a classroom tends to be high. Even when teachers and LSAs cooperate and do their utmost to accommodate all children, someone is inevitably left out. For instance, such activities as outings, group work inside and outside the classroom, textbooks and sometimes even some topics are sometimes not age appropriate and this makes it quite difficult for the LSA to come up with suitably differentiated materials. Another case in point is the endlessly controversial issue of the national examination system, which fails to accommodate students' diverse backgrounds and needs. Furthermore curricula are not designed on the basis of flexibility and often tend to be content-heavy. With such a rigid and extensive curriculum, students with individual educational needs are repeatedly excluded and marginalized and disadvantaged.

Inclusive education also contests the notion of streaming, setting and any other selective system which goes against all concepts of individualized teaching. Students require that the learning environment is adjusted so that their experiences are as close as possible to those of the rest of the pupils. In this context, adjustment refers to the removal of barriers that prevent participation in the classroom and in all the learning activities that happen in a school community. LSAs may find it difficult to eliminate such barriers at times especially when they are faced with school policies which do not tally with some concepts of inclusive and holistic education. Obstacles may include: lack of accessibility, lack of resources due to prioritized funding and budgets, ineffective collaboration with teaching staff, "a mismatch between the teacher's assumptions about how students learn and how they actually do learn" (Ashman & Elkins, 2008, p. 98), teacher attitude and lack of tolerance, and other whole-school and classroom factors. LSAs might also find lack of cooperation from parents, difficulties in dealing with prejudice and labelling, and the absence of shared goals.

LSA Fundamentals: Planning, Supporting and Evaluating

Within the framework of inclusive education, a large part of the LSA's job includes sensitivity to the barriers that might encumber a student's growth through the school years. Teachers, administrators and LSAs must actively engage in the shared responsibility of creating an environment that welcomes all students. A most important tool for the LSA and all the respective stakeholders is the *Individualized Educational Programme* (IEP). An IEP represents the programme that has been designed to meet a child's unique needs and it underpins the process of planning and intervention for the student. It is imperative that each student has an IEP which is a truly individualized document designed for him/her. The IEP creates an opportunity for teachers, parents, school administrators, related services personnel, and students (when age appropriate) to work together to improve educational results.

Every IEP should begin with the child's present level of educational functioning and behaviour. When the LSA is new with her student, the IEP can be done after four to six weeks of intense observation, assessment and gathering of information. Observation times and techniques must be carried out in a natural setting, in order to assess both the student's strengths and needs. The LSA can use a myriad of ways for observation, some of which might result in the need for a peer preparation programme.

When this information is collated, the IEP meeting should be organized. The parents are to be informed before about the IEP so that they themselves can come up with goals during the actual meeting. The discussion involves choosing the priorities and targets, together with detailed strategies, short term goals, activities, materials and equipment needed to achieve these targets. To be fully effective, the IEP must have a direct link to daily plans which incorporate class objectives and adaptations. Implementing the IEP also includes the actual support of the child which was discussed earlier in this Chapter. Finally, the IEP must be periodically reviewed and evaluated. Review dates are to be written down and all team members are responsible for evaluating its effectiveness. A copy of the document should be distributed to all the members who would have taken part in setting the targets for the child.

Success and Access – A Learning Journey

In order for inclusive education to be a success, teachers and students alike should be taught to understand diversity so that they have the knowledge and skills for positive participation in a democratic society. It will ensure that schools are supportive and engaging for all students, teachers, parents and caregivers. It will build communities that celebrate and respond to diversity. Inclusive education is underpinned by respectful relationships between all the persons who are involved with the children and it is also supported by collaborative relationships with the community and the Government.

The benefits of educating students with disabilities with their peers have been well established (Downing & Peckham-Hardin, 2007; Fisher & Meyer, 2002; Foreman, Arthur-Kelly, Pascoe & Smyth-King, 2004). Research also shows benefits for peers without disabilities when educated in inclusive classrooms

(Carter & Hughes, 2006; Dymond et al., 2006; Peck, Staub, Gallucci & Schwartz, 2004; Fisher, Sax & Grove, 2000).

We know that "...you can provide a supportive environment and useful assistance at home, but you cannot take away the disappointment and hurt that are almost an inevitable part of your child's school experience" (Ben-Ami & Stern, 1996, p. v). I have tried to challenge this statement by demonstrating that what we can offer the child with a disability by far exceeds what limitations the child may have.

Conclusively

For me, this has been a challenge. My own daughter has multiple learning difficulties and because of this I have struggled with notions of denial and resistance and finally found the energy to act. That my daughter has been both the resource and inspiration for my career almost goes without saying.

Thinking Point 1:
What are the most fundamental concepts that an LSA should learn and embrace before embarking on such an important career?
Thinking Point 2:
Read the *National Minimum Curriculum* and focus particularly on Principle 2 and Principle 8. These two principles are itemized in the document *Creating Inclusive Schools* (view at www.education.gov.mt/ministry/doc/inclusive_schools.htm). Use the general and specific indicators found in the second part and appendices of this document to determine whether the school you work in, or schools in general, are acting in accordance with these indicators.
Thinking Point 3:
Create a checklist whereby an LSA would be able to mark all the components which would have been accomplished for an IEP to be successful.

REFERENCES

Ashman, A., & Elkins, J. (2008). *Education for Inclusion and Diversity.* Australia: Frenchs Forest, N.S.W.: Pearson Education Australia.
Azzopardi, A. (2008). *Career Guidance for Persons with Disability.* Malta: Euroguidance
Bank-Mikkelson, N. (1969). A Metropolitan area in Denmark: Copenhagen. In R. Kugel & W. Wolfensberger (Eds.), *Changing patterns in residential services for the mentally retarded* (p. 227-254). Washington, DC: President's committee on Mental Retardation.
Carter, E.W., & Kennedy, C.H. (2006). Promoting access to general curriculum using peer support strategies. *Research and Practice for Persons with Severe Disabilities, 31, 284-292.*
Commission Staff Working Paper (2007). *Schools for the 21st century.* Brussels: Commission of the European Communities.
Directorate for Educational Services (2009). *Public Service Commission.* Malta: Department of Information.

Downing, J. E., & Peckham-Hardin, K. D. (2007). Inclusive education: What makes a high quality education for students with moderate-severe disabilities? *Research and Practice for Persons with Severe Disabilities, 32, 16-30.*

Dymond, S. K., Renzaglia, A., Rosenstein, A., Chun, E.J., Banks, R.A., Niswander, V., & Gilson, C.L. (2006). Using a participatory action research approach to create a universally designed inclusive high school science course: A case study. *Research and Practice for Persons with Severe Disabilities, 31, 293-308.*

European Agency for Development in Special Needs Education (2009). Identification of special educational needs – Malta. Retrieved from www.european-agency.org/country-information/malta/national-overview/ identification-of-special-educational-needs.

Fisher, D., Sax, C., & Grove, K. A. (2000). The resilience of changes promoting inclusiveness in an urban elementary school. *The Elementary School Journal, 100, 213-227.*

Fisher, M., & Meyer, L. (2002). Development and social competence after two years for students enrolled in inclusive and self-contained educational programs. *Research and Practice for Persons with Severe Disabilities. 27, 165-174.*

Foreman, P., Arthur-Kelly, M., Pascoe, S., & Smyth-King, B. (2004). Evaluating the educational experiences of students with profound and multiple disabilities in inclusive and segregated classroom settings: An Australian perspective. *Research and Practice for Persons with Severe Disabilities, 29, 183-193.*

Ministry of Education, (1999). *Creating the future together – National Minimum Curriculum.* Floriana, Malta: Klabb Kotba Maltin.

Nirje, B. (1985). Setting the record straight: A critique of some frequent misconceptions of the normalization principle. *Australia and New Zealand Journal of Developmental Disabilities, 11, 69-74.*

Peck, C., Staub, D., Gallucci, C., Schwartz, I. (2004). Parent perspectives of the impacts of inclusion on their nondisabled child. *Research and Practice for Persons with Severe Disabilities, 29, 135-143.*

Salend, S. (2007). *Creating Inclusive Classrooms.* USA: Prentice Hall.

Stern, J., & Ben-Ami, U. (1996). *Many ways to learn: Young people's guide to learning disabilities.* Washington, DC: Magination Press.

The Salamanca Statement (1994). *Proceedings of the World Conference on Special Needs Education: Access and Quality* (p. ix). Spain: Ministry of Education and Science.

UNESCO (2009). *Inclusive education: The way of the future.* Geneva: International Bureau of Education.

A TEACHER, A CLASSROOM, A SCHOOL:
A HOLISTIC APPROACH TOWARDS INCLUSION

ABSTRACT

Although much has been said and written about 'inclusive education', the construct of an inclusive curriculum along with its practical implications in Malta is still an emergent topic in need of further research. *Inclusive education* and *student diversity* are popularized concepts in educational discourse. These are becoming increasingly familiar terms however, it does not necessarily mean that these have become common knowledge and practice. In fact, Cheng (2000) emphasizes the social, rather than isolated, nature of learning. This Chapter also highlights inclusion as a value fostered by teachers and all stakeholders of the school community rather than an imposed policy.

Diversity: The Reality in Our Classrooms

Understanding the concept of inclusion requires that we reflect on the notion of diversity. Diversity's broad spectrum holds a wide range of possible differences that individuals might have. To mention just a few, students differ from each other by their cultural experiences, socio-economic background, interests, learning patterns and style preferences, gender, race and religion.

Inclusive education means that:

> schools should accommodate all children regardless of their physical, intellectual, social, emotional, linguistic or other conditions. This should include disabled and gifted children, street and working children, children from remote or nomadic populations, children from linguistic, ethnic or cultural minorities and children from other disadvantaged or marginalised areas or groups (UNESCO, 2001).

As cited in the Maltese *National Minimum Curriculum* (1999), Principle 8 (p. 36) sustains that all students should learn together in mainstream schools with appropriate networks of support. All students should learn together including students with specific or particular needs as they have an equal right to membership of the same groups as everybody else. A segregated education would restrict that right and limit opportunities for achieving self-fulfilment. People with disabilities, learning difficulties or social, emotional and behavioural difficulties do not need to be separated or segregated from each other. Concepts of inclusive practices focus on the fact that all students have a part to play in Society. An early start in mainstream educational is the best preparation for later on in life.

The fact that students come to school with a different 'baggage' is one of the realities that the educational system needs to cater for. The celebration of diversity is not just being aware of differences but it is the practice of creating an inclusive environment where diversity is not seen as a hindrance but an enriching opportunity for learning.

As Salend (2001), argues;

> Effective inclusion involves sensitivity to and acceptance of individual needs and differences. All students in inclusive schools are valued as individuals capable of contributing to society and should be taught to appreciate diversity (p. 7).

Inclusion as a Value

Research findings worldwide indicate that schools and teachers are in a continuous struggle to respond to the wide array of students (Wills & Cain, 2002). Inclusive Education seeks to address the different learning needs of students with 'a specific focus on those who are vulnerable to marginalization and exclusion' (UNESCO, 1994). School communities could be the most effective way of combating discrimination, creating welcoming communities, building an inclusive society and achieving quality education for all. Schools which do their utmost for all their children including children with specific needs have a strong value structure based on a commitment to valuing all students as being members of their school community. These values would therefore be reflected in all practical measures taken by the school to ensure that all the students experience success while accessing the curriculum. This may indicate that schools need to review their rationale and how to measure success. Broadening the way in which success is interpreted and avoiding the measuring of success solely with examination scores is one way to start. Effective schools are not standardized, driven by regulations but educators in these schools take action because it will help their students to learn. Dixon & Lois (2004), recount that throughout the years a lot has been said about inclusion, however, they emphasise that inclusion is not just a word, or a document or even an idea. It needs to be a way of life, something that eventually we do not have to consciously think about but that just is.

Positive Relationships in the Classroom

Harter (1985) recognises teachers as being influent significant others or role models in the lives of their students. He claims that irrelevant of our liking, since the behaviours we engage in are so frequently judged by them, teachers are an important source of feedback on our performance and can therefore have a serious influence on our self-worth. Thus the building of a healthy, positive teacher-student relationship is very important.

Rogers (1980), in his 'person centred approach' identifies three key conditions necessary for healthy relationships which could be directly applied to a healthy teacher-student relationship and healthy peer relationships. These are empathy, unconditional positive regard and honesty (Rogers, 1980).

As the social model discourse outlines, disability is caused by the society in which we live and is not the 'fault' of an individual disabled person, or an inevitable consequence of their limitations. As debated by Priestley (1998), disability is the product of the physical, organisational and attitudinal barriers present within society, which lead to discrimination. The removal of discrimination requires a change of approach and thinking in the way in which Society is organised. In the broadest sense the social model is nothing more than a concerted shift away from an emphases on individual impairments as the cause of disability, but rather onto the way in which physical, cultural and social environments exclude or disadvantage certain categories of people; namely, people who are labelled. Several theories have emerged explaining societal responses to individuals with accredited impairments (Priestley, 1998).

The Enhancement of Self-Esteem

Adopting a teaching style which is proactive in its approach towards all students is essential in having different needs met. Students having disabilities or specific difficulties experience many-a-times feelings of failure. Most of these students would have a very low self-esteem as regrettably they rarely experience success in their learning experience. As Maslow (1970) created the psychological model of human needs, self-esteem is put in a high standing in his hierarchy of needs. Maslow (1970) described two different forms of esteem: the need for respect from others and the need for self-respect, or inner self-esteem. Respect from others entails recognition, acceptance, status, and appreciation, and was believed to be more fragile and easily lost than inner self-esteem. According to Maslow (1970), without the fulfilment of self-esteem, individuals will be driven to seek it and unable to grow and obtain self-actualization.

Self-esteem (or self-regard, or self-worth), is an evaluative measure of our self-image, what Coopersmith (1967, p. 12) terms "a personal judgment of worthiness, that is expressed in the attitudes the individual holds towards himself". Salend (2001) describes that the teacher can establish a good learning environment by helping students develop their self-esteem through building and maintaining a rapport with the students.

Salend (2001) gives practical examples for achieving this good rapport namely:
- giving students the emotional support they need;
- letting students perform activities in which they excel;
- greeting students by their name;
- spending informal time with students.

As argued by Lawrence (1987), the teacher of any child is in a powerful position to influence the self-esteem of their pupil, through both the establishment of a caring relationship, and the use of certain systematic activities. Lawrence (1987), sustains that characteristically a child with low self-esteem represses their spontaneous ability to express themselves, through fear of punishment or feelings of guilt. A low self-esteem child finds it difficult to believe that they can safely reveal their true personality without risking disapproval or rejection from others.

A Collaborative Approach

An essential skill for supporting all students is the ability to collaborate with parents, teachers and other professionals. Consultative skills are first and foremost language communication skills; they are based on an awareness of how language works, how communication processes become effective, how one can ensure productive dialogue within a professional discourse. Steinberg (1989), outlines the fundamentals of a consultatively enabling joint problem-solving approach where colleagues need to be introduced to the skill of asking each other questions in such a way that the problem being explored can be looked at anew, so as to assist each other in finding their own alternative solution. A collaborative inquiry in order to deal with issues of inclusion in a school context helps in placing responsibility in the hands of the various stakeholders involved. This approach makes schools more responsive to family and community concerns.

Students Experiencing Social, Emotional and Behavioural Difficulties

Who are the students who are excluded from our classrooms and schools? Most of these are students whose behaviour is often described as 'disruptive and problematic' as it does not conform with the expected behaviour required by the schools. These are the students who most of the time are seen loitering in corridors and sitting outside the Head Teacher's office. Or, they could be the students who are always marked as 'absent' on the school Register, who sit down quietly without even muttering a word, who could be seen wandering alone in the yard during recess. As teachers, behaviour has a lot to tell us about the needs of our students. Camilleri, Cefai and Cooper (2008); a recent national study of students with social, emotional and behaviour difficulties in Maltese schools, give 9.7% as the prevalence rate of SEBD in Malta being close to the 10% cut-off point given by Goodman and his colleagues in the UK (Goodman 1997; Meltzer *et al.*, 2000). Cefai (2008), clearly states that these results strongly indicate that SEBD is a major issue of concern in Maltese schools.

Understanding Social, Emotional and Behavioural Difficulties (also referred to as SEBD) that students might be experiencing, shifts us towards a vision of education which celebrates rather than discourages diversity and to engage rather than ignore. Consequently, the roles of schools, teachers and educationalists is becoming more challenging and requires a broader sense of a flexible approach towards teaching in the mainstream setting. Social, emotional and behavioural difficulties widen the spectrum of our understanding to student diversity and inclusion.

Salend (2001) sustains that:

> Effective inclusion involves sensitivity to and acceptance of individual needs and differences. All students in inclusive schools are valued as individuals capable of contributing to society and are taught to appreciate diversity (Salend, 2001, p. 7).

Inclusion does not, however, only involve what students are learning or the substance of the curriculum. It also encompasses how learning takes place; which is the core practice within the classroom environment. How teachers apply themselves and how teachers expect students to behave and respond to the educational opportunities are very much dictated by the wider social and cultural norms very often informed and imposed by the dominant social group. Freire (1985), (cited in Ghosh, 1996, p. 42) says, "Besides being an act of knowing, education is also a political act; no pedagogy is neutral." Therefore, it is the inclusive school community that involves the creation of positive engagement for students with SEBD. My experience in working in the *Nurture Group* is that we work around one fundamental principle that is, addressing the needs of young students who are experiencing SEBD. The programme supports young students who are struggling in the mainstream class and we try to offer them a safe haven in a smaller group where individual needs could be addressed. The *Nurture Group* works wholeheartedly towards full re-inclusion in the regular classroom as it offers the best learning experience for students as they develop their self-esteem. *Nurture Groups* are a way of developing the necessary skills which are so much required to cope in the mainstream classes.

As cited by Cooper (2006), Sebba & Sachdev (1997), describe inclusive education as the process by which a school attempts to respond to all pupils as individuals by reconsidering and restructuring its curricular organization and provision as well as allocating resources to enhance equality of opportunity, (Sebba & Sachdev, 1997). Inclusion has in fact evolved from an aspiration linked to place, to one tied to participation, choice and relationships. This is supported by Bauer and Shea (1999), where they argue that inclusion is to be everywhere in Society not just in classrooms at schools. They state that when one mentions inclusion and diversity one has to keep in mind differences, such as; disability, cultural differences, language, ethnicity, style of interaction' learning style and rate, ways of gaining access to the environment and religion amongst other. Booth and Ainscow (2002), argue that inclusion is about making schools supportive, both for the students and the teachers. Giroux's (2003) recent appeal towards rejecting forms of schooling that marginalize students who are poor, black and disadvantaged, highlights the necessity for educators to reflect upon pedagogy and place it in the appropriate socio-cultural and political context. Oliver (1990) argues that an engagement with pedagogy involves a deconstruction of disabling pedagogies or pedagogies of disablement being responsible of the exclusion of people with impairments.

The concept of inclusion in the Maltese educational system is more than the right for every individual to belong to the mainstream. As argued in the document *Creating Inclusive Schools* (2002), it has become a responsibility of all schools to develop an evolving process of building inclusive cultures.

However, as Cefai (2008) points out, despite the promise of equal opportunity for all as stated in the *National Minimum Curriculum* (1999), some students are still attending schools with poorer physical and human resources. As Bartolo *et al.,* (2007) suggest, a barrier-free non-selective, inclusive educational system, with success and equal opportunities for all, would not only help to prevent SEBD, but strengthens the foundations for pro-social behaviour in students. Social, Emotional and Behavioural Difficulties as noted by Cooper (2006), in terms of values and attitudes, schools are often cited as a major influence on the development of SEBD. Schools are situated at the heart of an established community with its own values and cultures which are transmitted by individuals that make part of the school. Thus creating a school ethos which is inclusive in nature with regards to diversity can be challenging. As Cooper (2006) clarifies, in order to develop a whole-school approach, all stakeholders need to own such positive values rather than policies being imposed from outside the school.

Inclusion Requires a Flexible Pedagogy

In order to cater for such a diversity spectrum it is a great challenge. The teacher concerned with the education of students with such difficulties become aware that the work they programmed and activities prepared were not always going to work. A lot of adaptations need to be made and delivering effective teaching with these students needed to take place in a flexible learning environment. These realities in today's classrooms are embracing an even richer diversity of cultures; teachers are exploring novel ways of reaching out students with diverse needs. The *National Minimum Curriculum* (2000) recognises these new realities and therefore encourages 'pedagogy based on respect for and the celebration of difference' (p.30).

Cefai (2006), claims that classrooms should be like small communities with "*a social climate of mutual caring, respect and love*" (p. 16). Moreover, he argues that in such classrooms:

> pupils look happy, safe and secure ... teachers look satisfied and happy with their children (p. 16).

Positive relationships in the classrooms therefore are an important medium for supporting students' learning and socio-emotional development. Teachers must redefine their roles in order to enable rather than disable students. Teacher educators share responsibility for giving future teachers a lens through which to view every learner as ordinary and essential. As teachers are regarded highly as the key to change in education, their feelings of frustration and inadequacy are potential barriers to inclusive education. Such challenges are compounded where curriculum and assessment demands may appear inflexible.

> Educational policy has moved beyond the medical and dependency models ... to a new paradigm ... (that) requires that teachers possess positive attitudes towards inclusion (Brownlee and Carrington, 2000, p.104).

Thinking Point 1:
'Mainstreaming' vs 'Inclusion' - The concept of 'inclusion' grew out from the term 'mainstreaming'. It shares some of its philosophical terms, however, the terms 'mainstreaming' and 'inclusion' imply different concepts. Sometimes, the terms are used interchangeably. Discuss.

Thinking Point 2:
Diversity and Differentiation:- Students are not homogeneous. In order to meet the different strengths and needs of all the students, teachers need to be sensitive to student diversity. Due to diversity, the curriculum cannot be accessed by everyone in the same way. The curriculum can be differentiated *by content*; variation according to interests, *by process*; variation of delivery and method, *by product*; variation by showing what the student has learnt. Debate.

REFERENCES

Bartolo, P., Janik, I., Janikova, V. & Hofsass, T. (2007). *Responding to Student Diversity Teacher's Handbook.* Malta: University of Malta.

Bauer A, & Shea T, (1999). *Inclusion 101.* USA: Paul H. Brookes Publishers.

Booth, T., & Ainscow, M. (2002). *Index for inclusion: developing learning and participation in schools.* Bristol: CSIE.

Brownlee, J., & Carrington, S. (2000). Opportunities for authentic experience and reflection: a teaching programme designed to change attitudes towards disability for pre-service teachers. *Support for Learning,15(3), 99 -105.*

Cefai, C. & Cooper, P. (2006). Pupils with social, emotional and behavioural difficulties in Malta: An educational perspective. *Journal of Maltese Educational Studies, 4 (1),18-36.*

Cefai, C. (2008). *Promoting Resilience in the Classroom, A Guide to Developing Pupils' Emotional and Cognitive Skills.* London: Jessica Kingsley Publications.

Cefai, C., Cooper, P. & Camilleri, L. (2008). *Engagement Time: A National Study on Students with Social, Emotional and Behaviour Difficulties.* Malta: Resilience and Socio-Emotional Health. University of Malta.

Cheng, K.-M. (2000). Personal Capacity, Social Competence and Learning Together. *Unicorn, 26 (3).*

Cooper, P. (2006). *Promoting Positive Pupil Engagement. Educating pupils with social, emotional and behavioural difficulties.* Malta: Miller Publications.

Cooper, P.(2006). Awareness, understanding and the promotion of educational engagement. *Emotional and Behavioral Difficulties 11, (3), 151–3.*

Coopersmith (1967), Higgins (1987, 1989). (3rd Ed.). In *Psychology: The Science of Mind & Behaviour.* In Gross, R. D.. UK: Hodder & Stoughton.

Department of the Curriculum (1999). (Ed.). *National Minimum Curriculum.* Floriana: Education Division.

Department of the Curriculum (2002). (Ed.). *Focus Group for Inclusive Education, Creating Inclusive Schools.* Floriana: Education Division.

Dixon, G., and Lois, M.A. (2004). *Making inclusion work for children with Dysprexia.* New York: Routledge Falmer Press.

Freire, P. (1985). *The Politics of Education - Culture, Power, and Liberation,*Translated by Donoldo Macedo. New York: Bergin & Garvey.

Ghosh, R. (1996). *Redefining Multicultural Education.* Toronto: Harcourt Canada.

Giroux, H. A. (2003). Public Pedagogy and the Politics of Resistance: Notes on acritical theory of educational struggle. *Educational Philosophy and Theory, 35, (1), 5 -16.*

Goodman, R. (1997). The Strengths and Difficulties Questionnaire: A Research Note. *Journal of Child Psychology and Psychiatry, (38), 581-586.*

Harter, S. (1985). *Manual for the self-perception profile for children.* Denver, CO: University of Denver.

Lawrence, J. (1987). *Enhancing Self-esteem in the Classroom,* London: Paul Chapman.

Maslow, A. (1970). *Motivation and Personality,* New York: Harper Row.

Oliver, M. (1990). *The Politics of Disablement.* Basingstoke: Macmillan.

Rogers, C. (1980). *A Way of Being.* Boston, MS: Houghton-Mifflin.

Salend, S.J. (2001). *Creating Inclusive Classrooms: Effective and reflective practices* (4th Ed.). Upper Saddler River, NJ: Merrill Prentice Hall.

Sebba, J. & Sachdev, D. (1997). *What works in Inclusive Education?* London: Barnardo's.

Steinberg, D. (1989) *Interprofessional Consultation.* Oxford: Blackwell Scientific.

UNESCO. (1994). The Salamanca Statement and Framework for Action. In *Final Report of the World Conference on Special Needs Education: Access and Quality.* Salamanca, Spain.

UNESCO (2001). *Overcoming Exclusion through Inclusive Approaches in Education. A Challenge and A Vision.* Conceptual Paper for the Education Sector.

Wills, D., & Cain, P. (2002, 13th November). *Key competencies required for teachers to work in and foster inclusive school communities.* Paper presented at the Teacher Education for Inclusion, Edith Cowan University, Perth.

TEACHING STRATEGIES FOR CHILDREN
WITH DYSLEXIA IN THE CLASSROOM

ABSTRACT

Accessing the curriculum and being successful learners are basic human rights. Yet these rights are often inadvertently violated through lack of knowledge or true understanding of the implications of a profile of dyslexia on learners. This Chapter is meant to introduce readers to conceptualize what it means to live with a profile of dyslexia, and to grasp repercussions to what it really means to have difficulties with literacy in today's environments and contexts. Practical hints are also introduced in this Chapter. However, these hints cannot truly be implemented by educators unless there is respect for students with this profile and empathy of the experiences lived. Only if we truly understand, appreciate and respect experiences, can we be motivated to appropriately address the abilities and challenges that this profile brings along. After all, pedagogy and methodology are constructed on one's own philosophy and values.

Preamble

This Chapter has been inspired by my son, who has a profile of dyslexia. Before starting to write this Chapter, I asked him to point out difficulties he found when still making part of a class and what, according to him, made a good teacher. These are his views:

> Difficulties I found in the classroom:
> 1. Spelling tests
> 2. Taking Notes
> If the teacher indicates what to write (not necessarily a dictation) then it's easy to follow. It's hard if teacher keeps going, and even with all concentration it's still hard to take notes and follow class at same time. Often, if you take a few extra seconds to write better notes, i.e. add more material, insights, additional explanation etc... you find yourself spending the next five minutes to catch up and start following the lesson. As such, a section of good notes is usually followed by a section of bad notes. To get a complete set, reference to classmates' notes is often required.
> 3. Reading in front of other people, not excellent and I get nervous.

The questions that arise from these difficulties, is 'whether these can be avoided' and 'addressed in the classroom context'. This Chapter is meant to try to explore these two important concepts.

Accessing learning

All children have a right to be well-educated, productive, independent and effective citizens. In today's world, this also means being totally literate, as literacy is not only required for schooling but also for everyday life. Literacy is no longer an activity of the 'cultured' but a lifestyle. What happens to students for whom literacy is not easy? Very capable students are not given an opportunity to share their learning, their potential and their intelligence and are instead often perceived as lazy, stupid and very often even impossible to teach due to literacy challenges (Davis & Braun, 1997; Silver, 1984).

As Thomas Edison, recalls: "My teachers say I'm addled ... my father thought I was stupid, and I almost decided I must be a dunce" (The Gift of Dyslexia – a Site for Freethinkers – Quotes from *dyslexics*, retrieved 20/02/10).

Thomas Edison
Inventor 1847-1931

(Famous people with Dyslexia, retrieved 31/01/2010)

Children with literacy challenges (dyslexia) amount to 10-15% of the population, with a 1:1 ratio with respect to gender (Shaywitz *et al.*, 1999; Snowling, 2000). Dyslexia is present in every classroom and all teachers must understand this profile in order to address needs and abilities appropriately (Bender, 2001). Children with dyslexia need to be supported on three levels:
1.   Help them to learn how to read and write;
2.   Ensure that they can access the curriculum;
3.   Gauge and support their self esteem as needed.

We need to understand what it means to have a difficulty to access learning due to difficulties with literacy, as only after understanding and empathizing, can professionals truly cater for children with such learning difficulties.

Imagine moving to another country and going into a classroom where *you* have only been learning the country's new alphabet system for a few weeks and *you* are expected to cope with students who have been learning how to read for the last 4 years, and *you* are expected to read comfortably, effortlessly and heuristically. How would you feel? Possible scenarios:

- The lesson would seem to be going at breakneck speed;
- You will not understand what is going on;
- You feel disheartened;
- You feel frustrated;
- Your tolerance level becomes very low;
- You may start to sweat;
- You would probably shut down and daydream since you would not be coping with the situation;
- You would probably be perceived as in-attentive and unmotivated.

Should you have the opportunity to have this experience, it may be the closest that you may get to experiencing the life in the classroom of a student with dyslexia.

Every child has the right of access to the curriculum, yet we take away that right from so many students (Thomson, 2003). If children with dyslexia were to take a secretary to school, then most problems would be greatly minimized or removed. Since this is probably not feasible, the alternative is to ensure that the teaching provides access to the curriculum in spite of challenges to access print (Hegarty, 1993; Miles and Miles, 1983). It is totally unjust, I would dare say abusive, for educators to ignore that, in their classes, there are children who struggle with literacy. Yet this is the reality for a lot of children.

Frustration and failure are experiences in learning activities which lead to feelings of disappointment and a lowered sense of self-worth (Gross, 1997), especially in academic environments. Dyslexic pupils experience significant challenges and difficulties with regard to self-esteem and self perception (Humphrey & Mullin, 2002; Burden & Burdett, 2005). Thomson & Hartley (1980) and Humphrey & Mullin (2002) note that, given the school environment, dyslexic students come to equate happiness and intelligence with good reading, and consequently the lack thereof, with sadness and ignorance. Humphrey & Mullins (2002) further conclude that dyslexic persons also equate hard work with intelligence, effectively perceiving themselves as 'lazy'.

One must understand that literacy is pervasive in the educational system and dyslexic students are therefore continuously faced with hurdles to surmount, unless inclusive strategies and techniques are continuously and effectively used. Faced with situations beyond their control, and with continuous difficulties and failures, students with dyslexia may become helpless (Butkowsky & Willows, 1980), mostly because their efforts do not yield the expected results. Riley & Rustique-Forrester (2002) note that dyslexic students find school a profoundly sad and depressing experience, emphasized by the experience of shouting and retributions. As they put it:

> isolated children and shouting teachers. A recurring image is of school as a prison from which children continually try to escape…small voices crying for help, caught in a cycle of circumstances they felt largely unable to influence (p. 33).

Over a hundred years ago, Hans Christian Anderson recalled:

> The life I led during these days still comes back to me in bad dreams. Once again I sit in a fever on a school bench. I cannot answer; I dare not. The angry eyes stare at me, laughter and gibes echo around me. Those were hard and bitter times (Anderson, 1846).

"If only the teacher would read to me"; "if only the teacher would use pictures"; "if only the teacher would speak slowly"; "if only the teacher would just give me a handout instead of making me copy from the white board" - such requests are so simple yet often denied to children with dyslexia. These requests can be addressed by inclusive strategies which assume that educators:

1. Believe in Inclusive education and *Universal Design Learning* (Pugach 1995; Turnbull *et al.,* 2009);
2. Believe in child-centred learning;
3. Are prepared to plan for lessons, prepare resources, correct children's work, reflect upon teaching strategies beyond contact hours;
4. Understand that having difficulty with literacy does not mean inability to learn;
5. Understand that reading is not a gauge of 'intelligence';
6. Need to be in contact with students at all times;
7. Understand and respect challenges involved with literacy difficulties.

To further corroborate I have chosen to discuss five themes educators should consider in the learning process with regards to dyslexia; the learning process, copying activities and note-taking, accessing print, memory and multi-sensory techniques. These issues are by no means exhaustive.

The Learning Process

Since students with dyslexia have difficulty with learning from printed texts, alternative access to the curriculum must be considered (Riddick *et al.,* 2002). This implies alternative strategies in order for them to cope with the demands of the curriculum. Moreover, students with dyslexia also need alternative ways of learning if they are to succeed (Ryden, 1989; Davis, 1995). For example, students with dyslexia have difficulty with auditory sequential short-term memory, so the use of visuals in the learning and memory process is imperative in their learning. Students with dyslexia need to be offered alternative ways of learning. Tod (1999) refers to seven principles on which one should build learning strategies for students with dyslexia (Table 1). These strategies are not only beneficial to children with dyslexia, but also to all other students. In fact, all the strategies described in this Chapter are irrevocably meant for inclusive classrooms. Tod's seven principles of learning strategies refer to the importance of using as many modalities as possible in the teaching process and that learning should focus on understanding and allow for transfer to memory. Moreover, Tod (1999) refers to the importance of ensuring that each lesson is designed in such a way that all students can manage the learning and eventually master what is being taught. This implies that planning and implementation of all learning should be based on *Universal Design Learning* (Turnbull *et al.,* 2009). Tod also gives importance to motivation and the experience of success in the classroom.

Table 1: Tod's (1999) Seven-M Principles for Learning Strategies

1.	Multi sensory Techniques: The use of all possible senses;
2.	Meaningfulness: Using comprehension and meaning to circumvent memory challenges;
3.	Memory: Using active processing to enhance memory;
4.	Metacognition: Students' awareness of how they learn best;
5.	Manageability: Ensuring that there is no overloading in any one lesson;
6.	Motivation: Working towards motivation of self-directed learning and success in learning;
7.	Mastery: Students with Dyslexia often develop compensatory and coping strategies for their learning challenges. However, these are skills which need to be mastered and automatized, if the students are to progress.

Multi-Sensory Techniques in the Learning Process

Multi-sensory techniques actively stimulate all available senses simultaneously (Holley, 1994; Hulme & Snowling, 1997). This implies the use of concrete apparatus and visuals. A committed teacher would use multi-sensory techniques intrinsically, because it is the way we are born to learn. Babies start learning by putting things in their mouths, that it is way they access information. This paves the way for all multi-sensory learning (Furth, 1970). Humans learn best if all the senses are used to the max and this also helps improve memory. For example, when I was an early educator teaching six-seven-year-olds, I taught subtraction through drama. The class used to dress up and invent scenes where objects were decreased. These involved stealing, losing, eating, scoffing, hiding. Only after such drama lessons did pupils then move to the minus symbol and to pen and paper. All pupils in that class learnt subtraction, whatever their abilities or challenges. It made the minus sign tangible and part of the children's lives. Such an example also relates to Tod's (1999) Seven-M principles of learning strategies explained above.

Dyslexia and Memory

Very often, children with dyslexia experience auditory short-term memory challenges, which need to be catered for in class, if children are to be helped to learn, retain and be able to retrieve. If repetition is not varied or long enough, the learning will simply wash over students with dyslexia, as if it never happened. In order to address these challenges, teachers need to use multi-sensory approaches, to ensure that all possible modalities are used by children and that both hemispheres of the brain are being utilized in the learning and memorizing process (Davis & Braun, 1997; Reid, 1998). Again, these are inclusive strategies which can easily be implemented in the classroom context (Rose & Meyer, 2002). This concept is certainly not new and goes back to the ancient Greeks (Yates, 1966). Challenges children with dyslexia experience necessitate the use of strategies beyond the simple method of rote learning. Repetition and using a multi-sensory mode is the best strategy to use: ORAL (say), VISUAL (see), AUDITORY (Hear) KINAESTHETIC (Feel).

In other words, the use of mnemonics - systems to help memory, for example remembering the colour of the rainbow through *Richard Of York Gave Battle In*

Vain - is very important in the teaching and learning process. The seven *Rules of Thumb* for successful and permanent learning include:
1. The use of Visuals (e.g. Buzan, 2001)
2. The use of Structure
3. The use of Humour
4. The use of perceived 'Rude' themes by the child
5. Personalized learning
6. Made up by the child
7. Group work for students to come up with ways to remember
   With regard to memory and giving instructions, teachers must ensure that students have understood and retained every part of each instruction. It is always wise not to rely on the auditory only, but to back up by non-verbal and verbal visuals - drawing and writing on the board.

Accessing Print and Learning

Children with dyslexia may try to read fast, making a lot of errors and guesswork, and try to remember words as pictures, affecting comprehension. They may read by decoding extremely slowly, with a lot of hesitations and pauses and with great effort, such that so much energy is used for decoding and so much time elapses to read a paragraph that once again comprehension suffers.

In the classroom situation, such obstacles need to be addressed appropriately. Moreover, strategies that teachers use should be discussed with the students themselves. For example, on one occasion, I was suggesting the use of a tape recorder and the student refused as he felt that the tape recorder with the text would confuse him more. For him, the use of a computer was much more fruitful. Inclusive strategies to help access print include:
1. Have the text recorded so that students may follow print with auditory input. This can be done by the teacher-facilitator team, and one should also tap the computer programmes available (e.g. Read and Write - www.readwritegold.com/read&writedatasheets.html). The implication of this is that classrooms need recorders and computers.
2. Children with dyslexia may be able to access the curriculum through the printed word if the text were larger. Texts may therefore need to be enlarged. This includes any class work or test papers or examination papers. Such enlargement should not simply be through the use of a photo-copier, but adjusted on the computer and then printed on an A4 Paper.
3. Colour of paper may reduce reading difficulties (Irlen, 2005). This can be catered for in two ways: printing on the requested coloured paper, or use of coloured transparencies over text.
4. Fonts can make a huge difference for access to print. Research indicates that the *sans serif* font is the better font both for book and computer screen reading (www.dyslexia.com). *Sans serif* fonts use 'ticks' and 'tails' (e.g. Times New Roman or Georgia) and this may distort letter shapes. Furthermore ascenders (upper stem) and descenders (lower stem) of letters (e.g. b; p; h; y) also make a difference due to over-reliance on word configuration experienced by persons with dyslexia. If ascenders and descenders are too short, the shape of words may be more difficult to identify and readers are more likely to be inaccurate. In this respect, the best font, when taking into

consideration both the sans serif criterion and the ascenders/descenders criterion, tends to be Trebuchet MS (www.dyslexia.com). Other Sans serif fonts include Arial, Century Gothic, Comic Sans, Verdana and Geneva.

5. Students with dyslexia may prefer print similar to handwriting. In this case, the sans serif font comic sans would be the better option.

6. Whole pages of print may be disheartening:

(a) The use of a 'window' proves helpful for such a difficulty. This is simply created by cutting a square hole in a paper - size depending on the need of the students - and placing it on the book such that at any one time, students have in front of them either a paragraph of half a page or a single line, as the need may be. It may be wise for teachers to have prepared windows of different sizes and to ensure that the students have them as well;

(b) Preparing print interspersed with pictures;

(c) Preparing print that is not right justified. This is effective for two reasons. First the jagged right hand side of the paper gives less of a 'block' view for the reader and secondly, when print is non-right justified that spaces between rods and letters are constant and not ever-changing to suit the right justified line.

7. As noted also by my son in the introduction, many students with dyslexia do not like to read aloud in Class (Pollack & Wallwe, 1994). Some actually go to school, continuously fearing that they will be asked to read. Fear is one factor which inhibits learning; so because of anxiety, a lot of learning is lost (Ormrod, 2007).

Two strategies can be used:

(a) The teacher may prepare students by telling them beforehand what exactly to read. This length of the reading text should be negotiated with students, according to their abilities and challenges. It is then VERY important that teachers remember exactly which texts are given to whom.

(b) Teachers and students may have an agreement that students with dyslexia will never be asked to read aloud. As one student told me; "That was the best contract I ever signed. I felt so relieved and unstressed, that after two months I actually requested the teacher to give me a passage to read for the next day. I felt so safe" (11-year-old boy).

8. When preparing handouts, teachers need to use dyslexia-friendly principles. Apart from the hints provided above, bordering handouts will help students focus more. Such adaptations are of course good for the whole class and teachers should prepare handouts inclusive for all.

Other strategies include Buddy systems, Paired Reading, audio-visual aides, the use of the computer for accessing reading and writing, students' choice for presentation of work and method of assessment (e.g. use of presentation, use of orals).

Copying Activities and Note Taking

What is exactly happening when students are copying form the white board and what is the sequence of activities experienced? The following is the sequence of activities used:

Students:

1. Read the printed word/s on the board;

2.   Retain the printed word/s as sight moves away from the board and on to the copybook;
3.   Remember/visualize the word/s to be written;
4.   Write word/s down on their copybook;
5.   Do the above four process automatically and only focus on what should be copied.

Students with Dyslexia may have difficulties at any of the above four stages:
1.   When looking at the printed word, students may have difficulty reading the actual word. To compensate, students will copy one letter at a time, and not catch up with the class;
2.   Auditory short-term memory difficulties may impede remembering what word/s should be copied as sight moves away from the white board;
3.   Students with dyslexia may read and retain words to be written, but then have difficulty spelling the word. For example 'with' may end up being copied as 'wiht';
4.   Students with dyslexia may be doing neither of the above activities heuristically and therefore copying becomes such a difficult chore that a lot of energy is spent and by the time students have copied the material requested from the board, they are really exhausted and have no energy to start the task requested of them.

In the higher classes, teachers often assume that students can learn and take down notes. This is particularly difficult, or at times impossible, for some children with dyslexia, as they need all their energy to follow the language, and their writing may not be heuristic enough to cope with the complicated task of taking notes. In order to take notes, one is engaged with a number of 'activities and one cognitive activity (Table 2). Children with dyslexia may have to deal with more than one cognitive activity to the detriment of learning.

Table 2: Note Taking in the Classroom

Cognitive Activity:
•   Understanding the material presented
Heuristic Activities:
•   Attending to the task
•   Processing the language
•   Spelling
•   Reading from the board
•   Cursive handwriting
•   Spacing the letters on the page

Several strategies can be used to circumvent this difficulty. Notes can be prepared beforehand and precious time in the classroom may be used for discussion and understanding. For example, during a Geography lesson on volcanoes, instead of dictating notes on volcanoes or 'lecturing' on the topic and students trying to catch up with note taking, teachers could have notes prepared and organized and spend the lesson using non-verbal visuals and discussing the topic. This is simple and I am sure that a lot of teachers are using this strategy. But, I am also so tired and disappointed of listening to students who are upset because their lessons are boring with not even one visual.

Conclusion

There are many other aspects of the classroom experience that could not be addressed in this chapter. These include correction of work, addressing misbehaviour, language usage, alternative methods of performance, tests and examinations arrangements and dyslexia and organization. Hopefully you will empathize with this experience; understand that inclusive strategies are not rocket science but easily adapted in the classroom with regard to human and financial resources, expertise, time and availability; and be motivated to further research the subject. The crux is whether you believe that children with dyslexia have a right to access the curriculum, whether you understand, respect and accept the challenges students with dyslexia face. In this new millennium, everyone agrees that corporal punishment is abusive, but lack of understanding and empathy can also bring along abusive behaviour, whether intentional or not, when dealing with dyslexic students. A dangerous situation is when educators 'do not know that they do not know' and are therefore neither aware of the implications of their practise nor of a need for change!

My dream is that every class becomes totally dyslexia-friendly and that I am able to say that Table 3 below is a thing of the past as much as corporal punishment is.

Table 3: 200 Years On - Have We Improved?

1805	Author	Hans Christian Anderson: "Hard and bitter times"
1847	Inventor	Thomas Edison: "I almost decided I must be a dunce"
1879	Scientist	Albert Einstein: "Teachers..mentally slow..foolish dreams"
1937	Financier	Charles Schwab "I couldn't read. I just scraped by"
1950	Entrepreneur	Richard Branson spanked by teachers for bad grades and a poor attitude
1955	Maltese Artist	"One teacher... horrible, I called her the witch. She made my life hell"
2000	Maltese Pupil	"The teacher makes me copy and I cannot catch up"

In this Chapter I have attempted to help you understand the classroom experience of children with dyslexia. Only if we truly understand, appreciate and respect this experience can we be motivated to appropriately address the abilities and challenges that this profile brings along. We have a duty to help all children in the classroom learn, whatever their literacy abilities or challenges. This Chapter has tried to give some strategies to help professionals address these issues and it is hoped that it will be a platform for further reading and training for the reader.

> **Thinking Point 1:**
> The author states: "A dangerous situation is when educators do not know that they do not know!" Reflect on why dyslexia is often overlooked as a challenge in the classroom.
> **Thinking Point 2:**
> Reflect on how educators can become more sensitised to profiles of dyslexia.
> **Thinking Point 3:**
> In our local context, how are children with dyslexia being discriminated against, particularly with reference to certification?

RFERENCES

Anderson, H.C. (1846). *The true story of my life* Retrieved 6th June, 2010 from http://www.authorama.com/book/true-story-of-my-life.

Bender William, N. (2001). *Learning Disabilities: characteristics, identification a teaching strategies* USA: Allyn and Bacon.

British Dyslexia Association. Retrieved 31st March 2010 from www.bdadyslexia.org.uk/about-dyslexia/further-information/dyslexia-style-guide.html

Burden, R. & Burdett, J. (2007). What's in a name? Students with dyslexia: their use of metaphor in making sense of their disability. *British Journal of Special Education 34 (2) 75-79.*

Butkowsky, I. & Willows, D. (1980). Cognitive-Motivational Characteristics of Children Varying in Reading Ability: Evidence for Learned Helplessness in poor Readers. *Journal of educational psychology 72 (3): 408-422.*

Buzan, T. (2001). *Headstrong* London: Thorsons Publishers.

Davis, R. D. (1995). *The gift of dyslexia.* UK: Souvenir Press.

Davis, R. D & Braun, E.M. (1997). *The gift of dyslexia: why some of the brightest people can't read and how they can learn* UK: Souvenir Press Ltd.

Dyslexia.com *Typefaces for Dyslexia* Retrieved 31st March 2010 from www.dyslexic. com/index.asp?url=IND

Famous People with Dyslexia Retrieved 31st March 2010 from www.dyslexiaonline.com/famous/famous.htm#edison

Furth, H. (1970). *Piaget for teachers.* Washington: Prentice Hall.

Gross, A. H., (1997). Defining the self as a learner for children with LD [Electronic version]. *National Centre for LD.*

Hegarty, S. (1993). *Meeting special needs in ordinary schools.* UK: Cassell.

Holley, S. (1994). *A Practical Parents' Handbook on Teaching Children with Learning Disabilities.* UK: Charles C. Thomas Publisher.

Hulme, C. & Snowling, M. (1997*). Dyslexia, biology, cognition and intervention* British Dyslexia Association.

Humphrey, N. & Mullins, P.M. (2002). Personal constructs and attributions for academic success and failure in dyslexia.' *British Journal of Special Education, 29 (4), 196-2.*

Irlen, H. (2005). *Overcoming dyslexia and other reading disabilities through the Irlen method: Reading by the Colours.* NY: The Berkeley Publishing Group.

Kelly, K. & Ramundo, P. (1996). *You Mean I'm Not Stupid or Crazy?* USA: Simon and Schuster.

Miles, T. R. & Miles, E. (1983). *Help for dyslexic children*. UK: Routledge.

Ormrod, J. E. (2007). (5th. ed.). *Human learning*. N.J.: Prentice Hall.

Pollack, J. & Wallwe, E. (1994). *Day-to-day dyslexia in the classroom*. United Kingdom: Routledge.

Pugach, M.C. (1995). On the failure of imagination in inclusive schools. *Journal of Special Education 29, 219-229*

Read and Write - Retrieved 31st March 2010 from www.readwritegold.com/read& writedatasheets.html

Reid G. (1998). *Dyslexia: A practitioners' handbook* USA: John Wiley & Sons

Riddick, B., Wolfe J. & Lumsdon D. (2002). *Dyslexia: a practical guide for teachers and parents*. UK: David Futon Publishers.

Riley, K, & Rustique-Forrester, E. (2002). *Working with disaffected Students: why students lose interested in school and what we can do about it*. London: Paul Chapman.

Rose, D.H., & Meyer, A., (2002). Teaching every student in the digital age: universal design for learning. ASCD.

Ryden, M. (1989). *Dyslexia: How Would I Cope?* London: Jessica Kingsley.

Shaywitz, S.E., Shaywitz, M.D., Fletcher, J.M. & Escobar, M.D. (1999). Prevalence of reading disability in boys and girls. *Journal of the American Medical Association 264(3), 998-1002*.

Silver Larry, B. (1984). *The misunderstood child - a guide for parents of ld children* USA: McGraw Hill Book Co.

Snowling, M., (2000). *Dyslexia* UK: Blackwell Publishers.

The Gift of Dyslexia – a Site for Freethinkers – Quotes from dyslexics. Retrieved 20th February 2010 from www.thegiftofdyslexia.com/quotes_from_dyslexics,

Thomson, M. (Ed.) (2003). D*yslexia included: a whole school approach* London: David Fulton Publishers.

Tod, J. (1999). IEPS Dyslexia London: David Fulton Publishers.

Turnbull, R., Turnbull, A. & Wehmeyer, L. (2009). (6th Eds). *Exceptional lives – special education in today's schools*. USA: Merrill Prentice Hall.

Yates F. A. (1966). *The Art of Memory*. Chicago: University of Chicago Press.

RESPONDING TO STUDENT DIVERSITY
THROUGH DIFFERENTIATED TEACHING

ABSTRACT

Inclusive education entails the equal valuing of each student as a person and as a learner. This calls for the creation of a supportive environment that enables each student to participate actively and fully in the various activities of school. This Chapter describes how students can be enabled to participate in the academic curriculum as one of the main areas of school life. It highlights the diversity of students in today's classrooms and the challenge this raises for teachers as they try to reach out to each one of them. It describes how teachers try to get to know their students in order to meet their diverse strengths and needs. It then gives an account of the various ways in which teachers can differentiate first the learning environment and, secondly, the three main elements of lessons, namely learning content, learning process and learning product, in such a way as to ensure that each student feels part of the lesson and can engage in meaningful and successful learning.

One Size Does Not Fit All

Perceptive teachers are aware that the children or young people in their class are very different individuals. They differ in physical characteristics: some are tall and some are short, some are fat and some are slim, some have blue eyes and some brown, some fair hair and others black, some curly and some straight. They also differ in character: some may be impulsive and extrovert, others reflective and introvert; some have an active temperament and some are calm, some like staying on their own and some like to socialise all the time; some like cars and some like cats. They also differ in the way they learn: some like to experiment, some like to be told what the facts are; some like discussion and others like making things; some are competitive and others like cooperative activities. They also differ in their prior learning: some come to school already knowing how to read and write and use the computer, and others have never handled a book or a computer; some can already speak English and/or Maltese fluently and others have never said a work in English and/or in Maltese; some are very religious and belong to a faith and others have never been to any Church. They differ in the rate at which they learn: some can understand or do a task after one demonstration and others need three, ten, twenty explanations and examples; some finish their work in five minutes and others need a whole hour.

If students in a class differ in all these ways, even if they are of the same age or even streamed by their examination results, how can we expect them to fit into a one-size-fits-all lesson? How can we expect to engage them successfully through whole-class teaching only all the time, chalk and talk approaches only, single-grade exercises that students have to complete in the same time slot, reading and writing learning activities only, single-grade paper and pencil assessments only?

Effective teachers take account of student differences in motivation for (interests in and affect towards) learning, in their learning profile, and in the readiness levels by engaging in what has been termed differentiated teaching or instruction (Tomlinson, 2003; Bartolo *et al.*, 2007). Differentiated teaching was initially motivated by the need to challenge the high flyers, as this reflection by a Maltese primary school teacher illustrates:

> My inclination was about reaching all the children: all the children are in school, they have been accepted in the school, so all the children should be given a right to learn at the level they can learn. ... 'I have 29 children, ... different levels, I can't reach them all in the same way. What am I going to do about it?' So that is when I started then reading about differentiated teaching and what I have to do to reach everybody. Especially because, many a time, I used to concentrate more on the child with special needs, the struggling child, and I was leaving out the bright kids, and that sort of, all right, they were the ones who least needed my help, but I wanted them to move forward as well. ... I was leaving the average and the above average children out of my scenario. So this, differentiated teaching was my solution, of how to reach everybody (Ms. Tonna).

However, as we widen the concept of inclusion to apply to all students whatever their characteristics (Bartolo *et al.*, 2002), differentiated teaching has become a necessary tool for the implementation of inclusive education in the classroom as it enables each child to participate actively in regular classroom activities. A similar approach that arose from attempts in architecture to provide physical accessibility to buildings for all persons, and is thus more directly linked to the needs of persons with disability, is termed *Universal Design for Learning* (Rose & Meyer, 2002).

It may be useful to clarify here that differentiation on its own may not lead to inclusion. Differentiation is aimed at giving access to learning to all students. However, in the name of providing access, students have also been segregated into streamed groups in class or schools including special schools. Certainly in the context of this text, differentiation is seen as only one dimension in inclusive education, which lies mainly in the social dimension.

Inclusive education is seen here as the attempt to enable all children to feel that they are full members of the class and school. This membership is not limited to lessons, or even to the classroom, but is about being an equally valued member of the class and school during all activities, formal or informal. It is about the development of a democratic community where the presence and contribution of each student is equally valued.

Responding to Diversity

Thus, in an *EU Comenius 2.1 three-year Project (2004-07)* aimed at producing a *Differentiating Teaching Module for Primary Education (DTMp)*, it was decided to use the concept of *Responding to Diversity* as carrying wider implications on enabling full student participation in the life of the class and school. In *The Responsive Classroom* (www.responsiveclassroom.org) "the social curriculum is as important as the academic curriculum".

As part of the *DTMp Project*, we had asked five primary school teachers from each of the participating seven European countries what they did to reach out to their students. And they had indicated that differentiating the lesson was accompanied by wider inclusive actions on their part. They reported that they tried to create a supportive and inclusive community evident in three of five themes that resulted from an analysis of their interviews, namely:

1. The need for caring and inclusive attitudes and school ethos — all participants spoke of wanting to reach all students, believing and feeling accountable for each one's learning, caring about each one's progress and happiness, and enabling each one's participation. They mentioned the need for 'pedagogy conversations' in order to reflect and improve their responding.
2. The participants did not leave appreciation of diversity to chance but actively tried to develop inclusive and solidarity values in their students as they strived to build a classroom community.
3. In fact, participants also spoke of the need for building collaborative networks: firstly an interpersonal relationship with each of their students; secondly among their students; and finally with other school staff, parents and other professionals (Humphrey *et al.,* 2006, p.310).

We can call the above three themes the attempt to create an inclusive environment. This is a very important way in which teaching and learning can become personalised and respectful to student needs. For instance, when actually using different expectations and materials with different children, they were careful not to devalue those who were less advanced in their work as reported by these two teachers from the Netherlands and Malta:

When the children that are on a lower level finish early (because of this pretended head start) they can start their special extra work in couples. As a teacher I never wait until everybody is ready, but when about two thirds of the assignments are done the teacher can start to discuss them. In this way the slower children don't feel that they missed anything for instance the last six questions because they work slower, but because the teacher started too soon. In this way children don't doubt themselves (Ms. Hillevi).

My library is graded, that is there are some books which are very easy and some that are very difficult. ... But I don't emphasise if a girl that can read a lot has taken a book that is easy. I don't tell her, "No, that is not good for you because it is too easy" ... I know this girl reads a lot anyway. But I don't pinpoint it, because of the others. So I do not tell the others, "So this is an easy book, so I will not take it because it will show me up as one who takes the easy books only"... There's no need for me to tell him, "This is good for you," because he will realize that I am always giving him books that are easier than those read, for instance, by the one near him, and it makes - it hurts them (Ms. Teuma).

With regards to the importance of developing interpersonal relationships for differentiating the curriculum, stronger findings resulted from a study of teachers of Christian doctrine in informal evening classes for young children in Malta (Mizzi & Bartolo, 2007). The catechists' main way of adapting their teaching to individual needs was through building personal relationships with the students that enabled them to get to know the students' background cultures, activities and interests so that they then tailored their questions, work expectations and management of each student in ways that enabled them to be engaged meaningfully, actively, and successfully.

Thus it is within an inclusive learning environment that one can then effectively consider the more technical issues of how to differentiate the curriculum to match it to student characteristics. Figure 1 shows how, in addition to an inclusive learning environment, teachers can use differentiation of three major elements of the curriculum to reach all students:

1. The teaching content: which includes applying the content to student interests and readiness levels;
2. The learning process: which includes the use of learning activities that tap students' preferred styles and patterns of learning as well as adapting the use of individual and cooperative activities;
3. The learning product: which includes the kind of learning outcomes students have to show they have acquired and the kind of evidence that they will produce to show they have acquired them.

What we teach, *how* we teach it and *how and what* we assess as evidence of achievement are often inextricably mixed together: teaching children to enjoy reading a book, providing them with the experience of reading books, and observing their interest and how they handle books are intertwined. However, it is still helpful to consider each of the three elements of teaching separately.

Figure 1: Differentiating the Curriculum to Meet the Diversity of Strengths and Needs of Students

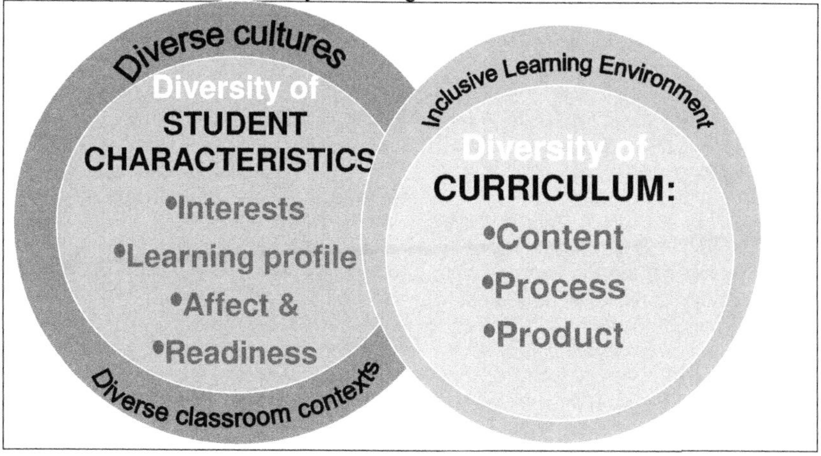

Differentiating Content

Content is the 'input' of teaching and learning. It's what we teach or what we want students to learn (Tomlinson, 2001, p. 72).

The teacher's challenge is to prepare the kinds of input that students are expected to be able to take up meaningfully and to find appropriately challenging.

One thing all teachers in most contexts can do is make content meaningful by relating it to students' interests. For example for boys interested in football, learning 'bigger and smaller than' can be much more meaningful if presented in the framework of the scores obtained by teams in the World Cup. A sure way of tapping individual interests is by making use of students' experiences. Personal experience carries meaning and emotional engagement (see Mizzi & Bartolo, 2007).

Content also needs to be within the student's zone of proximal development, that is that the student experiences it as a new challenge but at the same time it constitutes a next step for him or her and can be achieved with the support of the teacher. In order to do this, the teacher needs to see the whole curriculum as one of continuous progression:

One way of visualising the whole curriculum, including the curriculum for children with learning difficulties, is as a ladder in which broad steps are specified for all children. Within this ladder there are points at which, for some children and possibly for only some of the time, smaller intermediate rungs are needed. Like most analogies this ladder model has some weaknesses, such as of children's learning as necessarily hierarchical, clearly defined and sequential. However the ladder idea does emphasise the integration of curricula for all children, curricular progression and continuity (Lewis, 1995, p. 76).

It has been suggested that a practical way for teachers to adapt content to the different levels of readiness in a class would be to prepare activities that address the same content at two or more levels of complexity (sometimes called tiers) of content, possibly one for grade level, one above and one below (Tomlinson, 2001). This can be achieved through a *pre-assessment* that informs the teacher on the levels of knowledge and skills students have already acquired.

The teacher needs to understand what are the main or *big ideas* in the curriculum to be learned. Consider what are "the essential questions raised by this idea or topic" in addition to "what, *specifically*, about the idea or topic you want students to come to understand" (Wiggins & McTighe, 2005, p. 137). One can say that the big idea is the *top goal* of that specific part of the curriculum. For instance, what is the big idea in learning to read and write? Why do we learn to read and write? What couldn't we do if we didn't know how to read and write?

What comes to mind? Did you consider the possibility that the big idea behind literacy is *communicating through print*, or *getting the message from print*, or *giving messages through print*. If a teacher has the big idea in mind, he or she can more easily adapt the specific learning to the level of the student without feeling that it is not linked to the regular curriculum.

Particularly when there is a very big gap between what one student can do and the rest of the class, it becomes more important also to adopt a *holistic* approach to teaching. Holistic needs of development such as physical, social, emotional, spiritual and personal areas may be a more common link among students. Moreover, within holistic development, teaching children different things according to need also makes sense: for instance, while teaching the whole class mathematics, one may focus instead on teaching that particular child a social skill during the same lesson (Giangreco, 2007).

Differentiating the Learning Process

Another important way in which teachers can provide each student with access to required learning is through the use of differentiated learning activities (process or method of learning). "Teachers are particularly limited when the sole or primary instructional strategy is teacher-centred (such as lecture), or drill-and-practice (such as worksheets)" (Tomlinson & Demirsky Allan, 2000, p. 11). Effective teachers will use a variety of learning activities: brainstorming, problem-solving, observing an action or video and analysing it, audio or video recording of experiences as well as writing about them; exploring the use of objects, creating artefacts, project work; discussing ideas, singing, acting; working individually and in group tasks, working independently or with peer or teacher support; researching on the internet, practicing new skills possibly using role play, fieldwork. Creative teachers like to gradually extend their repertoire of activities.

In this way, each student can make use of his or her strengths in processing learning, according to one's particular intelligence strength, be it verbal, mathematical, visuo-spatial, kinaesthetic, musical, naturalistic, intrapersonal, interpersonal or spiritual – nine multiple intelligences described by Gardner (1999). There are various descriptions of different learning or cognitive styles and learning patterns that can help the perceptive teacher discover how the children in his or her class learn most effectively.

What is certainly useful is to become familiar and comfortable with a wide range of instructional strategies (Gregory & Chapman, 2006; Farrugia, 2003). Teachers find that when a variety of activities are used most students are evidently more stimulated. Certain methods appeal to a wider number of learners: role play, drama and storytelling are captivating; so are use of song and music; use of multimedia and now ICT; use of hands-on materials; use of fieldwork; project work and discussions amongst others.

One important dimension in the diversification of the learning process is the use of whole class, individual and group activities. Some learners are stimulated primarily in whole class interaction, others during individual and independent work whilst others during collaborative learning.

It has long been argued that collaborative learning leads to higher order thinking (Vygotsky, 1978), provides an opportunity for the learning of social skills as well as stimulates a higher level student engagement (Johnson & Johnson, 1998). In addition, group work frees teacher time for giving more individualised support in small groups. Indeed, it is difficult to imagine differentiated teaching without the use of some form of group work for at least some of the time. The organisation of cooperative group work requires the preparation of students to work collaboratively as well as the preparation of tasks that require each student to have a role in achieving the group goal.

One final important variation in the learning process that needs highlighting is the diversification of levels and type of *support*. Readers are probably familiar with the concept of *scaffolding*: that is the teacher's sensitivity to the level and amount of support each student needs in going through the process of acquisition of knowledge or skill. For all students it is recommended that one follows the process of first demonstrating, then guiding the student, and then letting the student work independently. Adaptation of support to each student's needs becomes more possible, and is doubled when there is a learning support assistant in the classroom: each student's needs can be known more individually, and it is possible to be helping two individual students or two groups simultaneously.

Support need not come directly from the teacher or other adult. One of the biggest resources a teacher can use, apart from his or her own competencies, is the learning and skills of students themselves. Peer tutoring is a recognised way of providing a wider support to students in class (Hall & Stegila, 2003). A student might even be able to help the teacher manage the use of the computer for certain tasks; another student might have more knowledge than the teacher about a topic that is being discussed. For instance, one teacher found that a student had visited the *Shakespearean Globe Theatre* in London and could recount personal experiences there to the excitement of the other students.

Within the concept of the social dimensions of learning, one has to consider that learning is not limited to the classroom (Wentzel, 1998). Working hand-in-hand with parents or guardians to extend students' learning is another essential aspect of the learning process. It is in fact at home that many students can experience very differentiated levels of support. There have been instances where teaching illiterate parents to read and write has had a great impact on their children's motivation for the acquisition of literacy skills.

The social dimension of learning extends to the whole community. Teachers sometimes find it useful to invite into the classroom or visit at work successful members of the community to serve as role models for their students. Inviting members of the different subcultures or ethnicities in the community can also serve as an aid to widening the understanding of the different multicultural perspectives on knowledge and skills and ways of living.

When teachers rely on only lecture type, whole class teaching, they are clearly denying their students much greater potential for learning in ways they may find more stimulating, meaningful and engaging.

Of course it must be pointed out, that merely providing a variety of activities is necessary but not sufficient: "it's crucial to remember that it's the quality and focus of what students do that is most important" (Tomlinson, 2001, p. 80).

Diversifying the Learning Product

The final element that teachers can differentiate in instruction is the learning product: what students end up doing to demonstrate their learning. Thinking deeply and creatively about learning products is important because this will have a wide impact on the students' long term learning outcomes, some products remaining with the students as a symbol of their learning and capacity for learning. Products of learning include the taking of tests, but go much beyond in helping students to extend and apply their learning.

Here again, particularly in all Maltese schools, there has been for a long time too much dependence on one-size-fits-all national examinations as evidence of student learning. These have also influenced classroom learning products becoming solely paper and pencil reproductions of information fed to students.

Within the new conceptualisation of assessment *for* rather than *of* learning (Black *et al.*, 2002), it is now understood that formative assessment is at the heart of effective teaching. It is an inclusive approach that intends that assessment should provide motivation for each student to learn rather than for the successful to be motivated at the expense of those who fail: "Feedback to any pupil should be about the particular qualities of his or her work, with advice on what he or she can do to improve, and should avoid comparison with other pupils" (Assessment Reform Group (ARG), 2002). And indeed, it needs to be realised that:

> Much of what teachers and learners do in classrooms can be described as assessment. That is, tasks and questions prompt learners to demonstrate their knowledge, understanding and skills. What learners say and do is then observed and interpreted, and judgements are made about how learning can be improved. These assessment processes are an essential part of everyday classroom practice and involve both teachers and learners in reflection, dialogue and decision making (ARG, 2002).

Teachers need to be creative by first of all ensuring successful learning for all: students need to have the teacher's confidence that they can learn and also the teacher's sensitivity to ensure that they can master the next step in learning they are challenged to tackle. When students make an effort, they will certainly have made progress in their knowledge and understanding, and the products they are asked to develop should allow for such progress to be evident and this should then be recognised by the teacher.

This can be better achieved if we allow students to use their strengths both in their learning and in their production of learning evidence. This is more often possible if use is made of:

a) *Authentic assessment*: demonstrating learning outcomes needs to be linked to real-life situations. For instance, if we are assessing language learning, then part of it is the ability to carry on a particular sort of conversation, and not only in doing written grammar exercises or writing an essay; the form of essays should also reflect forms of writing learners may be engaged in real life such as writing an email.

b) *Sharing of goals and evaluation criteria*: learners need to understand what it is they are trying to achieve - and want to achieve it. Understanding and commitment follows when learners have some part in deciding goals and identifying criteria for assessing progress...

c) *Self assessment*: Teachers should equip learners with the desire and the capacity to take charge of their learning through developing the skills of self-assessment (ARG, 2002).

Conclusion

Inclusive education is an attempt to enable each student to be a full member of his or her learning community. This implies valuing each student equally, and creating a supportive environment that enables each student to participate actively in the various activities of school life. One of the main areas of school life is the academic curriculum. Differentiated teaching is an attempt to ensure each student can see himself or herself as a learner like every other peer and be actively engaged in regular lessons.

This is a challenge for the teacher. Students differ in their interests and cultural and linguistic backgrounds, ways of learning and levels of achievement in each area of the curriculum. The first challenge is to enable students to respect each other as different but equally valued individuals and to create a learning environment where each is expected to be actively engaged and to make progress.

Secondly, the teacher will understand that one-size teaching, such as merely whole-class, chalk and talk, paper and pencil lessons cannot be engaging for all students. The responsive teacher reaches out to all students by differentiating the content, process and product of their lessons to meet the different interests, learning styles and attainment levels of their students.

This requires that teachers try to get to know their students and to appreciate and value each one equally as a person and as a learner. As they get to know their students, responsive teachers also engage in a continuous reflective process in search of making the curriculum accessible and meaningful to each one of them.

Thirdly, teachers gradually develop skills in preparing and managing their lessons in such a way that each student can use his or her strengths to engage actively and successfully with the curriculum. This requires tapping different student intelligences, and making use of peer-tutoring and cooperative learning that allow for differentiation of learning activity and support arrangements, giving an opportunity for the teacher to interact interpersonally with many more students.

As one of the strategies, teachers need to engage in assessment *for* learning, using assessment to provide feedback to their students on what they have managed to master and what is the next step in their learning. Each student is enabled to feel that he or she is making worthwhile progress and is indeed contributing to the learning of all.

Thinking Point 1:
Think of a unit of learning in the curriculum you are teaching. In what variety of ways can the content, process and product of the unit be varied to reach out to the various interests and motivation, learning profile, and readiness levels of your students?

Thinking Point 2:
Think of a student who is not engaged in your lessons. How can you differentiate the content, process or product of your lessons so that he or she too can be successfully engaged?

REFERENCES

Assessment Reform Group (ARG) (2002). *Assessment for learning: 10 principles - Research-based principles to guide classroom practice.* London: QCDA www.qcda.gov.uk/4335.aspx

Bartolo, P. A., Agius Ferrante, C., Azzopardi, A., Bason, L., Grech, L., & King, M. (2002). *Creating inclusive schools: Guidelines for the implementation of the National Curriculum policy on inclusive education.* Malta: Ministry of Education. (Available on line: www.gov.mt).

Bartolo, P.A., Hofsaess, T., Mol Lous, A., Ale, P., Calleja, C., Humphrey, N., Janikova, V., Vilkiene, V., Wetso, G. (2007). *Responding to student diversity: Teacher's handbook.* Malta: University of Malta. (Available online: www.dtmp.org).

Black, P.J., Harrison, C., Lee, C., Marshall, B., & Wiliam, D. (2002). *Working inside the black box: Assessment for learning in the classroom.* London: King's College.

Farrugia, M.T. 2003. Teaching and learning primary mathematics. In S. Gatt & Y. Vella (Eds.), *Constructivist teaching in primary school.* Malta: Agenda.

Gardner, H. (1999). *Intelligence reframed: Multiple intelligences for the 21st Century.* New York: Basics Books.

Giangreco, M. (2007). Extending inclusive opportunities. *Educational Leadership, 64(5), 34-37.*

Gregory, G. H., and Chapman, C. (2006). (2nd Ed.). *Differentiated instructional strategies: One size doesn't fit all.* Thousand Oaks, CA: Corwin Press.

Hall, T., & Stegila, A. (2003). Peer-mediated instruction and intervention. Retrieved from www.cast.org/publications/ncac/ncac_peermii.html.

Humphrey, N., Bartolo, P., Ale, P., Calleja, C., Hofsaess, T., Janikova, V., Mol Lous, A., Vilkiene, V., Wetso, G. (2006). Understanding and responding to diversity in the primary classroom: An *international study. European Journal of Teacher Education, 29 (3), 305–318.*

Johnson, R. T., & Johnson, D. W. (1998). (5th Ed.). *Learning together and alone: cooperative, competitive, and individualistic learning.* Boston: Allyn & Bacon.

King, A. (2007). Structuring peer interaction to promote higher-order thinking and complex learning in cooperating groups. In Gillies, R.M., Ashman, A.F. & Terwel, J. (Eds.). *The teacher's role in implementing cooperative learning in the classroom.* Netherlands: Springer.

Lewis, A. (1995). *Primary special needs and the national curriculum.* London: Routeledge.

Mizzi, E., & Bartolo, P.A. (2007). Creating inclusive environments: a supportive learning climate for children at the Society of Christian Doctrine in Malta. In Bartolo, P.A., Hofsaess, T., & Mol Lous, A. (Eds,), *Responding to student diversity, Teacher education and classroom practice (p. 267-94).* Malta: University of Malta.

Rose, D.H., & Meyer, A. (2002). *Teaching every student in the digital age: Universal Design for Learning.* Harvard: Harvard Education Press.

Tomlinson, C. A. (2003). *Fulfilling the promise of the differentiated classroom.* Alexandria: ASCD.

Tomlinson, C. A., (2001). *(2nd Ed.). How to differentiate instruction in mixed-ability classrooms.* Alexandria, VA: ASCD.

Vygotsky, L. (1978). *Mind in society: The development of higher psychological processes.* Cambridge: Harvard University Press.

Wentzel, K.R. (1998). Social relationships and motivation in middle school: The role of parents, teachers and peers. *Journal of Educational Psychology, 90(2), 202-209.*

Wiggins, G., & McTighe, J. (2005). *Understanding by design* (2nd Ed.). Alexandria: ASCD.

SUPPORTING THE INCLUSIVE EDUCATION OF STUDENTS WITH
SOCIAL, EMOTIONAL AND BEHAVIOUR DIFFICULTIES

ABSTRACT

One of the challenges to the success and effectiveness of inclusive education is the education of pupils with social, emotional and behaviour difficulties (SEBD). Teachers frequently express concern about students' behaviour and their major reservations about inclusion are usually related to challenging behaviour. This is the only group of students for whom punitive, exclusionary practices are permitted by law, practices clearly in conflict with the principles of inclusive education. The Author of this Chapter argues that as in the case of other individual educational needs, schools need to make the necessary changes to enhance the goodness of fit between the students' individual needs and their learning environment. Listening to what the students themselves have to say about their school experiences is one way of moving the inclusion project forward for these students.

Introduction

A recent international study amongst twenty-three countries, reported that one of the major factors which hampers teachers' effectiveness was misbehaviour in school, with an average thirteen percent of teacher time spent on maintaining order and correcting misbehaviour in the classroom (OECD, 2009). Maltese teachers participating in the survey said that students intimidating and verbally abusing other students (almost fifty percent of the teachers) or staff themselves (twenty per cent of the teachers) interfered with the quality of their instruction. It may come as no surprise therefore that classroom teachers tend to prefer students with other forms of difficulty such as physical or intellectual disability in their classrooms in contrast to students with SEBD, and are hostile to the inclusion of the latter in mainstream schools (Avramadis & Norwich, 2002; Kalambouka et al., 2007; Tanti Rigos, 2009). These are usually the least liked and understood students and the least likely to receive effective and timely support (Baker, 2005; Kalambouka et al., 2007; Ofsted, 2007). In their study of inclusion policy and practice in the UK, McBeath et al., (2006) reported that when teachers expressed concerns about inclusion, these were mainly related to behaviour issues.

In this Chapter I will argue that the use of punitive, exclusionary practices for students with *Social, Emotional and Behaviour Difficulties (SEBD)*[11] is in conflict with the principle of inclusive education itself, and that a more inclusive practice will be for schools to make the necessary changes to enhance the goodness of fit

---

[11] SEBD is a loose umbrella term encompassing behaviours and expressions of emotion among students which are experienced by adults and students as disruptive and/or disturbing, and which interfere with the students' learning, social functioning and development and/or that of their peers

between the student's individual needs and his or her learning environment. In the second part, I will then propose that one way of facilitating the inclusion of students with SEBD is to listen to what the students themselves have to say and include their suggestions in the classroom practice. The Chapter concludes with a task inviting the reader to reflect on the issue of mainstreaming and special provision for students with SEBD. Before continuing our discussion, it would be appropriate however, to provide a brief description of the Maltese Educational System.

Education in Malta is compulsory between the ages of 5 and 16, with six years of primary education followed by five years of secondary school. State schools cater for about two thirds of the Maltese school population, while the other one third goes to Church and Independent schools. Kindergarten (nursery) is provided for three and four year olds, with more than ninety percent attendance rate (Commission of the European Communities 2008). At the end of the primary cycle, pupils sit for the Junior Lyceum examination (11+) which streams children according to ability in two different types of secondary education, namely Junior Lyceum for those who pass the 11+ (presently the pass rate is sixty percent), and Area Secondary Schools for those who fail or do not sit for the examination. A recent development has been the clustering of state schools in the country into ten regional colleges, with all primary school pupils in a particular college going to one secondary school for boys and another for girls within that college (while primary schools are mixed, there is still single sex secondary education in state schools). A reform process has just been introduced with the aim of the gradual phasing out of the 11+ and streaming in primary schools. The vast majority of students attend mainstream schools, and less than one percent of the school population attend special schools. Only about 0.2 of the ten percent of students with SEBD receive their education in special schools (Cefai, Cooper & Camilleri, 2008).

Inclusion Versus Exclusion

Teaching students who are disruptive or defiant presents particular challenges for the classroom teacher. Challenging behaviour may not only disrupt the teaching and learning processes, but it may pose potential risks for the other members of the classroom. It may also be regarded as a direct threat to the teacher's own competence and authority, as well as to the school's attempts to improve educational targets and achieve academic excellence in a market led philosophy (Farrell & Humphrey, 2009). It is ironic however, that while there is virtually universal public support for the idea that students with Individual Educational Needs (IEN) should be educated in a supportive and inclusive context adapted to their needs, students with SEBD are often the subject of public debates on the use of exclusionist and segregationist practices. Jull (2008) makes a very pertinent point when he argues that SEBD is the only IEN category which exposes the student to increased risk of exclusion as a function of the identification of the IEN itself. Indeed, students with SEBD are the only group for whom punitive, exclusionary responses are still permitted by law (Cooper, 2001), a practice clearly in conflict with the policy of inclusive education. The identification of IEN within an inclusive system would imply that such needs, including those related to SEBD, should be addressed within the mainstream by adapting the system to fit the needs of the students concerned (Jull, 2008). Adapting the curriculum and its delivery to make it more flexible, meaningful and accessible, providing a safe classroom climate based on caring and supportive relationships, collaboration, reinforcement of positive behaviour, and opportunities to make responsible choices, would be in line with an inclusive approach to the education of students with SEBD (Cooper, 2001; Fletcher-Campbell & Wilkin, 2003; Visser, 2003; Ofsted, 2007; Cefai, Cooper & Camilleri, 2008; Mooij & Smeets, 2009). Such a learning environment would be an appropriate response to address the unmet social and emotional needs of the students, providing them with the tools and opportunities to become actively engaged in the social and academic activities of the classroom within a safe, caring and supportive climate and to develop a sense of belonging and classroom community (Cefai, 2008).

This approach is not much different from adapting the curriculum, pedagogy, and use of resources to the needs of a student with another form of disability or learning difficulty, such as a specific learning difficulty. In both instances, the objective would be to make the necessary changes in the educational context to enhance the goodness of fit between the student's individual needs and his or her learning environment (Jull, 2008). While in the case of a specific learning difficulty, exclusion, even in the form of segregation, is not usually an option, in the case of SEBD, schools may be more willing to consider exclusion as a way to resolve the problem. While there may be instances where exclusion cannot be avoided and may be the only way to solve the presenting difficulty, its use becomes problematic when it is seen as a way of responding to SEBD. It becomes a way of getting rid of the problem, indicating the school's failure to address the individual needs and support the inclusive education of students with SEBD (*ibid.*).

An Inclusive SEBD-Friendly Classroom

Listening to the voices of students with SEBD is gaining salience as one of the most useful ways to help create classroom environments which will make it easier for such students to participate actively in the academic and social life of the classroom, and less likely for them to be excluded or segregated (Flutter & Rudduck, 2004; Riley, 2004; Davies, 2005; Cooper, 2006; Lewis & Burman, 2008). What students with SEBD have to say about their learning and behaviour is not only valid and meaningful, but helps to provide a more adequate and useful construction of the situation, contributing to a better understanding and resolution of difficulties. They are able to throw light upon the causes and nature of learning and behaviour difficulties which might be overlooked or not mentioned by teachers (Rudduck, 2002; Fielding & Bragg, 2003). They are a source of knowledge and expertise, having unique and inside knowledge of what it is like to be a student in a particular school (Cooper, 1996). Students are also able to provide an accurate account of their own learning processes and how these could be enhanced by classroom teaching practices (Fielding & Bragg, 2003; Leitch & Mitchell, 2007). In a review of studies on the educational experiences of secondary school students with SEBD in Malta, Cefai & Cooper (2009) identified five major themes in students' narratives about their mainstream school experiences. These themes underline the basic issues of healthy and caring classroom relationships, democracy, engaging and meaningful curriculum and effective pedagogy, support in learning, and inclusion, and may serve as reminders for educators on what helps students with SEBD to remain engaged in their learning, connected with teachers and peers, and included in the classroom community[12].

Poor Relationships versus Connectedness with Teachers

One of the most common and frequently mentioned grievances by the students was the perceived lack of understanding and support by the classroom teachers. They felt humiliated and inadequate when teachers shouted at them in front of their peers, ignored them or refused to listen to their views. They complained about the punitive approach adopted by many teachers in their response to misbehaviour and argued that in many instances it can lead to an exacerbation of the problem. Relationships perceived as uncaring, autocratic and unfair are linked to student defiance and disaffection and consequently to disengagement from a system instilling a sense of failure, disempowerment and punishment in the students' quest for self definition, competence and autonomy (Daniels *et al.*, 2003; Kroeger *et al.*, 2004). The students underlined the common universal needs of young people, namely the need to be respected, listened to and treated with dignity and understanding (cf. Deci *et al.*, 1991). When teachers were understanding and took time to listen to them and their difficulties, the students felt comfortable and accepted, and found it easier to engage with what was taking place in the classroom. The close relationship with the teachers also provided a scaffold which helped the students to find stability in a sometimes disorganised and chaotic life, to believe more in themselves, and to find meaning in their school experiences.

Victimisation versus Sense of Fairness

Being treated unfairly and picked on by teachers and to a lesser extent by peers, was another concern expressed by the students. They defended their behaviour as a rightful and justified reaction to what they regarded as unfair treatment. They felt hurt and angry when they were singled out for misbehaviour, and even more when they were blamed and punished for their peers' misbehaviour. Bullying and teasing by peers added to perceived victimisation. Although some of the students had friends and some were even popular with their peers for standing up to the system, others said they were picked on by peers with little support from the staff. This led them frequently into trouble with both peers and staff, in many cases ending up in isolation and absenteeism. Schooling came to be perceived as a negative, destructive experience.

Oppression versus Democracy

The students felt they could do little at the school to change their predicament and get respite from their daily hassles. A sense of helplessness underlined their grievance that they had little say, with staff wielding the authority and making the decisions. They also complained about rules being imposed without consultation. While they appreciated that structure and discipline were necessary for learning to

---

[12] The following section presents a summary of these five themes, for a more detailed description the reader is referred to Cefai & Cooper (2009).

take place; the way many teachers dealt with challenging behaviour was described as autocratic and coercive, leaving them with no option but to fight the system or else disengage from it. Another 'disabling barrier' (Barnes *et al.,* 1999) was the imposition of the alien school culture on the students' own in some of the schools. Some students sought to resist the attempts of enculturation by refusing the values projected by the school, such as behaving and dressing in ways which conflicted with the culture in their communities and peer group. The students believed that if their views were given more consideration, it would have helped to improve both their learning, as teachers would know what helps or hinders students from learning, as well as their behaviour, as students would then have been treated with respect and responsibility. These voices strongly resonate with Oliver's (1996) assertion that social systems such as schools take little or no account of the needs of young people, eventually leading to the students' exclusion from engagement in the mainstream educational activities.

Irrelevant Curriculum versus Meaningful Learning Experiences

Many of the students found the curriculum boring and academic, unrelated to life and career. They had difficulty to engage in activities which appeared to have little relevance to real life situations and the concerns they had in their life and in their communities. They disliked traditional lessons based mainly on written academic work with little interaction and application to real life. This reflects the inextricable link between learning and behaviour frequently referred to in the literature, and how an irrelevant and inaccessible curriculum may lead to disengagement and absenteeism (Wise, 2000; Groom & Rose, 2004). On the other hand, when the subject was related to their needs and made sense to them, they found the experience worthwhile and meaningful. They especially liked to learn through practical, hands on activities. When they felt supported in their learning and provided with meaningful activities which they could follow and participate in, they became actively engaged in the learning process.

Exclusion versus Inclusion

The students felt excluded with staff being unwilling and/or unable to understand them and accommodate to their social and emotional needs. They found it difficult to thrive in a rigid system which expected them to change and adapt and left little space for flexibility and autonomy. Not having their learning needs adequately addressed, compounded their existing problems at school, leaving them excluded from the learning activities and vulnerable to exclusion from school itself. For instance, sitting for un-adapted, summative examinations in which they knew they will fail, had a demoralising effect on their self esteem. Lack of structure and support thus led to situations where they became more vulnerable and more likely to find themselves victims of labelling and stigmatisation. The label they ended up with as a result of lack of support to their educational needs in turn led to a self fulfilling prophecy where they stopped believing in themselves and considered themselves as failures, doubting their own capabilities and resources to face the challenges as young adults in society. In many instances, this led to disengagement, disaffection and absenteeism as students sought to detach themselves from a system which had a very negative effective on their view of themselves at such a delicate and vulnerable stage in their development. For some, disengagement became a self protective mechanism from an act of symbolic violence by a dehumanising, excluding system.

The students were quite clear on what would have helped to make their school experiences more rewarding and worthwhile. They underlined the need for a more humane, inclusive, democratic and relevant educational system. They warmed up to those teachers who showed them care and understanding, listened to their concerns, and supported them in their needs. They were ready to invest in teachers who respected them and believed in them despite their difficulties. They referred to the significance of caring relationships with teachers and the power of such relationships in realigning their development towards more positive pathways (cf. Cooper, 1993; Daniels et al., 2003; Kroeger et al., 2004). They yearned for a system where they would be treated fairly, where they would have a right of reply have a more direct say in decisions where they are not unfairly blamed (cf. Janhnukainen, 2001; Davies, 2005). They wished that what they had to do at school made more sense to their present lives and future career prospects, and helped them to develop their strengths and talents, rather than exacerbating their weaknesses. Instead of serving as an instrument of oppression and exclusion, the curriculum and its delivery would thus become a vehicle for opportunity and success. When they were given a second chance, such as going to another school which addressed their needs, they reported a more positive view of school and learning, which in turn led to a more positive view of themselves and their abilities, a process Cooper (1993) calls 'positive resignification'. Healthy student-teacher relationships, caring, and supportive teachers, flexible classroom management, meaningful engagement, inclusion, and support in academic and personal needs, would have prevented their negative signification and directed their educational experience towards healthy, successful pathways.

Conclusion

This Chapter has focused on how classrooms may be organised to become more welcoming and inclusive for students with SEBD by listening to what the students themselves have to say about what they would like to see in the classroom. There is a clear recognition however, that responding to, and preventing SEBD, needs to take place at various levels and various systems. Factors at whole school level as well as factors outside the school's sphere of influence, such as family makeup and parenting skills, socio-economic status and cultural values, have a direct influence on students behaviour at school (Cefai, Cooper & Camilleri, 2008). Classrooms do not operate in a vacuum and cannot, on their own standing compensate for the effects of wider social and economic inequalities. Their success will only be maximized when the relationships between SEBD and wider social and economic issues are acknowledged and acted upon. However, it is also clear that the classroom is one of the most influential systems in students' learning and behaviour, and that classroom processes remain at the core in seeking to address the needs of students with SEBD within an inclusive context.

Thinking Point 1:
Why is there such a resistance to the inclusion of students with SEBD in comparison to other IEN groups? What may help schools and teachers to become more SEBD-friendly?

Thinking Point 2:
The use of exclusion as a way to deal with SEBD is an admission that inclusion has failed and that the school has been unable to address the individual educational needs of the students. Why is exclusion not an effective long term strategy to deal with SEBD in school?

Thinking Point 3:
The inclusion of 'student voice' has been has been found to be a very useful way in facilitating the social and educational engagement of students with SEBD. How can teachers give more voice and choice to the students in their classroom, particularly when responding to students with SEBD?

Thinking Point 4:
Jull (2008) argues that the decreasing number of permanent exclusions from schools in the UK has been accompanied by a simultaneous increase in the number of placements at *Pupil Referral Units*, suggesting that the latter were operating as another form of exclusion. On the other hand, in their study of inclusive education in the UK, McBeath *et al.,* (2006) found that school staff expressed concerns about the capacity of mainstream schools to address the needs of students with complex emotional and behavioural needs. They also reported that such difficulties affected the ability of staff to provide an adequate education for these students besides leading to problems for other students as well. Cooper (2010) postulates that positive social, emotional and educational engagement are the goals of educational intervention for all students, and that educational placements should thus be based on decisions on where opportunities for such engagement can be found, rather than on where some people think they ought to be found. He argues that 'locational integration' is inclusion in name only and does not equate with social and educational engagement. Read Jull's (2008) and Cooper's (2010) papers and answer the following questions:

- Is the placement of students with SEBD in special provision another form of exclusion as suggested by Jull?
- Is the placement of students with complex emotional and behaviour needs in mainstream schools a futile exercise driven by 'heart' rather than 'head' as suggested by Cooper?
- How may these two positions be reconciled with regards to the education of students with SEBD?

REFERENCES

Avramidis, E. & Norwich, B. (2002). 'Teachers' attitudes towards integration/inclusion: a review of the literature'. *European Journal of Special Needs Education, 17 (2):129-149.*

Baker, P. H. (2005). Managing student behaviour: How ready are teachers to meet the challenge? *American Secondary Education, 33(3): 50-67.*

Barnes, C., Mercer, G. & Shakespeare, T. (1999). *Exploring Disability: A Sociological Introduction.* Cambridge, UK: Polity Press.

Cefai, C. (2008). *Promoting Resilience in the Classroom. A Guide to Developing Pupils' Emotional and Cognitive Skills.* London: Jessica Kingsley Publications.

Cefai, C. & Cooper, P. (2009). The narratives of secondary school students with SEBD on their schooling. In Cefai, C. & Cooper, P. (Eds.). Promoting *Emotional Education. Engaging Children and Young People with Social, Emotional and Behaviour Difficulties.* London: Jessica Kingsley Publishers.

Cefai, C., Cooper, P. & Camilleri, L. (2008). *Engagement Time: A national study of students with social, emotional and behaviour difficulties in Maltese schools.* Malta: European Centre for Education Resilience and Socio-Emotional Health, University of Malta.

Commission of the European Communities (2008). *Progress Towards The Lisbon Objectives in Education and Training. Indicators and Benchmarks 2008.* Brussels: Commission of the European Union.

Cooper, P. (1993) Learning from Pupils' Perspectives. *British Journal of Special Education, 20, 4: 129-133.*

Cooper, P. (2001). *We can Work it out: What Works in Educating Pupils with Social, Emotional and Behavioural Difficulties: Inclusive Practice in Mainstream Schools.* London: Routledge/Falmer.

Cooper, P. (2006). John's story: Episode 1 – Understanding SEBD from the inside: The importance of listening to young people. In Hunter-Carsch, M., Tiknaz, Y., Cooper, P. & Sage, R. (Eds.). *The handbook of social, emotional and behavioural difficulties.* London: Continuum International Publishing Group.

Cooper, P. (2010). Social, emotional and behaviour difficulties: The challenge for policy makers *International Journal of Emotional Education, 2 (1): 4-16.*

Daniels, H., T. Cole, E. Sellman, J. Sutton, J. Visser, & J. Bedward (2003). *Study of young people permanently excluded from school.* London: DfES.

Davies, J.D. (2005). Voices from the margins: The perceptions of pupils with emotional and behavioural difficulties about their educational experiences. In Clough, P., Garner, P., Pardeck, J.T. & Yuen, F. (Eds.). *Handbook of emotional behavioural difficulties.* London: Sage.

Deci, E.L., Vallerand, R.J., Pelleiter, L.G. & Ryan, R.M. (1991). Motivation and education: The self determination perspective. *Educational Psychologist 26: 325–346.*

Farrell, P & Humphrey, N. (2009). Improving services for pupils with social, emotional and behaviour difficulties: Responding to the challenge. *International Journal of Emotional Education, 1 (1): 64-82.*

Fielding, M. & Bragg, S. (2003). *Students as Researchers: Making a difference.* Cambridge: Pearson Publishing.

Fletcher-Campbell, F. & Wilkin, A. (2003). *Review of the research literature on educational interventions for pupils with emotional and behavioural difficulties.* Slough, UK: National Foundation for Educational Research.

Groom, B. & Rose, R. (2004). Involving students with emotional and behavioural difficulties in their own learning: a transnational perspective. In Garner, P. *et al.,* (Eds.). *The Handbook of Emotional and Behavioural Difficulties.* London: Sage.

Jahnukainen, M. (2001). Experiencing special education: Former students of classes for the emotionally and behaviourally disordered talk about their schooling. *Emotional and Behavioural Difficulties 6 (3): 150–66.*

Jull, S.K. (2008). Emotional and behavioural difficulties (EBD): The special educational need justifying exclusion. *Journal of Research in Special Educational Needs, 8 (1): 13-18.*

Kalambouka, A., Farrell, P., Dyson, A. & Kaplan, I. (2007). The impact of placing pupils with special educational needs in mainstream schools on the achievements of their peers'. *Educational Research, 39: 365 – 382.*

Kroeger, S., Burton, C., Comarata, A., Combs, C., Hamm, C., Hopkins, R., & Kouche, B. (2004). Student voice and critical reflection: Helping students at Risk *Teaching Exceptional Children, 36(3): 50-57.*

Leitch, R. & Mitchell, S. (2007). Caged birds and cloning machines: how student imagery 'speaks' to us about cultures of schooling and student participation in *Improving Schools, 10: 53 – 71.*

Lewis, R. & Burman, E. (2008). Providing for student voice in classroom management: Teachers' views. *International Journal of Inclusive Education 12 (2): 151–67.*

MacBeath, J., Galton, M., Steward, S., MacBeath, A & Page, C. (2006). *The Costs of Inclusion: A study of inclusion policy and practice in English primary, secondary and special schools.* Cambridge, University of Cambridge.

Mooij, T., & Smeets, E. (2009). Towards systemic support of pupils with emotional and behavioural disorders. *International Journal of Inclusive Education, 13 (6): 597-616.*

OECD (2009). *Teaching and Learning International Survey (TALIS).* Retrieved on 18th December 2009 from www.oecd.org/edu/talis/firstresults

Ofsted (2007). *Inclusion: Does it Matter where Pupils are Taught?* London: Office for Standards in Education.

Oliver, M. (1996). *Understanding Disability: from theory to practice.* Basingstoke: Macmillan.

Riley, K. (2004). Voices of Disaffected Pupils: Implications for Policy and Practice. *British Journal of Educational Studies 52 (2): 166-79.*

Ruddock J. (2002). What's In It for Us? Pupil Consultation and Participation. *The ESRC Network Project Newsletter No. 4.* Retrieved 15th May 2010 from www.consultingpupils.co.uk

Tanti Rigos, V. (2009). *Maltese Teachers' Causal Attributions, Cognitive and Emotional Responses to Students with Emotional and Behavioral Difficulties.* Unpublished M.Ed. dissertation, Faculty of Education, University of Malta.

Visser, J (2003). A Study of Young People with Challenging Behaviour. London: Ofsted.

Wise, S. (2000). *Listen to me! The voices of pupils with emotional and behavioural difficulties (EBD).* Lucky Duck Publishing Ltd.

THE ROLE OF SOCIAL WORK IN INCLUSIVE EDUCATION

ABSTRACT
This Chapter explores the relationship between social work and inclusive education. Historically social work has been concerned with giving oppressed minorities a voice, facilitating empowerment for the devalued, challenging discrimination for outsiders and supporting diversity within communities. On the face of it the inclusion of disabled children into mainstream schools fits well with this, however inclusion is both a complex and contested interaction of factors bound by history, culture, policy and social theory and social work in many ways is relativity new to education. Social work in the last twenty years has been undergoing profound changes in terms of its practice, values and ideology and this Chapter explores these in parallel to different models of disability.

Introduction

This Chapter will explore the relationship between the profession known as 'social work' and the community of practice known as inclusive education. Over the last twenty years social work in the UK as a profession has been experiencing a profound change in its discourse in terms of its practice, values and ideology. Discourse as discussed here is the system of beliefs and practices that aid the social construction of both social work and inclusive education. Historically social work has been concerned with giving oppressed minorities a voice, facilitating empowerment for the devalued, challenging discrimination for outsiders and supporting diversity within communities. Inclusion is both a complex and contested interaction of factors bound by history, culture, policy and social theory. In many ways the notion of developing an inclusive school community is comparable to the community care of the 1990s which was and continues to be problematic in its attempt to drive communities into caring about those who have been traditionally segregated. Education is a relatively new territory for social work, Openshaw (2008, p. 5) writes that:

> School social workers practice in a secondary setting-the primary purpose of schools is to educate students, not to provide social services.

This has presented a challenge to social work to itself be positively 'included' in this setting. To date there has been relatively little written on the role of social work and inclusive education in the UK but importantly they share or should share a strong ideology. In this Chapter a series of topics will be explored starting with a brief examination of social work and its ideological position, moving on to the assumptions around disabled children in education and finally the critical role of social work within inclusive education. Here 'disabled child' refers to both those children with learning difficulties and physical impairments. The Chapter will also raise a number of questions such as how should social workers work within inclusive education in the future? In addressing such questions the social construction of disability will be utilised, in particular the social model of disability born of the disabled people's movement (Oliver, 1991; 1996). The social model has a strong driver behind it projecting the rights of disabled people which can potentially align it with both social work and inclusive education. This could be realised through emancipation, respect and a direct challenge to disability as tragedy or invalidity.

Disability, Social Work and Inclusive Education

In understanding disability it is important to outline the two main social constructions which influence both theory and practice in the education of disabled children. Firstly, Hall (1997, p. 74) writes that:

> Whilst under medical domination, the process for distinguishing between different types and degrees of learning disability was quite naturally through the filter we have come to call the 'medical model'.

In describing the medical model of disability Hall (1997) includes therapy, charity, special labels and special places for those with such labels. For disabled children experiencing education these therapies can be diverse interventions, charities may support the acquisition of special equipment, special labels are a consequence of the statementing system, and the special places may be special schools and colleges. The emphasis under the medical model has historically been the pathology of treatment of the sick or the functionality of fixing what is deemed to be broken. Therefore disabled children become a problem to be normalized. Being 'normalized' should not be confused with Wolfensbergers (1986) 'normalisation' approach which later developed into Social Role Valorisation. Normalisation is not about making people normal but giving disabled people valued roles within society. Secondly, the social model of disability arose from the disabled people's movement as a direct challenge to the oppressive consequences of the medical model. Put simply the social model states that the problem is not with the child's impairment but the negative professional and societal response to the impairment. The social model has a tendency to be reduced to a belief that physical access is the main focus but attitudinal change is far more significant. In effect the social model challenges segregation, depersonalization, charity, oppressive use of language and has moved to notions of affirming disability identity (Swain and French, 2000). The social model explores and challenges the relationship between need, disability and education and attempts to remove the association of disability with passivity, dependency and the medical. It is important to recognise that in the last few years the social model of disability has importantly been criticised (Shakespeare, 2006) for in particular not taking account of disabled people's pain and everyday lived experience. The argument is made here that an evolving social model of disability must drive all practices in social work thus supporting professionals to challenge any oppressive engrained social relations within school settings. Corker and Davis (2000) argue that disabled children are not passive, vulnerable or the victims of impairment. Clare and Mevik (2008, p. 29) similarly promote that disabled children:

are not credited as competent social agents to be included as active participants in interventions in their lives; instead they are viewed as 'incompetents', passive recipients and consumers of services identified by others as in their best interest.

The *United Nations Convention on the Rights of the Child* emphasizes the importance of giving choice to children, but as Clare and Mevik (2008, p. 29) point out the reality is "many practitioners do not include children in the decision-making process".

What is required is for any profession working with disabled children to challenge these devaluing discourses. *Every Child Matters* (2004) reinforced the main drivers of increased protection and reduction in risk for any child within an agenda of general life improvement. A particular emphasis is made around the inclusion of children in care into education to reduce educational failure. *Every Disabled Child Matters* was a campaign in response to a policy that had little relevance to disabled children by a number of voluntary organisations. Specialist services have developed to deliver these goals for example *Children and Adolescents Mental Health Services* (CAMHS). In addition *Behaviour and Education Support Teams* (BESTs) evolved to work in selected schools and promote emotional well-being, positive behaviour and school attendance. Social workers along with psychologists, health visitors, nurses and other therapists make up these multi-disciplinary teams.

In the last twenty years very few professions have undergone the radical changes experienced by social work, with the push towards case management, the mixed economy of care and the restructuring of statutory provision (Banks, 2006). A brief look at the history of social work shows its trajectory over time and in turn where it may move to next. Brandon and Atherton (1997) describe social work from its early philanthropic roots through to its official recognition with the formation of the *British Association of Social Work* in the 1970s. The *International Federation of Social Workers* (IFSW) definition of social work is that it:

> promotes social change, problem solving in human relationships and the empowerment and liberation of people to enhance well-being. Utilising theories of human behaviour and social systems, social work intervenes at points where people interact with their environments. Principles of human rights and social justice are fundamental to social work (IFSW, 2007).

The school is such a point of interaction and the ideological purpose could be clear here, however social work has become a profession under threat. Over ten years ago Brandon and Atherton (1997, p. 15) wrote that:

> Social work became ever more bureaucratised; took on a local government identity, was more dominated by agency requirements; under immense pressure from hostile media attention, rocked by regular paedophile scandals. It was centrally riddled with angst and self-doubt in a world where the government was anti-professional, seeing them primarily as unnecessary cartels.

This has meant that social work has and continues to experience fragmentation and specialisation (Banks, 2006). There is evidence that this has left social workers with conflicts and ambiguity in their professional roles (Carpenter *et al.*, 2003 and Frost *et al.*, 2005). Tension and internal conflicts exist with the role of social workers as agents of the state, potential empowerers and protectors of the 'vulnerable'. If you take the example of a child in school with the label of 'challenging behaviour' the social worker may have conflict between protecting other children in the class from harm, advocating for the individual child's rights and supporting the removal of the child to a more 'appropriate' educational setting. Banks (2006, p. 13) outlines the ethical dilemmas for social work around individual rights, public welfare, equality, dealing with difference, structural oppression, professional roles, boundaries and relationships. These all are involved in contesting security, liberty, welfare, community and family. Banks (2006) suggests that the emphasis on social justice is much greater within social work than other professions. However as a discipline social work has been criticised; Oliver and Sapey (2006, p. 20) write:

> The failure of social workers to develop an adequate theoretical and practice base for their interventions has led to criticisms, notably by disabled people themselves, who have accused social workers of ignorance about disabling conditions, benefits and rights, failing to recognise the need for practical assistance as well as verbal advice, and to involve disabled people in the training process.

Oliver and Sapey (2006) go on to importantly argue that parents and children need advocates to represent them, and social workers are ideally placed to negotiate with all educational settings. However, Oliver & Sapey (2006, p. 174-175) are also sceptical:

> to professionalise social work on the basis of an expertise in impairment as a cause of social need would be an act of oppression as this would serve to reinforce theories of individual inadequacy and blame, whereas what is required is for social workers and social work to develop a commitment to the removal of disabling barriers, in partnership with disabled people.

Social work rests on a tripod of firstly, an authority to intervene around children's welfare, secondly to conduct therapies with children, and thirdly to advocate on their behalf. This is problematic not only as the three may be in conflict but also as the tripod stands on the shifting sands of changing policy, public opinion, media spin and the particular contested context of inclusive education. In recent years 'inclusion' has taken over from concepts such as 'community' and 'empowerment' as the fashionable social aerosol ideologically sprayed on social endeavours to promote excellence. In the past few years within education a concern has been raised that inclusion is politically driven and lacks evidence to support its continued championing (Warnock 2005). Inclusion is being spoken by everyone but in many instances it is not understood, or worse, being manipulated for political gain. Thomas and Vaughan (2009) make the argument that a sound ideology should be central to the ongoing support of inclusive education. Roaf & Bines (1989) state that conceptually 'needs' are fundamentally deficit-based and 'opportunities' and 'rights' are a better base for educational systems. They argue that the 'need' in *Special Educational Needs* (SEN) has been bastardised to become a pathological label. In turn the 'special' in Special Needs can be defined firstly as being 'exceptional: out of the ordinary', this is perhaps the normal usage in our language, 'special occasion', 'special treat' and 'special moments', all with positive associations. Secondly, it can be perceived as 'peculiar, specific not general'; unfortunately this is the meaning that has been used with regard to the special education system. In effect it donates separation rather than excellence, a 'special problem' rather than a 'special achievement'. Special education draws on the kudos of the first meaning but it's the second were its reality lies. It simultaneously reassures us and unsettles us as it is deeply complex and contested (Brandon, 1997). With reference to the work of Sharon Rustemier around special education; Thomas and Vaughan (2009, p. 23) write that:

> ...the central problem with the development of inclusive education in the UK is the continuing philosophical, financial and legislative support for segregated special schools and it demonstrates how this segregation is internationally recognized as discriminatory and damaging to individuals and to society as a whole.

The sum of her argument is that inclusion has to mean the elimination of exclusion and it is meaningless if it does not engage fully with this. Murray and Penman (1996) argue that practice is more problematic than principles. Murray (2000), as a parent of a disabled child, contends that parents have little power in relation to the power of professionals backed by legislation and the legislative process. Rogers (2007) suggests that there may be a problem that disabled children in mainstream school are being neglected, bullied and teased. Kenworthy and Whittaker (2000) suggest that in practice many teachers and schools disregard children's views and perspectives and inclusion is more than integration and its oversimplified placement of children.

In one form or another social work has been in schools for a long time under the guise of attendance or education welfare officers. Openshaw (2008) provides a detailed account of practice on how to do social work in American schools. Importantly she states:

> The goal of school social work should be to give all children the opportunity and resources to help them succeed academically and socially in a safe and healthy school environment (Openshaw, 2008, p.4).

Horner and Krawczyk (2007, p. xi) in turn write that social work in inclusive education should be formed from a social model of disability and that it:

> ...is about that small but very significant number of children and young people for whom schooling is potentially or actually difficult - whether that difficulty flows from their experiences of a disabling society.

They go on to suggest that the actual relationship between the professional activities of teaching and social work had been largely ignored and the focus of social work has been on discriminatory educational environments, children in care and in adverse family arrangements. What appears to be important for social workers in education is the current Labour Governments priority to address broader social issues beyond that of targeting school performance. Horner and Krawczyk (2007, p. xiv) therefore see a difficult but potentially healthy marriage between education and social work:

> No longer can social work and education operate along parallel lines. The two defined professional roles – that of social worker and teacher – have been progressively led into an arranged marriage.

Schools in turn are becoming increasingly multi disciplinary, for example, what can be termed an extended school operation at the school can consist of a social worker, assistant social workers, a school nurse, learning mentors, a school attendance and improvement officer and a team of special needs teachers led by an assistant head teacher. In an online article on *Bringing social work into schools* Head Teacher Neil Wilson talks on the role of the social worker in teams around plans for particular children:

> Communicating aspects of that plan to the staff with whom the young person comes into contact in school is a key part of the social worker's role. This might involve a particular approach to behaviour management, for instance, when the focus could be on developing a young person's understanding of the notion of responsibility for her or his actions and the consequences that flow from them.

Over ten years ago there was evidence (Bagley & Pritchard, 1998) that programmes involving social workers in schools were effective at reducing theft, bullying, truanting, fighting and the use of hard drugs.

Conclusion

This Chapter has presented the argument that social work is a contested discipline with internal conflicts of practice and strong external pressures. In turn both the concepts of 'disability' and 'inclusion' are not straight forward but challenging within the political agendas of educational settings. Kelly (2008) argues that all social work is local to the context of the particular school community. Schools are 'communities of practice' (Wenger, 1998) in that they are groups of people including teachers, social workers and children who share a drive for education and learn how to do it better through regular interactions. The role of social workers in these communities of practice is under researched and theorised. Very little is written specifically in this area so in a positive way if given the space this could allow social workers to develop a new and innovative way of working in the future. There could be a strong case for social workers to take on more of an advocacy role with disabled children's education. Social workers cannot be pure advocates (Brandon, 2000) due to the conflicts of having to work in children's best interests as agents of the state. Under similar constraints and they are invited they could take a positive role in 'Circles of Support' for disabled children. Newton et al (1996) write that Circles of Support are networks for any child within the structured setting of a school to gain confidence and develop strategies and practical solutions to help them learn and develop beyond the confines of education. Due to the wide conceptual and practical gap between education and social welfare social workers can feel unsure about telling schools how they should work with children. Professionals in children's social welfare are concerned with citizenship; educationalists are concerned with the achievement of academic results. These do not always sit well together, and questions the very nature of education. Interestingly Citizenship as a subject in itself is becoming more central to schools curriculum. Horner and Krawczyk, (2007, p. 100) write that the:

> Inclusion agenda does indeed often sit uncomfortably with the obsession with School Standards and Improving Performance Agenda, but social workers have a particular role to play as advocates within an evolving and dynamic system.

The Head of a School receptive to the wishes of a disabled child may well have to face the challenge of this duality. Looking to policy the future appears to have social workers as a one stop shops in coordinating children's care. Frost *et al.*, (2005, p. 195) writes that:

> Social work has long been central to joined-up thinking amongst child welfare practice. Arguably social work is the joined-up profession – a profession that seeks to liaise, to mediate, and to negotiate between professionals and between the professions and children and their families.

Theoretically, social work has a contested social construction in this challenging area of practice. So in the future whatever practical interdisciplinary role taken by social workers within inclusive education it is key that it is driven by the social model of disability, the principles of advocacy and provides support from a solid will considered value base.

Thinking Point 1:
Are all disabled children 'vulnerable' and how might this view be unhelpful and disempowering?
Thinking Point 2:
Is inclusive education a 'pure ideology', an 'ongoing process', an 'achievable goal' or all three? Can social workers, given the nature of their work truly advocate for disabled children?
Thinking Point 3:
Take Oliver's (1983) three defined roles for social workers working with disabled children and their families and describe for each a classroom situation where they would be applicable: 'Provision of emotional support'; 'Promoting access to relevant practical support'; 'Attempting to reduce the negative impact of having to deal with discriminatory organisations and bureaucracies'.

REFERENCES

Adams, R. (2008). *Empowerment, Participation and Social Work.* (4th Ed) Basingstoke: Palgrave.

Bagley, C. & Pritchard, C. (1998). The reduction of problem behaviours and school exclusion in at-risk youth: an experimental study of school social work with cost-benefit analysis. *Child and Family Social Work 3:219-226.*

Banks, S. (2006). *Ethics and values in social work* (3rd Ed) Basingstoke: Palgrave.

Brandon, D. & Atherton, A. (1997). *A Brief History of Social Work.* Cambridge: Anglia University.

Brandon, D. & Brandon, T. (2000). *Advocacy in Social Work* Birmingham: Venture Press.

Brandon, S. (1997) *The Invisible Wall.* Lancashire: Parents with Attitude.

Bringing social work into schools website 3719. Retrieved 16th January 2010 from www.teachingexpertise.com/articles/bringing-social-work-schools-3719.

Carpenter, J., Schneider, J., Brandon, T. & Woof, D. (2003). Working in Multidisciplinary Community Mental Health Teams: The Impact on Social Workers and Health Professionals of Integrated *Mental Health Care British Journal of Social Work 33:1081-1193.*

Clare, B. & Mevik, K. (2008). Inclusive Education: Teaching Social Work Students to Work with Children *Journal of Social Work, 8:28-44.*

Corker, M. & Davis, J. M. (2000). Disabled children – (Still) invisible under the law. In Cooper, J (Ed.). *Law, Rights and Disability* London: Jessica Kingsley.

Every Child Matters – Next Steps (2004). London: DFES Publications.

Frost, N., Robinson, M. & Anning, A. (2005). Social workers in multidisciplinary teams issues and dilemmas for professional practice. *Child and Family Social Work 10:187-196.*

Hall, J. T. (1997). *Social Devaluation and Special Education. The right to full mainstream inclusion and an honest statement.* London: Jessica Kingsley.

Horner, N. & Krawczyk, S. (2007). *Social work in education and children's services.* Exeter: Learning Matters.

IFSW (International Federation of Social Workers) (2007) *'International definition of social work'* available at www.basw.co.uk.

Kenworthy, J. & Whittaker, J. (2000) Anything to declare? The struggle for inclusive education and children's right. *Disability & Society 15(2):219-232.*

Murray, P. & Penman, J. (1996) *Let our children be a collection of stories.* Sheffield: Parents with Attitude.

Newton, C., Taylor, G. & Wilson, D. (1996). Circles of friends. An inclusive approach to meeting emotional and behavioural difficulties. In: *Educational Psychology in Practice, 11:41-48.*

Oliver, M. & Sapey, B. (2006). (3rd Ed.). *Social work with disabled people* Basingstoke: Palgrave.

Oliver, M. (1991). Social *work: disabled people and disabling environments* London: Jessica Kingsley Publishers.

Oliver, M. (1996). *Understanding Disability,* Basingstoke: Macmillan.

Openshaw, L. (2008). *Social Work in Schools: Principles and Practice* London: Guildford Press.

Rogers, C. (2007). Experiencing an 'inclusive' education: parents and their children with 'special educational needs.' *British Journal of Sociology of Education 28(1):55-68.*

Rose, S. (1990). Empowerment: an approach to clinical practice for social work *Journal of Sociology and Social Welfare 17:41-51.*

United Nations Convention on the Rights of the Child (1989).

Swain, J. & French, S. (2000). Towards an Affirmation Model of Disability. *Disability & Society 15(4):569-582.*

Thomas, G. & Vaughan, M. (2009). *Inclusive Education Readings and Reflections* Maidenhead: Open University.

Warnock, M. (2005). *Special Educational Needs: A new look.* Philosophy of Education Society of Great Britain.

Wenger, E. (1998). *Communities of Practice. Learning, meaning and identity* Cambridge: Cambridge University Press.

Wolfensberger, W. (1986). *The Principle of Normalisation in Human Services* National Institute on Mental Retardation, Toronto: NIMR.

DECONSTRUCTING STEREOTYPICAL
CONSTRUCTIONS OF SEXUAL IDENTITY

ABSTRACT

Sexuality is an area in which people with disability are disabled by social attitudes. The sexuality of people with disability has been feared, ignored and grossly misunderstood since the beginning of time, with any signs of sexual interest or arousal being potentially repressed. Stereotypical views of people with disability revolved around extremes of asexuality to hyper sexuality. The *Eugenics Era* intended to eliminate the reproductive capacity of people with disability by pursuing involuntary sterilization and institutional sex segregation and segregation from the rest of world, to avoid reproduction. While stereotypical images such as that of the *"eternal child"* portrays people with disability as perpetual children, thus assuming that children are not sexual. Their image as *asexual beings* also implies they have no erotic or romantic inclinations. *Disability movements* fought their way away from these notions and towards human rights, changes in legislation and demanded that people with disability live a normal life. As the *United Nations Economic and Social Council* declares; "Persons with disabilities must not be denied the opportunity to experience their sexuality, have sexual relationships and experience parenthood". Sexuality Policies undermine this assertion, encouraging sexual expression and underlining the need for sex education, the right to establish a relationship, marry or live with a partner, have children and chose one's own sexual orientation. Sexuality Policies reach out specifically towards people with disability in particular and deal with sex education and sexual abuse.

> Sexuality is often the source of our deepest oppression; it is also often the source of our deepest pain. It's easier for us to talk about – and formulate strategies for changing – discrimination in employment, education, and housing then to talk about our exclusion from sexuality and reproduction (Finger, 1992, p. 136).

Sexuality and People with Learning Disability

Malhotra & Mellan (1996), Kempton & Kahn (1991) and Whitney (2006), underline how the sexuality of people with disability has been feared, ignored and grossly misunderstood since the beginning of time. McCarthy (1999) explains that only up to a few decades ago, any signs of sexual interest or arousal were potentially ignored and repressed, and how the aberrant sexual interest of people with disability was thought to need social controls (Niederbuhl & Morris, 1993). Sobsey (1994), points out how people with learning disability have been targets of intervention intended to increase compliance or eliminate undesirable behavior, particularly sexual behavior. Research reports that Society perceives the sexuality of people with disability more negatively if the disability is a learning disability (Rodger, 2001; Katz, Shemesh & Bizman, 2000).

Still today Murray, MacDonald & Levenson (2001) recall stereotypical views of people with disability revolving around extremes of asexuality to hyper sexuality. Brown & Barrett (1994) point out that people with learning disabilities are often restricted in their sexual options by the prejudices and anxieties of carers, staff or the general public. Wheeler (2004) refers to sexuality as an area in which people with disability are disabled by social attitudes, such as society seeing people with disability as being asexual.

The History of People with Learning Disability and Sexuality

The Early Years (17th and 18th Century in Britain)

As from the medieval times to the late 19th century people with disability were supported by their family, as there was yet no other form of support. During the Victorian era (1837 to 1901) asylums were set up to house people with disability; these were intended to educate people with learning disability to reach their full potential. The Victorian era marked the height of the British industrial revolution when people with disability who could not produce goods as fast as a non-disabled person could, were looked upon with scorn. Segregation in institutions therefore was also a result of a productive industrial society that saw people with disability as worthless. Medical professions working in these institutions focused their work on diagnoses and classification rather than on social care and education. Sterilization and the repression of the sexuality of people with disability was a result of the values reflected in society at those times together with the concern of people with disability procreating and multiplying (Carnaby, 2002).

The 18th century followed a political democracy that contributed to society's responsibility to care for the less fortunate. The *1913 Mental Deficiency Act* in the U.K. was one of the first major pieces of State intervention for people with learning disability. This piece of legislation graded people with disability as "mental deficient", "idiots", "imbeciles" and "feeble minded". It permitted the detention of these people in institutions, segregated from their families and from society, but above all segregated them from the opposite sex Williams (1992). At this time the influential ideas of philosophers like Locke and Rousseau, contributed to the first "special education" programs for people with an array of disabilities. During this time it was assumed that people with learning disability were unable to learn so special education programs were run in the hope of developing their intellectual capacities.

The Eugenics Period (1880-1940)

Eugenics is the science of the genetic improvement of the human race. It was influenced by Darwin's theory of the importance of heredity in the evolutionary process (Block, 2000). Up till the early 20th Century "mental deficiency" was attributed to genetic mutations, the unfortunate result of "inappropriate breeding" on the part of defective parents. Eugenics then was a policy that is now considered outdated and above all discriminatory. Eugenics policy targeted a wide range of vulnerable adults, including those with learning disabilities. The infamous eugenics movement period (1880-1940) proposed as a solution to society's problems, to improve the human race through selective breeding. Eugenics intended controlling disability by eliminating the reproductive capacity (Sobsey, 1994). During this period the rights of people with disability were 'seriously violated' (Murphy & Claire, 2003). McCarthy (1999) reaffirms how hundreds of women with leaning disabilities, then labelled 'feeble minded', thought to be promiscuous, immoral and to reproduce extensively, having off springs of a similar intelligence, underwent involuntary castrations and ovariectomies. In the 1940s when institutions used to house a large number of people with disability, attempts by people with disability to have heterosexual contact, were severely punished, commonly by means of solitary confinement or the shaving of heads.

> Involuntary sterilization including hysterectomies was another means to avert sexual disaster. Laws permitting involuntary sterilization, variously defined to cover the mentally retarded, the mentally ill, epileptics, sexual perverts and habitual criminals (Kempton & Kahn, 1991, p. 94).

Sterilization seems to have decreased during World War II, as a counter reaction of the Nazi's eugenic sterilization movement. In Britain involuntary sterilization was not adopted but instead the trend was for institutionalization, as this was seen as the other solution to avoid reproduction, with segregated sexes and segregation from the rest of the world, (Murphy & Clare, 2004; McCarthy, 1999; Brown, 1994). Thus putting an emphasis on the fact that people with disability "were actually oppressed largely because of their sexuality" (Winifred Kempton & Emily Kahn, 1991, p. 94).

Stereotypes

Stereotypes are difficult to challenge as they are not perceived as harmful but rather as benign. The denial of sociosexual maturity increases the image of people with disability as being '*forever children*', influencing their sexual expression and behavior (Rodgers, 2001). This could in turn lead to being vulnerable to abuse or to acting in sexually inappropriate ways. Issues of this kind usually result from not being educated about the seriousness of inappropriate behaviour by another person in a sexually inappropriate or abusive way and from not being allowed to develop a sense of responsibility and respect for others.

> The misrepresentation of people with learning disabilities as innocent and childlike is as damaging to them as the more blatant charge of being 'oversexed' and menacing which fed the eugenics movement at the beginning of this century (Craft, 1994, p. 51).

The historically stereotypical image of the "eternal child" (McCarthy, 1999; Begun, 1996), portrays people with disability as having limited intellectual ability and retaining permanently the understanding of a child, thus assuming that children are not sexual beings and that people with disability were simply overgrown children (McCarthy, 1999; Murphy, 2004). Williams (1992) also refers to the eternal child stereotype when adults with learning disability are treated as perpetual children, being referred to as having a "mental age" of a child, not having their emotional maturity acknowledged, given pocket money instead of a wage and being "dressed in short white socks and sandals". Baxter (1994) affirms that people are generally influenced by the cultures of their families, and people with disability, who spend most of their lives in their family home, tend to be overprotected and unexposed to sexuality (Malhorta & Mellan,1996).

"Asexual" is another term closely related to the picture of the eternal child, used to describe the sexuality of people with disability or rather the lack of it. McAnulty & Burnett (2001), describe an asexual being as having no erotic or romantic inclinations.

Deinstitutionalization & the Normalization Period

The move from institutions to the community is known as the 'normalization' period. The normalization movement brought with it a movement towards human rights and a change in legislation. Normalization demanded that people with disability live a normal life and hold "*the rights to form relationships and experience an acceptable standard of living*" (Carnaby, 2002). The way people looked at disability changed both in terms of the opportunities offered, age appropriateness, services and quality of life. The right to have sexual relationships as well as sex education were all new issues (McCarthy, 1999; Murphy & Clare, 2004). Influential publications in the 1960s and 1970s emphasized the inadequate situation in institutions, and helped build professional and public awareness (McCarthy, 1999; Goffman, 1961; Morris, 1969). Some studies focused on the poor conditions, others gave a more in-depth reading of ill-treatment and atrocious living conditions (Carnaby, 2002). The 60's and 70's brought with it a sexual revolution for the general population, which in turn affected the population of people with disability as well (Lofgren-Marterson, 2004; Downs & Craft, 1996). Sexuality generally spread to the acceptance of people with disability as sexual beings, their sexual rights and the need for sex education (McCarthy, 1999). Reproductive rights and contraception also became a significant topic within the literature during this decade (McCarthy, 1999).

Policies and procedures provide ground rules for effective interaction; they are used widely in high-risk areas of care. Policies imply that discussion has taken place regarding the philosophy of the setting and the approach to be taken. Policies are used to coordinate responsibilities for care processes and for preventing and solving problems. They provide standards for assessing performance by identifying the roles and responsibilities of various individuals, while helping to identify potential obstacles to efficient and consistent performance (Levenson, 1995). Policies and procedures need to be developed specifically for each entity, although another source may be used to get a head-start, they always must be tailored to the individual setting.

Sexuality Policy

Malhorta & Mellan (1996) assert that when given the often taboo and emotive topic of sexuality, conflict between cultures or within cultures is bound to happen. Therefore in many settings, policies relating to sexuality, sexual expression and sex education have been developed (Downs & Craft, 1996). Policies are meant to formally guide service providers towards managing the difficult issues of sexuality (Cambridge & Mellan, 2000). It is clear that professionals and service providers working with people with learning disability have difficulty in addressing the issue of sexuality, and face complex challenges when establishing policy with regards to sexual expression (Conhan, Robinsona & Miller, 1993). Historically, service providers and staff have not been given clear instructions about their roles and responsibilities in regard to the sexual life of people with developmental disabilities (Conhan, Robinsona & Miller, 1993). The Policy can act as a guideline to staff working in services for people with disability, it elaborates on managerial responsibilities, including staff training and support. Some of these polices provide guidance for staff with respect to the recognition and reporting of sexual abuse. Others go into more detail and give advice on how to support service-users in friendships and relationships, physical contact, courting, personal hygiene, marriage and cohabitation, parenting, birth control and sexual relationship issues such as consent and abuse (Murphy, 1996).

Sexuality Policies can work hand in hand with other policies such as an 'Equality and Diversity Policy' or 'Gender Policy'. It can tackle issues of homophobia and assumptions of heterosexuality and prejudice on the grounds of sexuality (Whitefrairs Housing Group, 2008). Many service providers for people with disability issue their own Sexuality Policy specifically for people with learning disability. In most cases a Sexuality Policy would promote the rights and ensure that people with learning disability are supported to experience and express their sexuality. Clements *et al.,* (1995) argues that not to acknowledge the sexual personality of people with disability is to prevent them from stepping out of childhood and establishing themselves as adults. Such policies underline the need for sex education, the right to establish a relationship, marry or live with a partner, have children and chose one's own sexual orientation. Sexuality Policies also need to ensure the physical and emotional safety of person with disability. Many Sexuality Policies for people with learning disability include a *Sexual Abuse Policy,* possibly due to the fact that people with learning disability are more vulnerable to abuse and need to be protected from such circumstances, (McCarthy, Brown, Cambridge, Clare & Murphy, 1995).

Sex and Relationship Education Policy

Policy in the area of Sex Education usually covers the following; a rationale, aims, *Sex and Relationship Education* (SRE) framework, how SRE is provided and by whom, monitoring and evaluation of SRE, lesson aims, objectives and specific issues. The *Sex Education Policy* discusses the age of the students receiving *Sex and Relationship Education* (SRE), the parental involvement as well as the moral values involved (Norfolk County Council, 2008). Malta so far does not hold a *Sex and Relationship Education* (SRE) Policy. SRE policies are essentially formulated by teachers, school-governing bodies and parents (Harris, 2000). The *Sex and Relationship Education Guidance* issued by the DFEE (2000) in the U.K., advises governing bodies and Head Teachers, to consult with parents when developing sex and relationship education policy, to make sure that the policy developed reflects parent's wishes and the culture of the community they serve. The policy also refers to giving staff appropriate training and support, and on the other hand ensuring that the students' views are listened to.

Sex Education as Part of the School Curriculum

Contest Curriculum Stances - Converge Insider Perspective with Curriculum Discourses

Schwier & Hingsburger (2001) assert that from the very beginning parents need to play a key role in ensuring that their children with disabilities develop healthy attitudes towards their sexuality and their relationships. On the other hand societal attitudes may influence the opportunity of people with disability to receive sex education, as assumptions may be made that these issues do not need to be addressed, (Wheatley, 2005). Research reports that some parents might feel that their children have enough to cope with and that to raise the subject of sex is unnecessary and unkind (Guest, 2000; Davies, 1996; Brown, 1994). Parents may think that sexual activity will not happen, if it is not discussed, or that knowledge of sexuality and reproduction may present the disabled child with false hopes and expectations. Parents and support workers are often concerned that giving knowledge about sexuality to a person or young adult with learning disability will increase the likelihood of that person displaying inappropriate behavior. Robinault (1978) had also found that parents of people with disability, are typically faced with time and financial burdens and do not find sex education as a parental priority. Likewise, Squire (1989) reports that parents and staff give aspects of appearance, hygiene, health and social behavior more importance that sexuality and personal issues. Similarly Walter *et al.,* (2001), affirms that sexuality is not a discussed topic in family conversation and therefore parents need to be informed about the value of discussing sex at home and taught methods of bringing up the subject with their children. Other research (Wheatley, 2005) reports that professionals and parents working with people with disability, felt uncertain about how to address these issues (Cambridge & Mellan, 2000), as they feared for the children's vulnerability and their risk to be sexually abused, so that with the intention to protect people with disability, these fears lead towards not discussing sexuality and instead associating sex with negative issues.

Sex Education and People with Learning Disability.

The history of sex education for people with leaning disability is reported to have been characterized by neglect, distortion and toleration (Cambridge & Mellan, 2000). Malhorta & Mellan, (1996) assert that till the end of the 1980's there was a limited amount of direct sexuality work with people with learning disability in services. At the time of the HIV/AIDS epidemic era it was recognized that people with learning disability were very vulnerable and had no education about protection from this disease. The incentive of counter acting this epidemic, gave beginning to sex education work including HIV prevention work. Sex education was introduced in order to protect people with disability from abuse as well as to empower their sexual choice making (Murphy & O'Callaghan, 2004).

In Malta the *National Policy Document on Special Education* (1995), states that;

> It is the duty of the State to ensure the existence of a system of schools and institutions accessible to all Maltese citizens catering for the full development of the whole personality

Tabone (1995) brings to light that at the time of her research, neither personal and social education nor was sex education offered to people with learning disability. Micallef, (1996) suggests that sex education should be offered to people with learning disability, in state, church or independently run schools in Malta. He recommends that religious and ethnic views of the family are respected, and that there is the parents' acceptance and involvement. He emphasizes that this enables the parents to maintain responsibility and see that the teaching is according to their own principles. Unfortunately, not much has changed within the education system for people with disability with regards to sex education since the time of Micallef's recommendations. Although much improvement has been done in inclusive education in Malta in the last ten years, sex education has been overlooked for decades and still is. Even though there might be teaching staff willing to touch on the subject, adequate structures for training and resources are not available.

Providing comprehensive sexuality education to children and youths with disabilities is particularly important and challenging due to their unique needs. Although young people with intellectual disabilities experience puberty around the same time as their typically developing peers, they are likely to be delayed in the social and emotional maturity that typically accompanies this new stage of growth. Davies (1996) affirms that young people with disability need to be given sex education as they too have to cope with the physical changes in puberty, with menstruation and wet dreams, and with emotional changes. This dissonance between biological maturity and social/emotional maturity often requires additional attention (Walker-Hirsch, 2007). Because puberty is the bridge between childhood and adulthood, it stresses rather than ignores sex differences, therefore young people with disability will need reassurance, as they are likely to have anxieties about the form of relationships they can have.

Guest (2000) maintains that well-balanced and comprehensive sex education influences interpersonal relations and self-assurance. It is also an essential part of the character formation of people with disability. People with disability often have fewer opportunities to acquire information from their peers, have fewer chances to observe, develop, and practice appropriate social and sexual behavior (Murphy & O'Callaghan, 2004). Cambridge, Carnaby & McCarthy (2003) recommend that sex education is tailored to a person's cognitive capacity and known sexual experiences. They may not have reading levels that allow them access to information and may require special materials that explain sexuality in ways they can understand. They may also need more time and repetition in order to understand the concepts presented to them (Sugar, 1992). McCarthy & Thompson (1993) insist on the importance of using visual material such as pictures both to enhance understanding and to enable discussion. Cole & Cole (1993), discuss the importance of teaching children with disability the correct words so that they can express themselves appropriately regarding sexual matters. Since children with disabilities are particularly vulnerable to sexual perpetrators, they insist sex education can help a child recognize inappropriate behavior, abuse and violence.

Segregation, lack of sex education, limited opportunities for decision-making and barriers to appropriate sexual expressions all increase vulnerability to abuse (Hingsburger, 1995).

Parents, Professionals and Sex Education:
The Challenge of Professionalism and Professionalisation

There are widely varying views about sex education;
- Philosophical positions maintained on sex education include the belief that sex education is the responsibility of the parents and it should not occur at school (Reiss, 1995);
- Masters (1992) for instance accuses teaching professionals of having become seducers, who corrupt innocent young people, leading them to forbidden sexual experiences that guide towards teenage pregnancy, abortion, sexual disease and psychological and emotional problems;
- Guest (2000) sees parents as the principal source of sex education information and professionals as valuable collaborators providing complementary resources;
- While Stewart (1996) proposes that sex education for people with learning disability in special schools is carried out in parallel to sex education training for staff and parents.

Independently of the latter opinions there are reasons to think schools are the best place to supply this kind of education, the vast majority of parents and children look to schools to provide this education (Wellings, Wadsworth, Johnson, Field, Whitaker & Field, 1995). Archard (2000) claims that the default alternative (leaving it up to the parents) risks children receiving no, or inadequate, information about sex. He states that many parents will confess to the unwillingness to talk to their children about the subject. Moreover schools have the resources, the training, and the commitment to a common curriculum, which the home lacks. It must be taken into account that teachers may not have the skills needed to teach sex education and might have different values and beliefs from those held by parents. It is imperative that whoever is delivering sex education or counseling to people with disability must be aware of his own attitudes, beliefs and practices regarding sexuality (Baxter, 1996).

Thinking Point 1:
"The development of genetic engineering raises fears of a new eugenics movement, which gives priority to improving the human or national gene pool...." Williams (1992, p. 157). Nowadays eugenics can take a different form. Discuss.

Thinking Point 2:
Findings reveal that policy guidelines tend not to influence the staff's interactions with clients as; "Policies are filtered through staff beliefs" Murray, MacDonald & Levenson (2001, p. 2). What could be the differences between written policies and the practical strategies employed by staff in education or community services?

Thinking Point 3:
People with disability tend to internalize stereotypical attitudes towards them, resulting in barriers to self expression. How do these barriers manifest themselves in young people with learning disability? In what why would sex education help overcome these barriers?

REFERENCES

Archard, D. (2000). *Impact. Sex Education.* Philosophy of Education Society of Great Britain.

Baxter, C. (1994). Sex education in the multi-radical society. In Craft, A. (Ed.). *Practice issues in sexuality and learning disabilities.* London: Routledge

Begum, N. (1996). Disabled women's experience of general practitioners. In Morris, J. (Ed.). *Encounters with Strangers: Feminism and Disability.* London: Women's Press, p. 168-193.

Bezzina, F. (1995) (Ed.). *The Education of persons with disability in Special education in Malta, National Policy.*

Block, P. (2000). Sexuality, Fertility, and Danger: Twentieth – Century Images of Women with Cognitive Disabilities. *Sexuality and Disability. Vol. 18. No 4, 239-254.*

Brown, H. (1994). An Ordinary Sexual Life? A review of the normalization principle as it applies to the sexual options of people with learning disabilities. *Disability and Society. Volume 9, Number 2, January 1994, 123-144(22).*

Brown, H. & Barrett, S. (1994). Understanding and responding to difficult sexual behavior. In Craft, A. (Ed.). *Practice Issues in Sexuality and Learning Disabilities.* London: Routledge.

Cambridge, P. & Mellan, B. (2000). Reconstructing the Sexuality of Men with Learning Disabilities: empirical evidence and theoretical interpretations of need. *Disability and Society. Vol. 15, No. 2, 293 – 311.*

Cambridge, P., Carnaby, S. & McCarthy, M. (2003). Responding to Masturbation in Supporting Sexuality and Challenging Behaviour in Services for People with Learning Disabilities. *Journal of Learning Disabilities. Vol. 7, No.3, 251-266.*

Carnaby, S. (2002). *The Bigger Picture; Understanding approaches to learning disability.* Learning Disability Today.

Clements, J., Clare, I. & Ezelle, L. (1995). Real Men, Real Women, Real Lives? Gender issues in learning disabilities and challenging behavior. *Disability and Society, Vol.10, No. 4, 425-435.*

Cole, S. & Cole, M. (1993). Sexuality, Disability and Reproductive Issues Throughout the Lifespan. *Sexuality and Disability. Vol 11, No. 3, 189-205.*

Conahan, F., Robinson, T. & Miller, B. (1993). A Case Study Relating to the Sexual Expression of a Man with Developmental Disability. *Sexuality and Disability. Vol. 11. No.4, 309- 318.*

Craft, A. (1987). Mental Handicap and Sexuality: Issues for Individuals with Mental Handicap their Parents and Professionals. In Downs & Craft, (1996). Sexuality and Profound and Multiple Impairment. *Tizard Learning Disability Review. Vol. 1 (4).*

Davies, M. (1986), Sex education for young disabled people. *Adoption and Fostering, Vol. 10 No.1, 38-40.*

Department for Education and Employment. UK. (2000). *The Sex and Relationship Education Guidance.* Retrieved from *www.*publications.dcsf.gov.uk/default.aspx?PageFunction=productdetails&PageMode=publications&ProductId=DfES%200116%202000

Department of Health, U.K. (2000). *No Secrets*. Retrieved from www.dh.gov.uk/en/Publicationsandstatistics/Publications/PublicationsPolicyA ndGuidance/DH_4008486

Downs. C. & Craft, A. (1996). Sexuality and Profound and Multiple Impairment. *Tizard Learning Disability Review. Vol. 1 (2)*.

Finger, A. (1992). Forbidden Fruit, *New Internationalist, Vol. 233: 8-10*.

Goffman, E. (1961). Stigma: Notes on the Management of Spoiled Identity. In Hanh, H. (1981). The Social Component of Sexuality and Disability: Some Problems and Proposals. *Sexuality and Disability. Vol.4, (4), 220-233*.

Guest, G.V. (2000), Sex Education: A source of Promoting Character Development in Young People with Physical Disabilities. *Sexuality and Disability. Vol. 18, No. 2, 137-142*.

Harrison, J. (2000). Sex education in secondary schools. In Cumper, P. (2004). Sex Education and Human Rights – lawyer's perspective. *Sex Education. Vol.4, No.2, 124-142*.

Hingsburger, (1995). Just say Know! In Thompson, D. (1996). Sexuality and Sexual Abuse; Book Review. A Review of Recent Texts on the Sexuality and Sexual Abuse of People with Learning Disabilities. *Tizard Learning Disability Review. Vol.1 (4)*.

Katz, Shemesh & Bizman (2000). Attitudes of University Students towards the Sexuality of Persons with Mental Retardation and Persons with Paraplegia. *British Journal of Developmental Disabilities. Vol. 46, Part 2, No. 91*.

Kempton, W. & Kahn,E. (1991). Sexuality and People with Intellectual Disabilities: A Historical Perspective. *Sexuality and Disability, Vol. 9, No 2*.

Levenson, (1995). Centre for Adaptive Palliative Care. Accessed June 2008 www.64.85.16.230/educate/content/elements/developingpolicies.html

Lofgren-Martenson, L., (2004). "May I?" About Sexuality and Love in the New Generation with Intellectual Disabilities. *Sexuality and Disability. Vol. 22, No.3, 197-207*.

Masters, R. (1992). Sexual overload: the effects of graphic sex education on innocent minds. In Reiss, M.J. (1995). Conflicting Philosophies of School Sex Education. *Journal of Moral Education. Vol. 24, No. 4, 371-382*.

Malhorta, S. & Mellan, B. (1996). Cultural and Race Issues in Sexuality Work with People with Learning Difficulties. *Tizard Learning Disability Review. Vol. 1, Issue 4*.

McAnulty, R. & Burnette, M. (2001). *Exploring Human Sexuality*. US: Allyn & Bacon.

McCarthy, M. (1999). *Sexuality and Women with Learning Disabilities*. London: Jessica Kingsley Publishers.

McCarthy, M. & Thompson, D. (1993). *Sex and the 3Rs: Rights, Responsibilities and Risks*. Brighton: Pavillion.

McCarthy, M., Brown, H., Cambridge, P., Clare, I., & Murphy, G. (1995). *Sexuality and Sexual Abuse Policy*. Tizard Centre: University of Kent.

Micallef, M. (1996). *Sexuality and persons with mental disability*. A dissertation presented to the Faculty of Theology. University of Malta.

Morris, P. (1969). Put Away: A Sociological Study of Institutions for the Mentally Retarded. In McCarthy, M. (1999). *Sexuality and Women with Learning Disabilities*. London: Jessica Kingsley Publishers.

144

Murphy, G. H. & Clare, I.C.H. (2003). Adults' capacity to make legal decisions. In Bull, R. & Carson, D. (Eds.). *Handbook of Psychology in Legal Contexts.* Chichester: Wiley & Sons.

Murphy, G. (1996). *Working with Offenders: Assessment and intervention.* In Setterfield, M. (1996). Putting the Theory into Practice: A Case Study. *Tizard Learning Disability Review. Vol. 1 (4).*

Murray, J., MacDonald, R. & Levenson, V. (2001). Sexuality: Policies, Beliefs and Practice. *Tizard Learning Disability Review. Vol.6, (1).*

Murphy, G. H. & O'Callaghan, A. (2004). Capacity of adults with intellectual disabilities to consent to sexual relationships. *Psychological Medicine. 34, 1-11.*

Neiderbuhl, J.M. and Morris, C.D. (1993). Sexual Knowledge and the Capability of Persons with Dual Diagnoses to Consent to Sexual Contact. *Sexuality and Disability. Vol.11, No. 4.*

Norfolk County Council. www.schools.norfolk.gov.uk/myportal/ Accessed June, 2008.

Page, A. (1991). Teaching developmentally disabled people self regulation in sexual behaviour. *Australia & New Zealand Journal of Developmental Disabilities. Vol. 17, 81-88.*

Parallels in Time III the 17th & 18th Century. Accessed on 13th june 2010. www.mncdd.org/parallels/three/1.html

Powell, M. & Harwood, R. (2005). *Intimate Personal Relationships and Sexuality Policy.* Gloucestershire Partnership. NHS Trust.

Reiss, M.J. (1995). Conflicting Philosophies of School Sex Education. *Journal of Moral Education. Vol.24, No. 4, 371-382.*

Robinault, I.P., (1978*). Sex, society and the Disabled: A developmental inquiry into roles, reactions and responsibilities.* In Walter, L.J., Nosek, M.A., & Langdon, K. Understanding of Sexuality and Reproductive Health Among Women With and Without Physical Disabilities. *Sexuality and Disability, Vol. 19, No.3, Fall 2001*

Rodgers, J. (2001). The Experience and Management of Menstruation for Women with Learning Disabilities. *Tizard Learning Disability Review, Vol.6 (1).*

Schwier K. M. & Hingsburger, D. (2000). How to Teach "No". Sexuality – Your Sons and Daughters with Intellectual Disability. www.brookespublishing.com/store/books/schwier-4285/excerp.

Sobsey, D. (1994). Violence and abuse in the lives of people with disabilities: the end of silent acceptance. In Thompson, D. (1996). Sexuality and Sexual Abuse; Book Review. A Review of Recent Texts on the Sexuality and Sexual Abuse of People with Learning Disabilities. *Tizard Learning Disability Review. Vol.1 (4).*

Squire (1989) In Griffin, J., Carlson, G., Taylor, M. & Wilson, J. An Introduction to Menstrual Management for Women who have an Intellectual Disability and High Support Needs. *International Journal of Disability, Development and Education, Volume 41, Issue 2 1996, 103 – 116.*

Stewart, D. (1996). Sex education for students with severe learning disabilities. In Cambridge, P. (1997). How Far to Gay? The Politics of HIV in Learning Disability. *Disability and Society. Vol. 12, No.3, 427-453.*

145

Sugar, M. (1990). *Atypical adolescence and sexuality. In Sexuality education for children and youth with disabilities national information centre for youth with disabilities (NICHCY).* New Digest (1992).

Tabone, V. (1995*). A sexual education programme for adolescents with Down syndrome.* A dissertation presented to the Faculty of Education, University of Malta.

Walter, L.J., Nosek, M.A., & Langdon, K. (2001). Understanding of Sexuality and Reproductive Health Among Women With and Without Physical Disabilities. *Sexuality and Disability, Vol. 19, No.3, Fall 2001, 167-176.*

Walker-Hirsch, L. (2007). *Six components of sexuality education for people with intellectual disabilities.* Retrieved from www.brookespublisihing.com/newsletters/dd-article-0307.htm

Wellings, K., Wadsworth, J., Johnson, A.M., Field, J., Whitaker, L., & Field, B. (1995). Provision of sex education and early sexual experience: the relation examined. *British Medical Journal, 311. August 12; 311(7002): 417–420.*

Wheatley, H. (2005). Sex, sexuality and relationships for young people with learning disabilities. *Current Paediatrics. Vol. 15, 195-199.*

Wheeler, P. (2004). I count myself as normal: An explanatory study of men with learning disabilities telling their stories about sexuality and sexual identity. *Tizard Centre, University of Kent, Canterbury.*

Whitefrairs Housing Group. www.whitefrairshousing.co.uk Accessed June 08

Whitney, C. (2006). Intersections in Identity – Identity Development among Queer Women with Disabilities. *Sexuality and Disability. Vol. 25, No.1, 39-52.*

Williams, F. (1992). Women with learning difficulties are women too. In Hudson, A. (1992*) Women with Learning Difficulties.* UK: Routledge.

REFLECTIONS ON INCLUSIVE EDUCATION
AT HIGHER EDUCATION

ABSTRACT

Inclusive education stems from a constructivist pedagogy. Group work where problem-solving situations are presented is a teaching strategy that facilitates the implementation of inclusive education. The educator needs to give service to the 'other' according to the individual's needs. Through dialogue and collaboration with the senior administration team, learning support assistants and parents, the educator would be in a better position to help learners reach their full learning potential. Differentiation enables educators to present knowledge and skills in a reachable way to all students. Creating an environment which is conducive to learning improves classroom management and learners' motivation.

Introduction

A progressive, constructivist, critical pedagogy is the type of pedagogy that with conviction, theoretical background and practice, informs my practice. My daily practice as a teacher is to teach *Nutrition, Family and Consumer Studies* previously known as *Home Economics*. My experience in embracing and fostering inclusive education and mixed-ability teaching made me realise that inclusive education incorporates a wide spectrum of students' abilities. With the students' collaboration, I always attempted to discover how to accommodate and make learning accessible and possible to students with varying impairments and talents. In view of this perspective, I am going to focus on the importance of collaboration amongst different stakeholders, and advocating the possibility of implementing the emancipatory social model within inclusive education at Higher Education (HE).

The Effects of Group Work on Adolescent Psychology

As an educator, I try to encourage students to form a group since I am conscious that the inability to 'plug in' to a social network in adolescence is detrimental to students learning. On a positive note, Stasna (2000) corroborates that "studying with friends and co-operating with friends even if they are slightly different and have different needs is a contribution to help sow the seeds for future integration in the whole society" (p. 217).

Adolescents give relatively greater attention to social and personality characteristics and, eventually, belief systems, values, and thought processes. These differences come about partly because of cognitive changes, such as the shift to more abstract concepts that permit adolescents to infer traits that cannot easily be observed (Sprinthall and Collins, 1995). Group work helps all students to achieve and strive for achievement. Feldman, (1990) infers that the need for achievement is a stable, learned characteristic in which satisfaction is obtained by striving for and attaining a level of excellence. In return, the "feeling of self-efficacy" is generated. Results from practising newly developing skills and mastering challenging tasks that encourages a positive emotional experience (Stipek, 1998).

Giving a Service to the 'Other'

In teaching adolescents, I feel the need to develop sensitivity towards the needs of the 'other' by reflecting on how to become critically conscious of the students' needs, aptitudes, aspirations, strengths and weaknesses. Derrida (in Garrison, 2004) developed the concept of deconstruction which means "an openness towards the other". It welcomes in advance the excluded 'other'. Deconstruction urges recognition and respect for what is different, left out, or queer. It is this positive response to the 'other,' to those persons and situations different from the 'norm' that, he wants to urge educators to consider. Derrida (in Garrison, 2004) elaborates that "this is an ontological respect and openness to what one does not understand. Education is an ethical practice and ethical relations begin in respect for the particular, even if unknowable, being of other beings" (Garrison, 2004, p.97).

Social Constructivism

Students' strengths need to be celebrated and the weaknesses need to be challenged and overcome with the right and appropriate instruments that the educator together with learning support assistants (LSAs) and administrators are ready to provide. During the learning process, students need to be empowered to feel that they are developing.

These reflections echo social constructivist theory-based principles. Social constructivist ideas emphasise social interactions and scaffolded support for learning (Burton, 2003). The term 'scaffolding' has been developed by Bruner (2006). Bruner believed that teachers should try to encourage students to discover principles through active dialogue with the teacher. Thus, for Bruner, the teacher's job is to guide this discovery through structured support: for example, by asking focused questions or providing appropriate materials (Burton, 2003). Similarly, "The Zone of Proximal Development" (ZPD) so central to Vygotskian theory needs to be accounted for. ZPD is the gap between what one can do on one's own, unassisted, and what one can do with hints and aids from a knowledgeable other. Vygtoskian pedagogy works through the shielding a learner from distraction, by fore-fronting crucial features of a problem, by sequencing the steps to understanding, by promoting negotiation, or by some of the form of "scaffolding" the task at hand (Bruner, 2006). Thus, collaborative learning environments could motivate learners to face challenges. Scaffolding helps participants overcome what seemed before to be "innate" constraints and to develop the essential dialogue to get a deep understanding of their reality in context. Concepts could be explored following Bruner's "spiral curriculum". The idea is based that an educator oscillates from notions that are known to the students to ones unknown to them. Then the educator expands knowledge on a wider circumference using a multidisciplinary approach. This notion also encompasses the concept of "readiness" which is not only born but made. "The general proposition rests on the still deeper truth that a domain of knowledge can be constructed simply or complexly, abstractly or concretely," (Bruner, 2006, p. 145). By applying these teaching strategies, I feel that students are being empowered. Giroux (1999) states that "teachers can empower their students through what they teach, how they teach, and the means whereby school knowledge can be made worthwhile and interesting at the same time," (p. 107).

Classroom Management

Effective classroom management is also developed through mutual respect, trust and collaboration. The development of 'withitness' and a good peripheral vision students receive the message that the teacher knows the dynamics of the group. Kounin coined the term 'withitness' to refer to a teacher's awareness of what is going on in the classroom. Teachers with "eyes in the back of their heads" have withitness. Kounin emphasised that teachers increase the likelihood of students being on-task by demonstrating to students that they are with it and can accurately detect classroom events (Cangelosi, 2000). On-task settings which are smooth even during transitions in between activities enhance teaching and learning and eventually students' growth. Classroom management with an emancipatory style is essential for teaching and learning to take place. Giroux (1999) contends that emancipatory authority also provides the theoretical scaffolding for educators to define themselves not simply as intellectuals, but in a more committed fashion as transformative intellectuals. This means that educators are not merely concerned with forms of empowerment that promote individual achievement and traditional forms of academic success. Instead, they are also concerned in developing the ability to think and act critically to flourish the concept of social transformation. As transformative intellectuals, educators need to show commitment to a form of solidarity that addresses the many instances of suffering that are a growing and threatening part of everyday life.

Banking Concept Versus Problem-Posing Education

The aim of inclusive education is not to teach the students just content, replicating the banking style of teaching, but through problem-solving, an educator educates and facilitates learning to keep oppression and exclusion at bay as much as possible. Freire's "banking concept of education" indicates that "knowledge is a gift bestowed by those who consider themselves knowledgeable upon those whom they consider to know nothing," (Freire, 2000, p. 72). Problem-solving learning stimulates thinking and the building of concepts. It also permits appropriate differentiation to be applied to reach the abilities of all students. As Wisker (2008), states, "problem-based learning places the student at the centre of the learning process and is aimed at integrating learning with practice (p. 242). The effectiveness of problem-posing education represents itself as it:

breaks with the vertical patterns characteristic of banking education...Through dialogue, the teacher-of-the-students and the students-of-the-teacher cease to exist and a new term emerges: teacher-student with students-teachers. The teacher is no longer merely the-one-who-teaches, but one who is herself/ himself taught in dialogue with the students, who in turn while being taught also teach. They become jointly responsible for a process in which all grow (Freire, 2000, p. 80).

Differentiation

Appropriate differentiated learning objectives need to be identified so that appropriate questions techniques can be designed. Questions encourage students to reflect. Questions that require students to recall data can be targeted to low-ability students, questions that demand a comparison or analysis from facts are suited to average-ability students while questions in a hypothetical perspective or demand solutions or envisage possible limitations can be ear marked to high-ability students. Asking the right differentiated questions to students enables students to experience success rather than failure. Constructive feedback gives students information about how they are doing and motivates them to continue. A sequence in which feedback is sandwiched between praise, i.e. praise-constructive feedback–praise, is designed to provide encouragement and motivation, along with information to help the student improve the activity (Burton, 2003). Assertive feedback is characterised by openness, directness, spontaneity, and appropriateness (Cangelosi, 2000).

The Importance of Collaboration

Apart from learning difficulties, students may have physical impairments at varying degrees. The presence of an LSA is key to a more successful inclusive education. From grassroots levels, LSAs can help a teacher reach the social and academic targets. Collaboration with a teamwork approach is indispensable both from a systematic and an emotional perspective between the student, teacher, learning-support assistant and parents/guardians. Oliver & Barton (2000) recommend that:

> developing a constructive, collaborative working relationship with a range of colleagues resulting in co-operation over teaching and research, will be an extremely demanding task. Part of the relationship needs to be about clarifying values and providing insights into not only a theory of social change, but also how that can be brought about in practice. The generation of an ethos of mutual respect, lively and constructive debate and the establishing of realisable goals will all contribute to a more inclusive approach to research, teaching and learning outcomes (p. 13).

150

Although, the teacher has the ultimate responsibility for the teaching and assessment, through dialogue and teamwork the teacher and LSA can create the required learning and assessment instruments in a tailor-made fashion according to the individualised educational programme (IEP). As Freire (2002) argues:

> dialogue is meaningful precisely because the dialogical subjects, the agents in the dialogue, not only retain their identity, but actively defend it, and thus grow together. Dialogue implies a sincere, fundamental respect on the part of the subjects engaged in it, a respect that is violated, or prevented from materialising, by authoritarianism (Freire, 2002, p. 101).

Mutual cooperation with the fruition of an effective dialogue amongst the student, learning support assistant, teacher and parents/guardians have myriad positive impacts. Freire (2000) suggests that:

> Cooperation, as a characteristic of dialogical action – which occurs only among Subjects (who may, however, have diverse levels of functions and thus of responsibility) – can only be achieved through communication. Dialogue, as essential communication, must underlie any cooperation. In the theory of dialogical action, there is no place for conquering the people on behalf of the revolutionary cause, but only for gaining their adherence. Dialogue does not impose, does not manipulate, does not domesticate, does not 'sloganise'. This does not mean, however, that the theory of dialogical action leads nowhere; nor does it mean that he dialogical human does not have a clear idea of what she wants, or of the objectives to which she is committed (p. 168).

Improving Learning Environmental Through Collaboration

According to Dewey (1944, p. 19):

> we never educate directly, but indirectly by means of the environment. Whether we permit chance environments to do the work, or whether we design environments of the purpose make a great difference. Schools remain, of course, the typical instance of environments framed, with express reference to influencing the mental and moral disposition of their members." Similarly, Giroux (1999) notes that "it is important to note that while schools are not the sole sites for implementing social change, they do offer an important terrain on which to provide future generations with new way for thinking about the building of a more just society (p.65).

All stakeholders need to discuss ways how to make the environment more accessible according to the students' needs. Growing up in an inclusive environment, makes all involved more sensitive and conscious of each other's needs, limitations and abilities and together find ways how to live, accept and accommodate each other. This is the basics of developing democratic citizenship. However, psycho-social conflicts could emulate exclusion and oppression that influence an adolescent's maturing identity. This implies that an educator needs to have the right tactics on how to surface in a very salient yet progressive way each

151

spicy or mild ingredient within a group's dynamics. Adamantly an educator should be cognisant of the moral and ethical obligations s/he has towards the individuals under her/his care and their parents/guardians; the entity that employed them and society which attributed the responsibility for developing citizens who share democratic values.

Teaching is a Vocation

Being an educator is truly a vocation. The application of inclusive education is like a Head Chef who is accountable for developing her/his menu in the expected way through a multi-sensory and a multi-disciplinary teaching-learning approach. For instance a chef would denote from the sense of smell that something is just not right or with an amused glaze appreciates the work of her/his peers or learners. Similarly with ones sense of touch explains and manoeuvres all the educational tools to facilitate learning in mastering a skill or knowledge as well as with the sense of hearing listens attentively to the other's comments, queries, criticism and evolve them into a collaborative and a respectable dialogue. Moreover with the sense of taste hopefully the group would toast for each other's success. Success needs to be celebrated.

Conclusion

The inclusive educator should present her/himself as a learner who is experiencing transformation via his/her profession. Through a functionalist approach, it is essential to hope that every individual has a function and a meaningful place in society. The way society constructs itself, extrapolates the meaning of human diversity needs to be challenged. It is not a disgrace or a downfall that a class includes diverse students of different needs and abilities but an opportunity.

Some emerging problems that need to be analysed;
- At HE level the role of the parents/guardians with regard to their children's education needs to be reinstated;
- Some local HE institutions are selective and a number of qualifications are a prerequisite for entry to these institutions. This could limit the number of students with impairments to enter these Institutions. The question is whether concessions granted to some students for sitting the local Secondary Education Certificate (SEC) examinations are too stringent;
- If LSAs are present at a HE institution, they need to be trained to meet the academic rigour at such level;
- School policies at all levels of education might need to be revised and amended to reflect inclusive education in its broadest sense. The enforcement of such policies is essential. HE institutions need to be allotted the essential financial resources to do the necessary refurbishment to accommodate various disabilities;
- Unless students truly live inclusive education, disabled students could remain marginalised, excluded and possibly oppressed. The emotional and social impacts are great. Research could therefore provide evidence about how disabled students live their life at HE institutions;

- Formative assessment based on coursework would make learning more meaningful and give students the possibility to gain marks during the course of study;
- HE institutions should help students in their transition towards employment. Training would reduce the risk of statemented disabled students to be dependent on state welfare systems but become independent and contribute to our economy in a constructive way;
- Adolescence is a very delicate age group. Students at HE institutions could be mentored by adults who are ready to help them in growing up with a more reflective attitude towards life. The challenge is whether there is enough personnel ready to take under her/his care a number of students in a way that no one is excluded;
- There is the need that HE institutions would have a structured framework that is created to deal with the challenges of disabled students and improve the quality of inclusive education.

Thinking Point 1:
How can a progressive educator who believes and implements a constructivist pedagogy, with limited resources transform a classroom into a setting that dissipates teaching and learning? Analyse and list a number of practical solutions supported by appropriate theoretical perspectives.
Thinking Point 3:
Why is the notion of 'collaboration' amongst different stakeholders, so essential in making inclusive education work?

REFERENCE

Bruner, J. S. (2006). *In Search of Pedagogy Volume II – The selected works of Jerome S. Bruner.* London: Routledge Falmer.

Burton, D. (2003). Ways pupils learn. In Capel, S., Leask, M., & Turner, T. (Eds.), *Learning to Teach in the Secondary School.* London: Routledge Falmer.

Cangelosi, J. S. (2000). *Classroom Management Strategies – Gaining and Maintaining Students' Cooperation.* (4th Ed.). New York: John Wiley & Sons, Inc..

Dewey, J. (1944). *Democracy and Education – An Introduction to the Philosophy of Education.* New York: The Free Press.

Feldman, R. S. (1990). *Understanding Psychology.* London: McGraw-Hill Publishing Company.

Freire, P. (2000). *Pedagogy of the Oppressed.* New York: Continuum.

Freire, P. (2002). *Freire – Pedagogy of Hope.* London: Continuum.

Garrison, J. (2004). Dewey, Derrida, and the 'the Double Bind'. p. 95-108. In Pericles Trifonas, P. & Peters, M. A. (Eds.) (2004). *Derrida, Deconstruction and Education – Ethics of Pedagogy and Research.* Oxford: Blackwell Publishing.

Giroux, H. A. (1999). Border Youth, Difference, and Postmodern Education. In Castells, M. *et al., Critical Education in the Information Age.* Oxford: Rowman & Littlefield Publishers, Inc.

Sprinthall, N. A., & Collins, W. A. (1995). Adolescent *Psychology – A Developmental View.* (3rd Ed.). London: McGraw-Hill, Inc..

Stastna, V. (2000). Examples of good practice from Czech higher education institutions in overcoming the social exclusion of people with disabilities. In Thomas, L. & Cooper, M. (Eds.), *Changing the Culture of the Campus: Towards an Inclusive Higher Education.* Staffordshire: Staffordshire University Press.

Stipek, D. (1998). *Motivation to learn – from theory to practice.* (3rd ed.). London: Allyn and Bacon.

Wisker, G. (2008). *The Postgraduate Research Handbook.* (2nd ed.). New York: Palgrave Macmillan.

Barton, L. (2003). Inclusive education and teacher education- A basis for hope of a discourse or disilusion. www.leeds.ac.uk/disability-studies/archiveuk/archframe.htm [Accessed on 26/8/2009].

POVERTY, DISABILITY AND EDUCATION:
DEBATING INCLUSIVITY IN THE MAJORITY WORLD

ABSTRACT

Around 600 million people are disabled globally, and some 80% of these are said to live in the so-called majority world, often in disproportionate levels of a multidimensional poverty, impacting socio-economic spheres including education. While the subject of disability in the majority world has gained some momentum, notably through the international development sector, the debate remains embryonic. Furthermore, concerns related to broader poverty, neoliberalism and its historical antecedents, and the social, economic, cultural and political contexts of a post/neocolonial global South, remain subsumed under or reframed through Western discourses (e.g. disability and development studies). In light of this, this chapter seeks to discuss issues around disability and poverty in the so-called majority world, in an effort to outline and discuss critical concerns around education in neoliberal times, and the implications for inclusive education in the global South.

Introduction

This Chapter seeks to discuss issues around disability and poverty in the majority world[i], with a view to highlighting critical concerns around education in neoliberal times, and the implications for an education we may (or may not) call inclusive. Poverty has become a common currency, but there is no single definition of this deceptive term. While poverty is often associated with lack of income (generally calculated according to some predefined threshold, for example a poverty line) or consumption (e.g. of food), there is much more to poverty than this. This is further complicated by the fact that the understanding of poverty (and conversely of what it means to be non-poor), varies in accordance with the social, cultural and historical contexts in which it is placed. The implication, is that no single dimension can account for the multiple aspects of deprivation, and poverty is multidimensional and includes among others: lack of income and consumption, access problems to adequate facilities (e.g. sanitation), infrastructure and basic needs (e.g. to housing, sanitation, water, clothing and health), low capabilities (e.g. the opportunities to achieve desired and acceptable functionings), unemployment and economic exclusion, poor nutrition, unsafe living and working conditions, powerlessness, vulnerability, disability and ill-health and physical weakness, social isolation and social exclusion, low educational opportunities, voicelesness, powerlessness and political and institutional exclusion, inequality, lack of respect, and low self-esteem.

It is also important to differentiate between absolute and relative poverty. Absolute poverty is the notion that people are poor if they fall below a predetermined threshold (e.g. a poverty line such as the $2 a day) namely, an absolute level. Relative poverty on the other hand does not depend on a predetermined level, but is measured according to that which is considered poor in a particular society. For example, while a person may not be poor in absolute terms (e.g. earns well more than $2 a day), he may be considered relatively poor if he/she earns or consumes less than the average person in his/her community or if he/she does not have access to certain goods and services to which the majority benefit from.

Poverty: Manifestations and Antecedents in the Neocolonial

Poverty remains a critical and serious concern, and the situation is indeed more of a global crisis, but still concentrated in the global South: more than 1 billion people (1 in 6) live in extreme poverty (less than $1 a day) and between 320 and 443 million are trapped in chronic and intergenerational poverty; 1.1. billion (17% of the global population) lack access to safe water; 840 million live in chronic hunger; 2.6 million lack access to adequate sanitation; 1.8 million people (90% of which are children under the age of 5) die every year from diarrhoeal diseases (including cholera); around 42 million are infected with HIV/AIDS (disproportionately women) - more than 2 million die every year; more than 500,000 women die in pregnancy and childbirth (one every minute); and around 75 million primary school children are out of school) (UNDP, 2006; CPRC, 2008). Despite the measures and statements of good intent, including the *Millennium Development Goals* (MDGs), poverty is indeed here to stay - it is estimated that 900 million people will remain poor ($1 a day) even if the *Millennium Development Goals* (MDGs) are to be met (CPRC, 2004).

Positioning poverty necessitates a historical view of its antecedents and its more contemporary manifestations, and the linkages of both. Colonialism not only initiated the mechanisms of pillaging, cultural, economic and political domination of the colonised 'other' (the 'uncivilised native' to be civilised by the mechanics of the colonial empires-Christianisation, slave labour, violence and so on). Importantly, the lineages and dynamics of colonialism, continue to operate into the present day, unabated and unashamedly renewed and re-enacted in contemporary forms of colonisation (social, economic, political, and ideological), in other words, neocolonialism. The 'formal' decolonisation post World War 2 has not meant freedom from the clutches of empire. This is in fact one of the criticisms often wavered at postcolonial theory, that through its polemical prefix 'post', and its fixity on the colonial period, appears to imply that colonisation has come to an end. As McClintock (1992) states:

> post-colonialism is unevenly developed globally....Can most of the world's countries be said, in any meaningful or theoretically rigorous sense, to share a single 'common past', or single common 'condition', called the 'post-colonial condition' or 'post-coloniality' and goes to remind us that 'the term 'post-colonialism is, in many cases, prematurely celebratory (p. 87).

Indeed, the Western domination, power, control and exploitation, not only continued unabated following decolonisation, but also found new powers sustaining the asymmetrical relationship between the metropole and the periphery: 'colonialism became historically illegitimate', but 'global power relations did not disappear; they transmuted' (McMicheal, 2008, p. 274). This is witnessed in the rise of the US as an international hegemonic power through the domination of international markets and imperial foreign policy in the 20th century, and the consequent political, economic and military interventions in many regions to maintain economic, political and cultural control (see for example the US funded and initiated atrocities in Guatemala and more recently Iraq). These efforts were consolidated following decolonisation through the establishment of the development industry and its agencies (for example the World Bank, the WTO and the IMF) and associated trade and monetary policies that not only meant 'development' came to be conceptualised in Western terms, for all and sundry, and using specific strategies - notably the neoliberal globalisation project, but also strengthened the relegation of countries in the global South further into the peripheries. Measures such as the Structural Adjustment Programmes imposed by the IMF on countries in crippling debt, maintained foreign intervention an impending reality, created unprecedented inequality between and within countries[ii], impoverished, and above all continues to regenerate the hegemony of the West, reinforcing and creating new forms of imperialism - the neoliberal global-centrism - where racial differentiation and perhaps also citizenship continue to sustain the logic and trail of domination and control.

Disability Matters: Encounters with Poverty

Many are those that suffer the brunt of poverty, but some are more vulnerable to its clutches, often trapped in its folds, intense and intergenerational- chronic poverty. Vulnerability is a dimension of poverty, and does not refer to what a person has in her/his hand, but how well he/she can weather stresses and shocks when they strike. For people living in poverty, with little if any disposable incomes, and even less formal safety nets (e.g. government benefits, access to health care and medication), where life is lived on the brink of subsistence (often in remote and dispersed rural areas), and where every day is a struggle for survival, anything that rocks the survival boat can have tragic outcomes for themselves and their households (e.g. droughts, floods, food insecurity, conflict, ill-health and so on).
    Disability is a major concern in such circumstances, because those in dire poverty simply cannot afford it. Survival, where hard physical labour is critical, and where access to formal support systems is often absent or fragmented, is not only the prime concern, but means poor people often can only depend on each other. This means that making demands on each other's scant resources, also implies that benefits are limited, and translates into spiralling poverty for whole households and communities. The risk of impairment is also a major one in the majority world, especially for those living in poverty: malnutrition, unsanitary and unsafe living and working conditions, communicable diseases, inaccessible or unavailable health care including pre- and ante-natal and health related information, unassisted or unsafe births, accidents, natural disasters (e.g. the earthquakes in Haiti and Chile), violence and conflict, HIV/AIDS, and unsafe methods of transport among others. In fact, it is estimated that some 50% of impairments in majority world contexts are preventable, and a direct result of poverty (DFID, 2000).
    Disability is a major concern in the majority world, when 80% of the 650 million disabled people worldwide, are located in the countries of the global South, and make up more than a mere minority amidst the broader poor, especially when one considers the impacts on whole families and communities. And the rates of

disability are set to increase, especially in the global South, with some forecasting an increase in the numbers of disabled people by over 120% over the next 30 years as opposed to the North which will increase by some 40% (EDF, 2002). Reasons include among others: increasing levels of poverty, poor nutrition, increased life expectancy and associated age-related impairments reductions in infant and maternal mortality rates enabling survival of disabled people; increase in violence, conflicts and wars; HIV/AIDS; natural and other disasters; lack of environmental management itself a symptom of development; better detection systems; increased commercialization of the health sector affecting accessibility especially for the poorest; and inadequate access to rehabilitation, education, clean water and sanitation, employment and income security, and increase in prevalence of chronic as opposed to infectious diseases.

Disabled people are also often said to be amongst the poorest of the poor, an argument often used for the inclusion of disability in a development sector that at least in theory is concerned with poverty and its reduction. Although accurate statistics of the poverty situation of disabled people are absent and research about the dynamics operating in the disability and poverty relationship is sparse- especially at country levels, it is suggested that some 82% of disabled people in developing countries live below the poverty line (EC, 2003), encountering barriers in a number of life spheres: employment, education, rehabilitation and assistive devices, the physical environment, costs both direct and indirect, and sometimes negative attitudes and exclusion. But this does not mean that disabled people have garnered the same attention as women and ethnic minorities in poverty reduction efforts and the development sector, and in practice remain excluded at research, policy, and programme levels (Grech, 2009).

Education in the Folds of Poverty:
What Chances for the Disabled Poor?

Education is often considered one of the basic mechanisms through which people can be lifted out of poverty, not only through its impacts on employment and income, but also through positive effects on other life spheres including health, information, self-esteem and sociability among others- therefore it is suggested that it may be a portal to various types of capital (social, financial, natural, political and so on). Despite the proclaimed benefits, the poor remain disproportionately disadvantaged in accessing education- globally around 72 million children are out of school, with seven out of ten of these children residing in the poorest countries of Sub Saharan Africa (SSA) and South and West Asia (UNESCO, 2008).

Disability is trapped in a double bind, since disability (and associated barriers), impacts the opportunities for education, and education often marginalises or excludes disabled people, especially when disability and education are mediated by poverty. Guesstimates highlight that of the 120 million or so disabled children, only 1% to 5% (the most common figure cited is that of 2%) have access to any form of education (Miles, 1999), with those who manage almost exclusively through special schools and occasionally charitable organisations, rather than mainstream facilities. But even special education is scarce in regions like Central America, and is haunted by other problems: the propagation of isolation of disabled children from the mainstream; the inability to cater for those with multiple impairments; concentration in urban areas and cities; and prohibitive costs especially for poor families- special education is largely provided by the private sector. Overall, the lack of educational opportunities, affect future prospects of employment (especially those requiring technical skills), and consequently disabled people are thrown into deeper poverty, even when compared to other poor people. Furthermore, barriers propagate their marginalisation and dependency, deprive them of opportunities for socialising (and hence to acquire social capital) and to build self-esteem and confidence, and prevent a shift in an educational landscape where the sight and presence of disabled children in schools continues to often not be normalised.

But the problems disabled people face need to be positioned within the broader barriers confronting all poor people, with the implication that we perhaps need to first question whether education is inclusive for the poor at large. Again, this does not undervalue the fact that disabled people may encounter more barriers in comparison to their non-disabled poor peers, especially women, those residing in rural areas and people with specific impairments (e.g. sensory). Disabled people indeed face most of the barriers encountered by other poor people. These may, or may not include, and to varying levels and not exclusively (see Grech, 2008):

- geographical dispersion and remoteness;
- the absence of schools (especially in rural areas);
- overcrowded classrooms;
- competing demands (e.g. when children have to contribute to harvesting crops and other key stages in the agricultural cycle);
- low quality education;
- inadequate or absent policies for including disabled people in mainstream schools and insufficient funding, monitoring and enforcement when implemented;
- devaluation of disabled people (e.g. by policy makers and schools), especially when investing in disabled children's education is perceived to translate into less returns for the household or the economy as a whole (people are seen as economic tools to economic ends);
- negative attitudes by teachers and peers;
- inadequate resources to cater for educational and other costs (e.g. books, uniform and transportation) especially when these compete with more basic household demands;
- architectural barriers and absent or inadequate transportation (affecting mobility);
- lack or absence of affordable assistive devices and other equipment (e.g. wheelchairs or leg braces);
- overprotection by parents;
- untrained teachers especially in disability issues; and unavailability of specialised teaching materials (e.g. Braille) and under-resourced schools (human and financial resources).

The issue of competing demands is extremely important since in conditions of poverty, it means that the willingness of parents to send their children to school, will depend on what the opportunity costs of education are, that is the value of the activities children could be performing and that need to be foregone if they go to school. Furthermore, the perceived value of education depends on whether or not education will translate into material or other benefits for the household economy at least in satisfying some of the basic needs. This does not mean a lack of desire to send children to school, but simply that in light of persistent and more basic concerns (food, shelter, health care, the need to work the land etc.) and activities (e.g. collection of water and firewood), and in the absence of formal social protection measures, basic survival takes over, and any other activity outside this scheme of things, may have to be dropped. These aspects of education, and problems encountered in the provision of an inclusive education, not only do not lend to simplification, but above all call for the need to question and problematise our own epistemologies and solutions, especially when these are fixed in a specific space, time and context- generally the Western one.

Neoliberalism and the World of Unequals

The above issues also (and again) need to be positioned within the hegemonic neoliberal globalisation agenda, that continues to dilute the power and role of national and local governments in the lives of their people, where multinationals rule the game on their own terms, and where profit making individuals, autonomous and self-determined, compete in a field 'regulated' solely by the unfettered market. Mass-based privatisation, cuts in public sector expenditure, and reductions or elimination of what are seen as market distortions (import tariffs, subsidies and price controls), imposed by the World Bank and IMF on the fragile economies of the global South, with the purported aim of opening markets to induce economic growth, continue to reap havoc, suffering and magnify poverty and inequality. This is what is called 'development'. As Esteva & Illich (1986, p.5-6) state, development means:

> Having started down a road that others know better, towards objectives others have achieved... Development signifies sacrificing possibilities, solidarity, traditional interpretations and customs, on the altar of the experts whose assessments are always changing. Development promotes getting rich but for the majority it only signifies the modernisation of their poverty and growing dependence on the guidance and administration of others *(my translation)*.

Education has not been spared, as governments invest less and less in this sector, and the private sector takes on the task of providing it - hence excluding poor areas and people unable to pay for it. The little public education they can access is marked by severe problems in funding, quality and coverage (especially in the poorer rural areas) among others. With disability, in a world guided by economics and numbers, disabled people continue to be devalued, when the worth of human life is judged by what it produces and how much this output is worth, and more often not in the global South, on the terms defined by the powerful West including what is considered work, and hence productive.

The neoliberal strategies above have other implications for disabled people. For example the shift from household and subsistence based activities that have and continue to enable people to survive towards market-based activities targeted at export, translates into migration to urban areas or across country borders especially by those who are younger and healthier, and in turn depriving disabled people of their support mechanisms, and broad fragmentation of households and communities. This shift, also means that the diverse activities performed in the household economy (e.g. those in small gardening and small scale agriculture and other subsistence activities), and that provide tasks for most household or community members including disabled people, are traded in, and depriving most of their sources of livelihood. This is further compounded by the flooding of local markets with artificially low priced imports upon liberalisation of markets, pushing out of business local producers, hence impacting their livelihoods and those of their households and communities, while the emphasis on non-traditional exports such as flowers as opposed to traditional agriculture, reduces the supply of subsistence crops and food, relocates employment to often exploitative industrial sectors (e.g. sweatshops), impacts traditional social relationships and networks, and importantly threatens other spheres such as health (e.g. through reduced food consumption).

Conclusions

The quest for inclusive education has many barriers to contend with in the complex and heterogeneous majority world, historically, socially, culturally and politically. Importantly, and as outlined in this chapter, the quest for inclusive education, cannot be disassociated from the broader educational needs of all poor people. While disabled people face more barriers, it remains perhaps unrealistic to address the educational needs of disabled people, without catering for those of poor people at large, especially since the complex dynamics of poverty act as the principal and often unmoveable barrier. Many have been and remain the policies and statements of good intent, both international and national, that remain a paper on a shelf when confronting the complex dynamics of poor people's lives on the ground, especially when these are quick fix and often Western one size fit all solutions un-adapted to context, culture or socio-economic situation. At the most basic level these contexts defy any attempt at simplification- simply because poverty is complex, often permanent, causes are structural and renewed in constant power differentials, and hence any strategies require attacks on multiple fronts. Inclusive education is hence only one part in the complex puzzle. Measures such as the quota system introduced in many countries, for disabled children to be in schools remains perhaps a good example, where the impacts, if any, are often negligible in impoverished areas. This is especially the case where schools are overcrowded, underfunded and policies are not monitored, teachers are untrained, training materials are un-adapted or unavailable (e.g. Braille material), poor people face competing demands *(see above)*, and when even basic architectural barriers and the absence of adequate/adapted transportation preclude access. Positive steps can only be taken if we start addressing the causes of barriers, structural and their historical antecedents, rather than dealing with symptoms - this is necessary at least for initiatives to be relevant, effective and sustainable, and which in turn necessitates a shift away from the Western deficit view of the global South, towards confronting its own role historically and more contemporarily in the maintenance of a hegemony that keeps the fire of colonialism continuously alive, through poverty, inequality, deprivation, health and also education.

> **Thinking Point 1:**
> To what extent do we need to understand poverty and its dynamics in order to engage with education in the majority world?
> **Thinking Point 2:**
> How important is it to address the barriers imposed by poverty, and what are the implications of these for education and for disabled people?
> **Thinking Point 3:**
> How important are historical aspects, and the role of the West in the majority world, and what are the implications of these for education, and more narrowly for an inclusive education?

REFERENCES

CPRC. (2008). *The Chronic Poverty Report 2008-09: Escaping Poverty Traps.* UK: PRC.

CPRC. (2004). *Chronic Poverty Report 2004-2005.* Manchester UK: IDPM.

DFID. (2000). *Disability, Poverty and Development* . UK: DFID.

EC. (2003). *Guidance Note on Disability and Development for European Union Delegations and Services* . Brussels: European Commission.

EDF. (2002). *Development Cooperation and Disability.* Brussels: European Disability Forum.

Esteva, A., & Illich, I. (1986). *El Desarrollo: Metáforo, Mito, Amenaza.* Mexico: Tecno-política.

Grech, S. (2008). Living with disability in rural Guatemala: exploring connections and impacts on poverty. *International Journal of Disability, Community & Rehabilitation, 7 (2).*

Grech, S. (2009). Disability, poverty and development: critical reflections on the majority world debate. *Disability & Society, 24 (6), 771-784.*

McClintock, A. (1992). The Angel of Progress: Pitfalls of the Term "Post-Colonialism". *Social Text , 31/32, 84-98.*

Miles, S. (1999). *Strengthening Disability and Development Work.* London, UK: Bond.

Sachs, J. (2005). *The End of Poverty: How We Can Make it Happen in Our Lifetime.* London: Penguin Books.

UNDP. (2006). *Human Development Report 2006: Beyond scarcity: Power, poverty and the global water crisis.* New York: UNDP.

UNESCO. (2008). *Education for All: Global Monitoring Report.* Oxford: Oxford University Press.

---

[i] The term majority world is used interchangeably with 'developing countries' to emphasise countries where the bulk of the world's population reside & where poverty is largely concentrated. The term is employed to delineate the power & resource differentials with rich countries that host a smaller percentage of the world's population but where wealth is largely concentrated & controlled, & which exert influence & power (economically, politically, socially, & culturally) over poor countries.
[ii] While in 1820, the gap between the richest economy at the time (the United Kingdom) & the world's poorest region, Africa, stood at four to one, in 1998, this gap between the US & Africa had widened to a staggering twenty to one (Sachs, 2005). Globalization, & the free market accumulation has benefited pockets of countries (rich ones), & bypassed or often worsened the conditions of those (in the global South) unable to participate on equal terms, pushing them deeper into poverty. The rich are richer & the poor are poorer, since poverty reduction depends not only on economic growth, but on his growth is (re)distributed.